Margaret Stokes

Early Christian Architecture in Ireland

Margaret Stokes

Early Christian Architecture in Ireland

ISBN/EAN: 9783337027032

Printed in Europe, USA, Canada, Australia, Japan

Cover: Foto ©Lupo / pixelio.de

More available books at **www.hansebooks.com**

Drawn by George Petrie. Engraved by Swain.

Dún Aengus.

EARLY CHRISTIAN ARCHITECTURE IN IRELAND.

BY

MARGARET STOKES.

ILLUSTRATED WITH WOODCUTS.

THE TEMPLE AS REPRESENTED IN THE BOOK OF KELLS.

LONDON:

GEORGE BELL AND SONS, YORK STREET,

COVENT GARDEN.

1878.

CHISWICK PRESS: CHARLES WHITTINGHAM, TOOKS COURT, CHANCERY LANE.

TO

EDITH CHENEVIX TRENCH.

You will remember that about two years ago Margaret Freeman, asking our aid for the sufferers in Servia, reminded us of a passage in the "Vision of Piers Ploughman"[1] which, I think, workers in other fields may use. The poet tells us of a certain company journeying on a pilgrimage in search of Truth. Ignorant of the path, they ask for aid and guidance of the ploughman, whose answer is that they must wait till he has "eeried" and sown his half acre e'er he can "wende" with them "and the way teche;" and a veiled lady in the company answers—

"This were a long lettyng!
. . . .
What sholde we wommen
Wercke the while?"

This question, asked some five hundred years ago by one who had the strength to wait, now stirs in the hearts of many of us women in the present day, and it may be well for us to think over the answer that was given. These "lovely ladies with their long fingers" were to work their "churches to honour," while also to take heed how the needy and the naked do lie, and to cast them clothes. "For so commaundeth Truthe," and so "for the Lordes love of Hevene" doth the woman help man to work "wightliche."

With this humble yet lofty aim of helpfulness we women need not fear stepping outside our sphere. Many and various are the ways by which we may help, not only in the honouring of our Church, but in the giving of food and raiment. Our Church, in its past and present,

---

[1] *Passus* vi.

needs something more than manual labour, and there are forms of hunger and of thirst other than for mere material food. No country stands more in need of clothing of honour, and of that food by which the soul is fed than does our own beloved Ireland. These things you have felt with me. May I, then, dedicate to you this my imperfect effort to be the helper, not the hinderer, of such men as have striven, and still do strive, to work wisely in her cause?

MARGARET STOKES.

CARRIG-BREAC, HOWTH, *April*, 1878.

LIST OF WOOD ENGRAVINGS IN THE LETTERPRESS.

	DRAWN BY	ENGRAVED BY	PAGE
Pilaster	George Petrie	Hanlon	35
Finan's Oratory, doorway	Margaret Stokes	Swain	36
Ground plan, Tempul Gel	Lord Dunraven	Swain	38
Arch	Lord Dunraven	Swain	47
Diagram of Interments, Kilkenny Tower	Graves	Oldham	59
Killenda Tower	George Petrie	Branston	61
Ireland's Eye, Church on	George Petrie	Branston	61
Tamlaght Finlagen, ground plan	George Petrie	Branston	62
Killossy	George Petrie	Branston	63
St. Michael-le-Pole	George Petrie	Branston	64
Dinkelsbühl	F. W. Burton	Hanlon	65
San Giovanni Battista	O. Jewitt	O. Jewitt	65
Notre Dame, Maestricht	James Fergusson		67
St. Maurice, Epinal	S. Ferguson	O. Jewitt	68
Gernrode in the Hartz	James Fergusson		69
St. Gertrude, Nivelles	James Fergusson		69
St. Geneviève			70
Mungret	George Petrie		71
Deerness, Orkney	George Petrie	Branston	72
St. Magnus, Egilsha	George Petrie	Branston	72
St. Patrick's Church, Isle of Man		Hanlon	73
Kelletstown	George Petrie	Branston	75
St. George de Bocherville	Turner	Hanlon	78
King David	MS. illumination	Swain	79
Female Bell Ringer	Illuminated MS.	Swain	79
Bell Ringers	Illuminated MS.	Swain	81
Belfry	Illuminated MS.	Ellacombe	82
Bell of St. Patrick	Ellacombe		83
Clog Beannaighte	Ellacombe		83
Ancient Bells	George Petrie	Swain	84
Killmallock Church and Tower	George Petrie	Branston	90
Churches and Towers in MSS.	George Petrie	Hanlon	102
Seir Kieran	James Graves	Hanlon	107
Old Church on Seal	Hanlon	Hanlon	110
Old Church on Capital	Hanlon	Hanlon	110
Tullaherin Church and Tower	George Petrie	Branston	111
Capitals, Inchagoile	W. F. Wakeman	Hanlon	115
Capitals, Clonaltin	W. F. Wakeman	Hanlon	115
Capital, Banagher	George Petrie	Swain	116
Capital, McCarthy's Church	J. Rogers	Swain	116

vi *List of Engravings on Wood.*

	DRAWN BY	ENGRAVED BY	PAGE
Capital, Trim	*George Petrie*	*Branston*	116
Bases, sections of	*O. Jewitt*	*O. Jewitt*	117
White Island, doorway of church	*George Petrie*	*Swain*	118
St. Farannan's Church	*George Petrie*	*Swain*	119
Mouldings in St. Farannan's Church	*George Petrie*	*Swain*	120
Arcade in Ardmore Church	*O. Jewitt*	*O. Jewitt*	121
Ardmore, Arcade in	*O. Jewitt*	*O. Jewitt*	122
Scroll on bronze ornament	*Margaret Stokes*	*Swain*	124

LIST OF ENGRAVINGS ON WOOD AT THE END OF THE VOLUME.

PLATE	FIGURE		DRAWN BY	ENGRAVED BY
		Dún Aengus (*frontispiece*)	*George Petrie*	*Swain*
I.	1	Dún Aengus, doorway of	*F. W. Burton*	*Swain*
II.	2	Caher Gel, county Galway, steps in	*W. F. Wakeman*	*Hanlon*
II.	3	Dún Oonacht, steps	*H. Burchett*	*Swain*
II.	4	Portion of wall, Caher Gel, county Kerry	*Dr. Graves*	*Gray*
III.	5	Caher Gel, on Lough Corrib	*W. F. Wakeman*	*Hanlon*
III.	6	Clochàn, doorway of	*Margaret Stokes*	*Swain*
IV.	7	Scelig Mhichil	*Robert Callwell*	*Swain*
V.	8	*Ib.*, Way of the Cross	*Margaret Stokes*	*Swain*
VI.	9	Oilen-Tsenaig	*Margaret Stokes*	*Swain*
VII.	10	*Ib.*, doorway of Cell	*Margaret Stokes*	*Swain*
VII.	11	Finan's Cell, interior	*Margaret Stokes*	*Hanlon*
VIII.	12	Brendan's Oratory	*Margaret Stokes*	*Swain*
IX.	13	Tempul Brecain, cross at	*F. W. Burton*	*Swain*
X.	14	Macdara's Church, window in	*Margaret Stokes*	*Swain*
X.	16	*Ib.*, doorway of	*George Petrie*	*Hanlon*
X.	15	Kill Enda, window in	*Margaret Stokes*	*Swain*
XI.	17	St. Caimin's Church, Inismain	*Margaret Stokes*	*Swain*
XI.	18	*Ib.*, window	*Margaret Stokes*	*Swain*
XII.	19	Trinity Church, Glendalough	*W. F. Wakeman*	*Swain*
XII.	20	St. Caimin's Church, Inismain	*George Petrie*	*Swain*
XIII.	21	Kilmoremoy Church, window	*F. W. Burton*	*Hanlon*
XIII.	22	Kilfrauchen, doorway of	*W. F. Wakeman*	*Oldham*
XIV.	23	Brecan Church, window	*Margaret Stokes*	*Swain*
XIV.	24	Kilcrony, doorway	*George Petrie*	*Branston*
XV.	25	Mungret Church, doorway	*George Petrie*	*Hanlon*
XV.	26	Killannin, doorway	*George Petrie*	*Hanlon*
XVI.	27	Altannin, window	*George Petrie*	*Hanlon*
XVI.	28	St. Kevin's Church	*J. Parker*	*O. Jewitt*
XVI.	29	*Ib.*, interior	*J. Parker*	*O. Jewitt*
XVI.	30	*Ib.*, doorway	*J. Parker*	*O. Jewitt*
XVII.	31	Killcananach, doorway of	*W. F. Wakeman*	*Hanlon*
XVII.	32	Temple Martin, doorway of	*Margaret Stokes*	*Swain*
XVIII.	33	Banagher, doorway of	*George Petrie*	*Hanlon*
XVIII.	34	*Ib.*, exterior of doorway	*George Petrie*	*Hanlon*
XIX.	35	Maghera Church, doorway of	*George Petrie*	*Swain*

List of Engravings on Wood.

PLATE	FIGURE		DRAWN BY	ENGRAVED BY
XX.	36	Scattery, doorway of Tower	George Petrie	Branston.
XX.	37	Aran, doorway of Tower	George Petrie	Branston.
XXI.	38, 39	Lusk Tower, windows in	George Petrie	Branston.
XXI.	40	Clondalkin Tower, window in	George Petrie	Branston.
XXI.	41	Taghedoe Tower, window in	George Petrie	Branston.
XXII.	42	Lusk Tower, doorway in	George Petrie	Branston.
XXII.	43	Drumcliff Tower	George Petrie	Branston.
XXIII.	44	Aghavuller Tower	George Petrie	Branston.
XXIII.	45	Ib., doorway in	George Petrie	Branston.
XXIV.	46	Killree Tower	George Petrie	Branston.
XXIV.	47	Ib., doorway in	George Petrie	Branston.
XXV.	48	Inisceltra Tower	Watkins	Swain.
XXV.	49	Ib., doorway in	Watkins	Swain.
XXVI.	50	Meelick, doorway of Tower	George Petrie	Branston.
XXVI.	51	Kevin's Church, Nave of	O. Jewitt	O. Jewitt.
XXVII.	52	Monasterboice Tower, window in	G. Du Noyer	Hanlon.
XXVII.	53	Temple Finghin, herring-bone masonry in	O. Jewitt	O. Jewitt.
XXVII.	54	Roscrea Tower in 1835	George Petrie	Swain.
XXVIII.	55	Cashel Tower	George Petrie	Branston.
XXVIII.	56, 57, 58	Dysert Aengus Tower, windows in	Gordon Hill	G. Jewitt.
XXIX.	59	Ib., doorway of	George Petrie	Branston.
XXIX.	60	Ib., Church and Tower	O. Jewitt	O. Jewitt.
XXX.	62	Kilkenny Tower, doorway in	George Petrie	Branston.
XXX.	61, 63	Devenish Tower and Section	O. Jewitt	O. Jewitt.
XXX.	64	Glendalough	Margaret Stokes	Swain.
XXXI.	66	Kells Tower, doorway of	George Petrie	Branston.
XXXI.	65	Disert O'Dea Tower, doorway of	F. W. Burton	Branston.
XXXII.	67	Kells Tower, window of	George Petrie	Branston.
XXXII.	68	Kells Tower	George Petrie	Branston.
XXXIII.	71	Ardmore Tower	O. Jewitt	O. Jewitt.
XXXIII.	69, 70	Ib., Corbels in	O. Jewitt	O. Jewitt.
XXXIV.	72	Timahoe Tower, window in	O. Jewitt	O. Jewitt.
XXXIV.	73	Kildare Tower, doorway in	George Petrie	Branston.
XXXIV.	74	Tory Island	George Petrie	Branston.
XXXV.	75	Dromiskin Tower, doorway in	George Petrie	Branston.
XXXV.	76	Dromiskin Tower	George Petrie	Branston.
XXXVI.	77	Kilbannon Tower	George Petrie	Branston.
XXXVI.	78	Dinkelsbühl and Abernethy Towers	George Petrie	Branston.
XXXVII.	79	Kilmalkedar	George Petrie	Swain.
XXXVII.	80	Ib., doorway of	Margaret Stokes	Swain.
XXXVIII.	81	Iniscaltra, ground plan of Monastery	G. Brash	Swain.
XXXVIII.	82	Ib., capitals in	Swain	Swain.
XXXVIII.	83	Ib., doorway of Church	G. Petrie	Hanlon.
XXXIX.	84, 85	Rahen, capitals in	Margaret Stokes	Swain.
XXXIX.	86	Inchagoile, doorway of	George Petrie	Swain.
XL.	87	Cormac's Chapel, interior	M. Stokes, after George Petrie	Swain.
XLI.	88	Cormac's Chapel, doorway of	J. Deane	Swain.
XLII.	89	Ib., Chancel of	O. Jewitt	O. Jewitt.
XLII.	90	Ib., exterior of	O. Jewitt	O. Jewitt.
XLIII.	91, 92	Killeshin, doorway of	Photograph on wood	Swain.
XLIV.	93	Freshford, doorway of	Photograph	Swain.
XLV.	94, 95, 96	Dervorgilla's Church, Clonmacnois	Jewitt	Swain.
XLVI.	97	Cronan's Church, Roscrea	George Petrie	Swain.

List of Engravings on Wood.

PLATE.	FIGURE.		DRAWN BY	ENGRAVED BY
XLVII.	98	Mona Incha	George Petrie	Swain.
XLVIII.	99	Killeshin, moulding in	Margaret Stokes	Swain.
XLVIII.	100	Tomgrany, moulding in	Margaret Stokes	Swain.
XLVIII.	101	Aghadoe, doorway of	Margaret Stokes	Swain.
XLVIII.	102	Annadown, moulding in	J. Rogers	Swain.
XLIX.	103	Dervorgilla's Church, base of pillar	J. Rogers	Swain.
XLIX.	104	Clonmacnois Cathedral, bases in	J. Rogers	Swain.
L.	105, 106	Clonmacnois, corner projections	J. Rogers	Swain.
L.	107	Ib., impost of west door	J. Rogers	Swain.
L.	108	Tomgrany, quoin shaft.	J. Rogers	Swain.
LI.	109, 110	Tuam Cross	George Petrie	Swain.
LII.	111	Corner shafts of churches	Margaret Stokes	Swain.

INTRODUCTION.

THE special interest which attaches to the study of Ecclesiastical Architecture in Ireland before it ceased to be essentially Irish, is not that it possessed, as some have vainly asserted, any unequalled antiquity or beauty as compared with works of ancient art in other countries, but rather that, owing to the fact that the remains of a great number of monuments belonging to the period between the sixth and twelfth centuries of the Christian era have survived, untouched by the hand either of the restorer or of the destroyer, and that in them we may trace the gradual development from an early and rude beginning to a very beautiful result; the dovetailing, as it were, of one style into another, till an Irish form of Romanesque Architecture grew into perfection.

The first examples of architecture in Ireland are the Pagan forts and dome-roofed Sepulchres, built without cement, and showing the same ignorance of the principle of the arch which is common to the primitive builders of all countries. The sepulchres are of such dignity and importance that the reader may ask why they are not as closely described as the forts in the beginning of this work. The answer to this is, that, while the forts can be distinctly connected with the first Monasteries and Cashels of the early monks, no such link exists between these ecclesiastical remains and the sepulchres. On the contrary, in the one thing which sets any stamp of individuality on such architecture, that is, the character of the designs in their decoration, nothing is more remarkable than the difference in principle which exists between the ornaments on the walls of these pagan tombs and those which appear on monuments known to be of Christian origin. Interlacings, knots, conventional forms, and the double line or divergent spiral never appear among these pre-Christian carvings, but rude attempts at imitation of natural forms, so strangely absent from our early Christian art, such as outlines of leaves, are found instead. In the fern leaf carved on the wall of New Grange we find a perception of nature which will be sought in vain in the works of the early monks, and such designs are found along with single line spirals and other linear patterns, differing in no sense from the rudest and first efforts in the graphic art of primitive man throughout the world.

The tombs in which such stone carvings are found were pre-Christian, so far as they were the burial-places of a race who practised heathen forms of interment, as is proved by the discovery of vessels containing offerings, or perhaps provisions, placed near the skeleton, or of urns which held the ashes of the dead. That the custom of burning the dead continued in use for some time after the partial Christianization of the island cannot be doubted. However, no record or tradition exists proving these tombs to have been devoted to Christian uses at any time, whereas many such survive regarding the forts which were in numerous instances given up to ecclesiastical purposes, when the king or chief, on his conversion to Christianity, presented to God his *Dún* or fortress, within the shelter of whose walls the missionary and his attendant monks erected their little cells and oratories.

To judge from the existing remains of the earliest Christian monasteries in Ireland, it would appear that the monks merely adopted the method of building then practised among the natives, making such modifications in form as their difference of purpose and some traditional usage required. The earliest ecclesiastical buildings in Ireland are the monasteries consisting of two or more oratories together with the dwellings of the monks, enclosed by a wall termed *Caisel*, pronounced Cashel, *i.e.*, stone fort, a word derived from the Latin *castellum*. The remains of these circumvallations so strongly resemble the pagan fortresses, that Dr. O'Donovan was inclined to regard them as having been such originally. However, a comparison between the two proves that, while their similarity in structure seems to point to the same degree of knowledge in the builders, yet differences do exist which mark their independent purpose.

It may be surmised that the island monasteries were often used as places of temporary retreat, from the many incidental references to them as such in the legendary lives of the saints; for instance, in the Martyrology of Donegal, p. 65, it is said of Kieran of Scirkieran, "It is he that used to go to the sea rock that was far distant in the sea . . . . and used to return again." And the founders of these hermitages were generally men at the heads of large and important schools of religion and learning, such as Clonfert, Devenish, Ardfinnan, and others, who either used them as places of probationary effort at an early period of life, or visited these retreats at rare intervals, or in their old age retired thither to die in quiet. But they were men of "hard hands and tender hearts, sustaining themselves by their labour," men of indomitable courage and no mean skill, who crowned these storm-beaten cliffs with their uncemented but still enduring walls.

Monasticism and the love of an eremitic life, which are the natural growth of a fervent religious spirit in any period, became especially so while the Eastern influence, in which asceticism formed so large a part, still permeated the Western Church. They were an essential portion of the ecclesiastical system of these ages all over Europe, and such monasteries and cells as are described in this work were probably not peculiar to Ireland at the time in which they were erected. This is proved by the existence of similar remains in the islands off the coast of Scotland and Wales and Brittany; and if on such heights as those of Mont St. Michel, in the bay of Avranches, or St. Michael's Mount, off the coast of Cornwall, no such rude and primitive remains are now visible, yet, nevertheless, they may have once existed, and may have been superseded by the works of the greater architects of the eleventh and twelfth centuries. The student of ecclesiastical history must then turn to the islands off the west coast of Ireland if he would see the outward and visible signs of this system in the sixth and seventh centuries. He will see the dwellings and the sanctuaries of men who lived and died upon these barren rocks; but how they lived is a question he will not be able to answer. Only in such a scene as lies before him in the church of St. Michael on the Skellig can a thoughtful mind realize to the full the strength of that spirit which drove man, in his undying struggle with the powers of evil, into these solitudes.

In the next period of Irish architecture a very perceptible advance takes place, the marked features of which are the gradual introduction of cement in some form or other, the addition of the chancel with the chancel arch; and, thirdly, while the ancient features of the horizontal lintel and inclined sides are preserved in the doorways, the introduction and growth of a richly decorated style anterior to that of a Romanesque style in Ireland. The greater number of these buildings, not omitting the smallest and most primitive, show marks of tooling, and the decorations in four of them are mouldings and ornaments elsewhere held to mark a late period in architecture. Small as these buildings sometimes are, we shall call them churches, to distinguish them from those uncemented oratories previously described. Besides, they generally stand alone, and do not form the centre of a group of monastic cells enclosed in a cashel such as did the first oratories.

Whatever faith may be placed in the traditionary evidence of the antiquity of these simple churches of one chamber, it is clear that those buildings which have the addition of a chancel, and in which this feature is coeval with the rest of the building, and not the work of a later date, must belong to a period far removed from that of the founders of these churches, who lived in the sixth and seventh centuries. There is but one example of a chancel arch built in the primitive style—one stone overlapping another till the sides meet at the apex—and this is at St. Kevin's, Glendalough. The true arch, with radiating joints, seems to have been introduced with the chancel, and it is curious that, long after the knowledge of the arch was thus spread through the country, the horizontal lintel was preserved in the doorways.

The point of greatest interest in the development of architecture at this stage is the gradual growth of the use of ornament, not only on the principal features, but on the walls of the buildings also. At first such ornaments seem often introduced without reference to the general effect or beauty of the building, however they may add to its significance; the cross is often found on the soffit, not on the face of the doorway, and the other fragmentary decorations are scattered about the walls of the buildings without any principle of arrangement that we can discover, and yet evidently are not insertions of a later period. These churches thus decorated preserve all the archaic character of the earliest Christian remains with rude and massive masonry, and little, if any, cement; the primitive east window is seen adorned, perhaps only on one side, by the fillet moulding; the corner stones are carved with scrolls; the eave rests on dragons' heads; and from the walls which bear

"The grey and grief-worn aspect of old days,"

strange human heads project

"With wild bewildered gaze,
Of one to stone converted by amaze."

English writers on architecture seem to hold that, where any mouldings are thus found, they are the best and safest guide to the history of the building, both as to the period when it was erected and the people by whom it was constructed. As regards England, it is true that the architecture of the Norman style of the eleventh and twelfth centuries, and of the earlier variety of Romanesque, commonly called Anglo-Saxon, may be characterized by certain mouldings and ornaments which are not found to have existed in that country before the introduction of the round arch; and it seems probable that such ornament was of foreign origin, while in Ireland the decoration of the Romanesque doorway of the twelfth century is but the repetition in stone of the illuminated pages of the scribe of the seventh century, who, in his turn, repeats the graceful and varied designs of the pre-Christian worker in bronze and gold. The history of the development of art in England and Ireland is so different, that no arguments founded solely on English experience can lead to any safe conclusions as to the date of similar work in Ireland.

At one period in the history of Britain there was a school of Celtic decorative art existing in the country characterized by a peculiar spiral pattern. From this source forms of infinitely varying beauty might have been drawn, yet it seems as if all traces of such native art had died out during the long occupation of the country by the Romans, and the power of free and graceful design, shown in the decorated bronzes and other relics of the late Celtic period, no longer lives in the art of the Anglo-Norman time. But the events which happened in England so early as from the second to the fifth centuries, and which led to the disappearance of the Celtic style of decorative art, do not find their parallel in Ireland till the end of the twelfth and beginning of the thirteenth centuries, when, after the settlement of the Normans, a foreign school of art gradually superseded the native style. The date of Irish ornamented buildings cannot be arrived at, therefore, by means of any comparison with English examples. These monuments must be viewed with a larger vision than that of writers who bind themselves by rules merely founded on local experience.

Dr. Petrie, who was the first great investigator of the history of Irish architecture, though in his early life holding that most of these churches were the work of their founders, yet at a later period saw the difficulty of assigning to them so early a date;[1] and the more he learned of other examples of Romanesque architecture in Western Europe, and the further he advanced in the science of Comparative Archæology, the clearer it became to him that he had antedated many of our buildings. This learned antiquary gladly assisted in the further investigations which he felt must clear the way for truth, and welcomed the light he saw arising, while his own torch declined, even as

"All great men who foreknew
Their heirs in art, for art's sake have been glad
And bent their old white heads as if uncrowned
Fanatics of their pure ideals still,
Far more than of the laurels which were found
With some less stalwart struggle of the will."[2]

---

[1] See Archæological Essays, by the late Sir James Simpson, Bart., edited by John Stuart, LL.D., vol. i. pp. 67, 87, 116. Notes by Dr. Petrie.
[2] Elizabeth Barrett Browning. Casa Guidi Windows, p. 26.

Whatever his followers may discover, he will remain the Pioneer who guided our footsteps in the all but interminable and tangled jungle which must be cut through before we can even hope to arrive at the brink of that gulf which divides us from the Past.

It is not till we reach the tenth century that any historical basis on which to fix the date of these buildings can be found, and with the church and belfry of Tomgraney (County of Clare) begins that first series of buildings in Ireland the age of which can be estimated with any certainty. The belfry of this church was erected in the year 965, by the Abbot Cormac O'Cillene, who also built a church at Clonmacnois, where another tower of the same nature is said to have been commenced that year.

A great restoration of monasteries took place between the years 996 and 1008, when King Brian Borumha secured a temporary peace from the incursions of the Danes, by whom, as we read in the annals, "the whole realme was overrunn and overspread. The churches, abbeys, and other religious places were by them quite razed and debased, or otherwise turned to vile, base, servile, and abominable uses. . . . But King Bryan was a meet salve to cure such festered soares, all the phissick in the world cou'd not help it elsewhere, in a small time he banished the Danes, made up the Churches and Religious houses, restored the nobility to their Antient patrimony and possessions, and in fine brought all to a notable reformation." [1]

To this period and the two following centuries the erection of the Round Towers, half strongholds and half belfries, may be safely assigned; and Lord Dunraven has already proved that the type chosen was not so peculiar to Ireland as has been supposed.[2] One of the earliest forms of campanile in Italy appears to have been a tall cylindrical tower with a conical roof; and various instances to be hereafter given of such structures in Ravenna, Switzerland, France, and the British Isles, will prove that such a type existed in the eleventh century in Western Europe, although, having elsewhere been superseded by forms of greater beauty, few examples are now left standing save in Ireland.

In the Carolingian period, as we are informed by M. Viollet-le-Duc, " Les constructeurs carlovingiens, préoccupés avant tout d'élever une défense surmontée d'une guette et d'un signal sonore, ne songèrent pas tout d'abord à décorer leurs clochers,"[3] and in another place

---

[1] Annals of Clonmacnois, A.D. 1002.
[2] Memorials of Adare, pp. 218, 232.
[3] Dict. de l'Arch^{re}. Française, Viollet-le-Duc, tome iii. p. 288.

he remarks, "On peut donc considérer les plus anciens clochers autant comme des monuments destinés à faire reconnaître l'église au loin comme un signe de puissance, que comme des tours bâties pour contenir des cloches. Des motifs étrangers aux idées religieuses durent encore contribuer à faire élever des tours attenantes aux églises. Pendant les incursions normandes sur les côtes du Nord, de l'Ouest et le long des bords de la Loire et de la Seine, la plupart des églises furent saccagées par ces barbares; on dut songer à les mettre à l'abri du pillage en les enfermant dans des enceintes et en les appuyant à des tours solides qui défendaient leurs approches. Ces tours durent être naturellement bâties au-dessus de la porte de l'église, comme étant le point le plus attaquable. Dans ce cas, le placement des cloches n'était qu'accessoire; on les suspendait au sommet de ces tours, dans les loges ou les combles qui les couronnaient. C'est en effet, dans les contrées particulièrement ravagées par les incursions périodiques des Normands que nous voyons les églises abbatiales et même paroissiales précédées de tours massives, dont malheureusement il ne nous reste guère aujourd'hui que les étages inférieurs." [1]

There appear to have been five varieties of campanile in Ireland, the first and most common that which stands apart from the church, the second that which is attached to its side, the third a smaller tower springing from some portion of the roof, and, though circular, yet generally rising from a square base, while the fourth and fifth are square, the first bearing a strong resemblance to the early Scottish square towers, such as may be still seen attached to St. Diarmid's Church on Inis Cloran in Lough Ree, and the last belonging to a later and more ornate type, such as the towers at the junction of the nave and chancel at Cormac's Chapel, Cashel. The lofty detached tower appears to be the oldest type in Ireland, and its singular character of solitude is clearly to be attributed to the fact that the Irish churches before the Cistercian period were invariably low and small, while the continental buildings reach nearly to the height of the tower beside which they stand.

Speaking of these towers, Mr. Wilkinson remarks: "Such designs could have originated only with people whose minds were familiar with the large structures of the country from which they emanated; there is a character and bold design in their outline, and indeed in every part, which bespeak them as the production of a vigorous mind; nothing is superfluous, nothing indicating doubt and experiment, but

---

[1] Dict. de l'Arch^{re}. Française, Viollet-le-Duc, tome iii. p. 286.

with a bold and preconceived outline they at once advance their lofty form."[1]

Although the apertures of some of these monuments suggest that they belong to a period earlier than that in which the knowledge of the true arch had reached Ireland, yet some, most probably erected in the eleventh and twelfth centuries, have beautifully ornamented round arched doorways, and among these are some of the earliest examples of Irish Romanesque. The limits of this introduction permit a very faint indication of those points in which this style differs from the Anglo-Norman.

In an essay[2] on the origin and growth of Romanesque architecture by Mr. Freeman, this writer points out that the two great systems of Architecture, when arranged according to their leading principles of construction, are the Entablature and the Arch. Each of these systems has been, in its own time and place, the animating principle of a style of architecture. It is apparently in the blending of these two styles—the lingering of the older, that of the entablature, and the engrafting of its forms on those of the Round Arch—that the local character to which we give the name of Irish Romanesque consists.

The first style, characterized by the horizontal lintel, had already reached to a very high type of beauty (as we may see in the doorways of Maghera and Banagher churches), when the round arch was first introduced; and there appears still to have been a clinging to the idea of horizontal extension in the minds of the Irish builders even after they had universally adopted the round form. In the Irish doorway the idea of a group of columns is conveyed by rounding off the angles and channelling the jambs into bowtels or little clustered shafts. And instead of capitals, which each crown a separate column, one long and level entablature unites the whole at the top. At each end of this a woman's head is often carved, whose streaming hair, intertwined in long locks, seems to bind the group of columns into one, and forms an interlaced ornament on the face of the entablature. The feeling that gives rise to such preservation of ancient forms is very different from blind imitation or retention. The constancy that will not part from that which has already borne noble fruit belongs to some higher principle than ignorance or blind idolatry.

It may be that the most important achievement of Irish architec-

---

[1] Practical Geology and Ancient Architecture of Ireland, p. 90.
[2] The Origin and Growth of Romanesque Architecture, Fortnightly Review, No. LXX. New Series. Oct. 1, 1872. See also History of Architecture, by Edward A. Freeman, p. 199. London, 1849.

ture was the discovery of a method of stone roofing at once enduring, lofty, and picturesque, which seems a natural growth as a defence in a climate exposed to rain, and snow, and tempest. The later examples of these buildings mark the transition from the period of the round to the pointed arch; but there are early stone roofs of simpler and ruder form, and there still remain a number of these buildings in Ireland which can be so arranged as to show in a regular series the striving after, and final achievement of, the pointed arch. These churches all form studies of the deepest interest owing to this fact, but it will suffice for our present purpose to name four: Gallarus; Friars' Island, near Killaloe; St. Columba's House at Kells; and Cormac's Chapel at Cashel. The first evinces no knowledge of the principle of the arch; but the *form* of a pointed arch was obtained by one stone projecting beyond another till they met at the apex. This roof was liable to sink at the sides from the great weight of the stones, and the second church on our list shows that the method adopted for counteracting this was as follows:—The lower story of the building was roofed by a barrel vault built on the radiating principle;[1] on this was raised the high pitched stone roof, at first, as in the church on Friars' Island, constructed of rectangular slabs of various thicknesses laid in courses each overlapping the preceding one, and dressed inside and out to the rake of the roof. Under the ridge is a space left, the primary purpose of which was to lighten the weight on the vault, but which afterwards, and in larger buildings, served as a chamber. In the oratory or house of St. Columba, at Kells, the construction of the upper arch is less rude, and the builders were evidently striving to rise from the false pointed to the more perfect form of the radiating round arches; the stones are laid in horizontal layers half-way up, and then radiate towards the top. The open space above the barrel vault is divided by cross walls into three portions, the shape being a triangle having two sides formed to a rude curve, these sides not being arched but built of thin stones and thick beds of mortar, the courses projecting as they rise. The process followed seems to have been this: that the walls were brought up to the level of the springing of the arch, that then dry stone cross walls were built, supported on which a rough centring was made, and upon this the arch was formed by building flat stones on their edges with a rough approach to radiation by the use of thick mortar beds, and finished at the top by selecting a thicker

---

[1] The barrel, waggon, tunnel, or cradle roof, a cylindrical vault resting on the tops of the side walls, with its axis in the longitudinal direction of the building, was a common and ancient method of roofing.

or thinner stone, as the case might require, for keying; then, having brought the external walls up to the level of the eaves, they proceeded to form the roof, carrying it up in masonry resting on the back of the arch as far as they judged it safe to go, and building the remainder with a hollow space to reduce the weight, introducing cross walls for support. In the roof of Cormac's Chapel a further advance is seen. Here the coverings in both stories are true arches constructed with radiating joints, and the upper one is in every respect a pointed arch, and as Mr. Wilkinson observes, speaking of another similar roof at Killaloe, "this is only one of the several examples of the kind in which pointed arches were used, and the date of whose erection is probably prior to the existence of buildings in England containing the pointed style." The boldness with which the heavy stone roof of Cormac's Chapel was placed 50 ft. above the ground upon a structure little more than half that width, as well as the skilful manner of its execution, are very striking.[1]

The theories held by some that the pointed arch was first derived from copying forms produced by the intersections of branches of trees, or of apertures made by two stones meeting at the top, or from the intersection of round-headed arcades, seem all founded on insufficient basis, since they merely show how the external form might have been suggested, as if architecture arose from copying some visible outward feature, and were not in itself the expression of some inner necessity. The discovery and progression of newer and more perfect forms in this art must emanate from some want, and spring from the effort to supply some defect in a previous style which may have rendered it less fit for its purpose. The object of the Irish builder being the formation of an extremely steep roof, the method which combined loftiness with lightness was sought after until the pointed arch was attained, and proved the perfect form on which to rest his superstructure. It is probable that the first cause which led to the prevalence of the pointed arch throughout the north of France, the west of Germany, and the Netherlands, in the eleventh and following centuries, was the method of vaulting churches. Mr. Fergusson in his "History of Architecture" speaks of the mode of double roofing which originated in Ireland, comparing it with that adopted in the south of France in the same age, and adds that "it enabled the Irish to make the roof steeper than could be effected with a single vault, and in so rainy a climate this may have been of the first importance.

---

[1] See Wilkinson, Practical Geology and Ancient Architecture of Ireland, p. 145. See Monograph of Cormac's Chapel.—A. Hill.

Had the Irish been allowed to persevere in the elaboration of their own style, they would probably have applied this expedient to the roofing of larger buildings than they ever attempted, and might in so doing have avoided the greatest fault of Gothic architecture. Without more experience it is impossible to pronounce to what extent the method might have been carried with safety, or to say whether the Irish double vault is a better constructive form than the single Romance pointed arch. It was certainly an improvement on the wooden roof of the true Gothic style, and its early abandonment is consequently much to be regretted."[1]

The study of these buildings and the questions that they raise may be of wider import than has been yet acknowledged. To the Irishman it may minister to his self-respect to feel that he belongs to a race who could originate and develop, to a result of great excellence and beauty, a native school of architecture. To the student of art in its widest sense it is a matter of deepest interest, that enough yet remains through which he can trace step by step the progress of this style from the simple source from which it sprang. To copy the work of a former age is one thing, to search out its vital principles and strive to trace them to their source is another; and if we are to be the begetters of new beauty, and our work to be a living growth and no mere imitation, no work of ancient art will be too humble for our study.

It would appear that Irish Romanesque, though influenced by foreign art, yet was somewhat pre-existent to Anglo-Norman architecture, and entirely independent of it. It was a native style springing from a people possessed of original power and mind, lowly in aspect when placed beside the grand monuments of Norman art in England, lowly, but not therefore unlovable. No one can stand before the doorway of Maghera or the chancel arch of Queen Dervorgil's church, or gaze upon the Chalice of Ardagh, without feeling that there was "a true instinct of composition" and a pure vital principle at the source of art so noble and so chaste, for in them a certain classic character is visible, and these works give evidence of the existence of a spirit which, could it be called back to life, might help us to better results than we have yet attained. "None but a master may dare such simplicity."

The quality here alluded to is not in any way a proof that Irish Architecture is imitated from the Greek, nor is there any evidence that it could be its offspring. This art was of native growth, and a

---

[1] See History of Architecture, James Fergusson, vol. ii. p. 110.

style the leading characteristics of which were gradually developed features of primitive forms which may be termed the architecture of necessity, springing, as it were, from the wants and instincts of man in a natural state, yet gifted with artistic feeling. Such, also, was the case in Greece, though with an infinitely greater result; and there the original idea of the Entablature never was abandoned, even when architecture reached its highest point. The interesting thing to note is, that a result, similar in some important details, is arrived at by schools entirely ignorant of each other's works; and a classic character marked by a certain simplicity and repose, as well as by a delicate perception of fitness in ornament, with a noble reserve in its use, has been attained by both.

However, while it can be proved that Ireland may lay claim to the possession of a national and individual style, this was but a branch of the great order of Architecture then prevailing over Western Europe, which has been termed *Ur* Romanesque, and is the earliest form after the introduction of the round arch. On its first springing from Italian models, it varied less in different countries than the Norman and other later styles which supplanted it, yet it had in all places its local character, and in Ireland this character is marked with a peculiar strength as well as beauty, because, when the Romanesque wave reached our shore, there was already a style of architecture here which had attained to very noble results, and from the blending of the former with the latter emanated that form which we need not feel ashamed to claim as Irish Romanesque. It becomes a matter of deep moment now to fix the period at which this art touched its highest point. For now it is for us to say whether the story told by past and present writers on her history be true. We are told that Ireland had long fallen from that high state when her faith "burnt like a star in Western Europe;" that her people "when the Normans took charge of them, were, with the exception of the clergy, scarcely better than a mob of armed savages," who, as a nation, "have done nothing which posterity will not be anxious to forget," who "have little architecture of their own, and the forms introduced from England have been robbed of their grace;" "imaginative and poetical, yet unable to boast of one single national work of art."[1]

For errors such as these the antiquaries of Ireland, who have claimed a too early date for her monuments, are as much to blame as those who would assert that no stone churches were built, or chiselled work was executed, till the eleventh or twelfth centuries. Nothing

---

[1] Froude, The English in Ireland, vol. i. pp. 14, 15, 22, 23.

Introduction.

but calm and patient inquiry, with careful balance of evidence and opinion, will ever place our feet on solid earth ; and let us not forget that the place where History stands with veiled face is holy ground, and the veil will only rise before the large eyes of Love, that love which "bids touch truth, endure truth, and embrace truth,"[1] but which, when the veil is lifted, "grows fairer than at first, more strong, far greater."[2]

In conclusion, a few words may be added in explanation of the circumstances under which the following essay was written. It was merely intended as a summary of the conclusions to be drawn from the study of the series of monuments, military and ecclesiastical, prehistoric and historic, which were described and photographed in the work of the late Earl of Dunraven, entitled "Notes on Irish Architecture." The writer has to acknowledge the kindness of his son in allowing her the use of many of the woodcuts in this publication, and references to the Photographs with which that work is illustrated will constantly be given in the following pages.

---

[1] Browning, Turf and Towers, p. 273.
[2] Shakespeare, Sonnets, No. CXIX.

CHAPTER I.

Pagan Forts.

AS the traveller on the west coast of Ireland crosses the Bay of Galway and reaches the Islands of Aran which lie at its mouth, he there finds remains of the earliest examples of architecture known to exist in Western Europe, excepting those whose primary object was sepulchral. Landing on Aranmôr, the largest of the three islands, and commencing his walk at the southern end, he should keep along the edge of the cliffs, which gradually increasing in height as he advances seem to form a grand barrier to the ocean that beats for ever at their feet. They are of limestone, and are marked by long parallel horizontal lines or fissures, so that where they break they seem to shape themselves into huge masses, squared as if by giant hands. Here and there, where in bold promontories they advance into the sea, they have become separated from the land and rise like towers from the waves. The ruins of some ancient city with its broken pinnacles and shattered towers and riven walls seem to lie before him, and Nature is the giant builder here.

Passing upward and onward toward the highest point, the traveller will begin to perceive that this precipice is crowned by a circular wall, "grey, weather-beaten and wasted," whose broken and serrated edge stands dark against the sky. That it is indeed a wall and not a part of the rock on which it is founded, seems at the first glance doubtful, so little does it differ in colour from the cliff itself; yet, on gazing steadily, the masonry comes out like some fine mosaic work as contrasted with the enormous slabs from which the cliff would seem to have been formed. And so, still ascending towards the building, the traveller reaches at length the highest point of the range and enters the fort of Aengus.

The solitude and grandeur of the scene are unspeakable. To the north and west lies the ocean, while to the south are dimly visible the cliffs of Clare, shining in silvery whiteness through a summer mist. To the east the eye also reaches the horizon, but over a dreary desert of limestone flags. No human habitation is to be seen, not even a tree or plot of grass; grey and silent, the monotony of the scene is only broken, while its strange sadness is increased, by the ruined fortress that stands in the foreground as it has stood for centuries, like

> "one upon a rock,
> Environ'd with a wilderness of sea,
> Who marks the waxing tide grow wave by wave."

Then turning from the broken cliff to the ruined wall, the traveller will ask, who was the builder here?

Dún Aengus is in some respects the most striking example we have seen of those great uncemented stone forts of Ireland, held by tradition to belong to that time which forms the culminating point of Irish heroic story. The legend (said to have been handed down orally during the first centuries of the Christian era) of the early builders of such strongholds in the islands of Aran is the story of the wanderings and final destruction of a hunted and persecuted race, whose fate would seem to have been mournful and strange as the ruined fortresses of the lost tribe which now stand before us. Coming to Ireland through Britain, they seem to have been long beaten hither and thither, till, flying still westward, they were protected by Ailill and Maeve, who are said to have reigned in Connaught about the first century of the Christian era. From these monarchs they obtained a grant of land along the western coast of Galway, as well as the islands of Aran, where they remained until their final defeat by the heroes Cuchullin, Conall Carnach, Ross, and Keth. Thus their forms seem to pass across the deep abyss of time like the white flakes of foam drifted by the hurrying wind over the wild and wasted ruins of their fortresses.

Legend has in like manner connected the other uncemented stone fortresses found in the north and west of Ireland, not only with these heroes who surrounded the thrones of Ailill and Maeve in Connaught, but also with the Knights of the Red Branch, who formed the guard of Conor Mac Nessa, King of Ulster, when he reigned in his palace at Emania. If in the opening of an essay which, of necessity, deals with many material remains of an unknown and certainly prehistoric age, the writer be thought to linger too long in the labyrinths of Irish legend, it is by no means with the intention that these tales should in any sense be taken as history. Their authors, who, while recording others' names have left their own unsung, will doubtless appear as unreal as the heroes whose deeds they have perpetuated in their song; but since so it is, that for untold centuries these primitive strongholds have been associated with the ancient heroes of the Irish people, we have no more right to discard such tales as in all senses worthless, and to destroy all memory of such connection, than we have to accept them in any way as history. Who can dwell in the forest of Arden and not feel that its scenes are hallowed by a solemn interest, and have gained another elevating power, because associated by our greatest bard with those fair and noble forms whose memories still seem to haunt its "desert inaccessible," and linger 'neath its "shade of melancholy boughs"?

LEGEND OF THE MIGRATION OF THE SONS OF UMOR.[1]—When Cairbre Niafer reigned in Leinster, at or about the time of the birth of Christ,[2] and Conor Mac Nessa, his father-in-law, still reigned in Ulster, there lingered on the western shores and islands of Scotland a branch of the same Belgic race who, centuries before, had migrated to Ireland through Britain. Pressed by the superior forces of the Picts, a number of them are said to have again sought refuge in Erin, where they made application to Cairbre Niafer, King of Leinster, and from him received a tributary territory. But as it came to pass that they could not support the heavy tribute laid upon them for this subject soil, they moved westwards and sought the protection of Maeve, who with her husband, Ailill, then ruled in Connaught. This was the migration of the sons of Hua More, for Aengus, son of Hua More,

---

[1] The Irish before the Conquest, Mrs. Ferguson, pp. 129, 131. The Editor has also to acknowledge Mrs. Ferguson's kindness in giving her the use of her MS. lectures on Irish bardic poetry, read before the Ladies' Literary Society of Alexandra College, Dublin.

[2] O'Curry, Lectures on the MS. materials of ancient Irish history, p. 483, n. 34.

was their king in the east. They obtained a grant of lands and protection from Maeve, who thus appeared at the head of her armies:—
"A woman, comely, white-faced, long cheeked and large; gold yellow hair on her; a short crimson cloak on her; a gold pin in the cloak over her breast; a straight carved-backed spear flaming in her hand."
Welcomed by this Amazonian queen, the followers of Aengus Hua More fortified themselves along the western coast in Mayo, Galway, and Clare, and in the islands of Aran, at the mouth of Galway Bay.[1]

But the doomed race were not long to remain in safety. When they first settled in the east of Ireland, they had made a covenant with the Irish king, Cairbre Niafer, and four of his noblest heroes, Knights of the Red Branch, had stood surety for them; Cuchullin, Conall Carnech, Ross, and Keth. Seeing how the tribe of Aengus had broken faith with him, the king called upon his knights who had thus pledged themselves either to compel their return or to challenge them in battle. The fugitives accepted the challenge, and on their side chose four of their mightiest champions to meet the Knights of the Red Branch. They were named Conall the Mild, who was son to their chieftain Aengus, Kemi Kethir Kenn, King, and Irgas of Many Battles. But the champions of King Cairbre were victorious. The followers of Aengus Hua More were driven backwards to the cliffs and rocky islands of the Atlantic, to seek shelter in those stupendous stone fortresses and ramparts which they had thrown up for the protection of their tribes and of their cattle. Dún Aengusa and Dún Conor and the fort of Muirbhech Mil still preserve the names and memory of the chieftains of this early race.

LEGEND OF CUROI, SON OF DARÉ.—When Conor Mac Nessa reigned in Ulster at his palace of Emania, there dwelt a beautiful maiden, named Blanaid, in the sea-girt isle of Mana, off the coast of Scotland. Her palace was richly stored with gold and silver, and with priceless gems. The Knights of the Red Branch, headed by the hero Cuchullin, gathered their forces to ravage this island, and Curoi, son of Daré, having heard that the heroes were about to start on this expedition, disguised himself as a grey-coated clown and came to the assistance of the knights, and said he would himself take possession of the fort if he were given choice of the jewels it contained. The fort was plundered and Blanaid borne away. When

---

[1] Dún Aengus still bears the name of their chieftain, while among their other leaders was Cutra, who has left his name at Lough Cooter near Gort; Adhar at Moy-Adhair, or the Plain of Adhar in Clare; Measca at Loch Mask in Mayo, &c.

the knights came to divide the spoil, the clown in the grey garb said, "Blanaid is the treasure I must claim." "Take thy choice of all the other jewels except Blanaid," said Cuchullin; but the clown gave answer, "I will take no exchange for her." Then Curoi surprised the maiden unperceived, and bore her away under an enchanted mask.

But Cuchullin loved the maiden and followed on their track to Munster. Worsted in his encounter with Curoi he renewed his search in the following year, and guided by a great flock of dark birds coming over the sea from the north, he came to Munster, and found her alone on the banks of the Finnglas or white brook, in Kerry.[1] There she told the hero that she loved him before all other men, and implored him to come at the season of All Hallows with an armed force to carry her away. And a signal was agreed upon between them. Encamped with his forces in the neighbouring forest he was to watch the waters of the stream, and when he beheld them turning white he was to attack Curoi's abode.

Then Blanaid persuaded Curoi to build for himself a fortress upon the summit of the mountain, which should surpass all the kingly forts of Erin, and to disperse his knights and warriors to seek through Ireland for the greatest stones wherewith to build it. The guard being thus removed and Curoi alone and defenceless, Blanaid brought pails of milk and emptied them into the stream. Cuchullin seeing the waters whitened rushed upon Curoi and slew him. Cuchullin returned to Ulster with Blanaid, but the death of Curoi was soon avenged. His bard Ferkertni pursued them to the north and found her on the promontory of Kenn Barra with Conor Mac Nessa and Cuchullin and a great company around them. But the bard seeing Blanaid approach the edge of the cliff came up behind, and twining his arms around her sprang with her locked in his fatal embrace into the wild sea beneath.

All evidence now tends to prove that the dawn of letters in Ireland began between the third and fourth century of the Christian era; and Oghamic writing, the origin of which is still hidden in darkness, seems to have preceded the introduction of Roman letters, while the language of such inscriptions is known to be a very early form of Irish. On the covering stone of an ancient cromlech which still stands on the side of a mountain in Kerry, crowned by the fort of Curoi

---

[1] This stream rises close beneath the wall of the fort, the ruins of which may still be seen.

alluded to in the above legend, an Ogham inscription has been discovered, with its correlative in the debased Latin character of the early Christian period. The Ogham inscription, which has been translated CONNAIT, SON OF CUROI, conveys the name of the hero who lies buried below. While the Latin, FECIT CONURI, tells that the grave was erected by his father, Curoi.[1]

A similar monument has been discovered connected with the memory of Queen Maeve. At Rathcroghan in Roscommon, where her palace is said to have stood, there is an old pagan cemetery, and a remarkable cave, which is called traditionally Queen Maeve's Treasury. The materials for the artificial portion, or ante-grotto, of this cave, appear to have been taken from the adjoining burial-ground, two of the roofing-stones bearing Ogham inscriptions, which must have been sculptured before the stones were built into their places. On one of these, we learn from Mr. Ferguson, the name Maev, in an ancient spelling (Medf), certainly exists.[2] In such cases as this we seem to find a link connecting the fort and the cromlech and the Ogham inscription with the culminating period of heroic legend in Ireland, and all three with the dawn of letters and of art. The works in gold and bronze which have been from time to time discovered in Ireland, all witness to like conditions as are indicated in these bardic legends. A certain splendour in dress and armour giving evidence of skill in various arts, many examples of which are characterized by the sense of beauty exhibited in the delicacy and grace of the ornamental design with which these objects are covered.

It may be claimed for these legends that there is some amount of actual knowledge incidentally conveyed in them bearing on early conditions of society. Mr. Ferguson, referring to the Knights of the Red Branch, who surrounded the throne of Conor, has shown that we find in this order of knighthood a companionship forming part of the old social economy of the kings of Ulster—an association much of the same nature as the warrior fraternities which existed among the Celtic and Germanic tribes in other countries; and in the tales of these knights and their adventures, such as the single combat between Cuchullin and his loved friend Ferdiah, we find ample signs of a quite mediæval spirit of chivalry; while the pictures of the gallant boy hero

---

[1] See Proceedings of the Royal Irish Academy, vol. i., ser. ii., p. 52, a letter on this subject by the Rev. Ch. Graves, D.D., Bishop of Limerick, also Christian Inscriptions of Ireland, G. Petrie, vol. ii. p. 3.

[2] Congal, p. 212, note 54; also a paper by Mr. Ferguson on this Ogham in the Proceedings of the Royal Irish Academy, vol. ix. p. 161.

Setanta[1] recall the stories of the youthful Cid. As regards, too, the pagan remains of Ireland, they are endowed with a gradually increasing and a deeper interest as link after link comes to light, serving to connect them not only with such legends, but "with a period of critical transition and the dawning of the religion of peace upon a race, barbaric it may be, but far indeed from savage."[2] In the bardic legends of the heroes who surrounded the thrones of Conor Mac Nessa and of Ailill and Maeve, the first chords are struck which announce the advent of Christianity. King Conor, amazed by the darkness which covered all the earth at the hour of the Crucifixion, inquires from the Druids for the cause; they reply that Jesus Christ, the Son of the living God, was at that moment suffering at the hands of the Jews. "What crime has he committed?" said Conor. "None," replied they. "Then they are slaying him, being innocent?" "It is so," said the Druids. Thereupon Conor, bursting into uncontrollable fury, drew his sword, and rushing into the neighbouring forest began to hew and hack the trees, crying aloud: "Beautiful the combat that I would wage for Christ, who is being defiled! I would not rest though my body of clay had been tormented by them. It crushes my heart to hear the voice of wailing from my God, and that this arm does not come with true relief to arrest the sorrow of death." Then was his frenzy so great that a ball, once flung from a sling and long embedded in his skull, burst forth, and he fell dead upon the spot.

It does not seem too much to hope that the study of such records, both legendary and monumental, may help us to solve those problems which are at the root of all history. "The first question," says Dr. Arnold, "in the history of every people is, What was their race and language? the next, What was the earliest form of their society, their social and political organization?"[3] In seeking to arrive at a true estimate of the rise and progress of Christian architecture in Western Europe, it is in the first place essential that we should search out and discover the nature of the original soil on which it was planted, and what the estate of these races when the new faith penetrated to their shores—how far beyond the mere animal condition of a sunken and degraded savage was the noble barbarism of these early people, beholding,

---

[1] See Congal, a poem by S. Ferguson, page 224. Setanta was the original name of the hero Cuchullin.
[2] Aubrey de Vere, Legends of St. Patrick. Pref. p. xi.
[3] Arnold, Hist. of Rome, vol. i. p. 20.

> "The race, in feud of clan with clan,
> Barbaric—gracious else and high of heart,
> Nor worshippers of self, nor dulled through sins."[1]

The early legends go on to show how the bards, always gifted with prophetic power, foretell the advent of Christianity to Ireland. It is revealed to Ossian in a vision that his soul must tarry in the flesh for 300 years, until the messenger of Christ shall come. The Druids Locree and Luchat prophecy the coming of a missionary across the sea with new rites and doctrine, who will overthrow their ancient gods. King Cormac, dying three hundred years before the coming of Patrick, refuses heathen burial,

> "Spread not the beds of Brugh for me
> When restless death-bed's use is done,
> But bury me at Rossnaree,
> And face me to the rising sun.
>
> For all the kings who lie in Brugh
> Put trust in gods of wood and stone;
> And 'twas at Ross that first I knew
> One, Unseen, who is God alone.
>
> His glory lightens from the east,
> His message soon shall reach our shore,
> And idol god and cursing priest
> Shall plague us from Moy Slaught no more."[2]

The seven centuries that elapsed between the mission of St. Patrick and the English invasion under Strongbow form the epoch within which any historical account of the native art of Ireland must be confined. The ecclesiastical remains of this time are so numerous that their sequence can be traced from the primitive cell of the early founders of Christianity to the exquisite chapel of King Cormac on the Rock of Cashel, and the contemplation of the various signs of development in the rise and progress of this art may lead us to those points in its history at which cement was first used, or the lofty ecclesiastical towers of Ireland were erected, and when the knowledge of the true arch was introduced.

The cashels, or ecclesiastical forts as they may be termed, of Ireland are connected by tradition with the introduction of Christianity, which the legends of Ireland thus place between 200 and 300 years after the culminating point of the heroic period. However, the first

---

[1] Aubrey de Vere, Legends of St. Patrick, p. 9.
[2] Lays of the Western Gael, S. Ferguson, p. 55.

Christian monuments, by their exact similarity to the pagan, tend to prove either that this heroic period has been antedated, or that the interval between the first and fourth century of the Christian era was one of comparative stagnation; or, thirdly—and, indeed, this may be the truest hypothesis of all—it may teach us by what slow and gradual evolution change was wrought in the first stages of human progress.

Many traditions exist which imply that St. Patrick was not the first missionary who visited Ireland. The earliest place of Christian worship here would seem to have been the subterranean cave, such as that the existence of which was revealed to the saint when his servant, Ailill, required of him sacred vessels for the service of his church; then, "the holy prelate, divinely instructed, pointed out to the presbyter, in a certain stone cave of wonderful workmanship, an altar under ground, having on its four corners four chalices of glass." This altar must have been the remains of the devotion of one of those ancient and isolated congregations of Christian worshippers, which the Apostle was to gather into regularly organized congregations.[1] Then we see that the body that really formed the nucleus of the Church of Ireland was contained in the little ship, said to have found its way from Gaul, which first touched the sands of Inver Dea, and then sailed northwards, past the swelling outlines of the purple hills of Wicklow, and beneath the wild cliffs of Howth, to the little island that still bears the Apostle's name. The church which was to prove to North-Western Europe (like Lerins in the South), the central school of the monastic system, is next seen within the Barn of Dichu.[2]

> "There, garnered, lay
> Much grain, and sun-imbrowned; and Patrick said,
> 'King Dichu, Give thou to the poor that grain,
> To Christ, our Lord, thy barn.'"[3]

And, lastly, the four great stone fortresses, that of the old Belgic hero Muirbhech Mil in Aranmór, the Dún of Lugaidh, that of the chieftain Conall, and the palace of the kings of Ulster, were, on the conversion of the native chieftains, given over to Christian uses, and the saint with his little community of monks erected their cells and oratory within the shelter of their walls.

These ecclesiastics who founded the Irish Church present themselves to our mind under three different aspects—as teachers, mariners,

---

[1] Todd, St. Patrick, pp. 222, 226.
[2] Saul in the county of Down. See Reeves, Ecclesiastical Antiquities, pp. 40, 220.
[3] Aubrey de Vere, p. 31.

and anchorites: 1st, Heads of the great schools which were frequented by crowds of students from Britain and the Continent. 2nd, Toilers by sea and land,[1] the labours of navigation or agriculture occupied a large portion of their lives; and, lastly, as Hermits they stand prominently forth among the most striking figures of the time.

> "Raise thine eyes to yonder mountain head
> That 'twixt us and the eastern sky uplifts its glittering cone;
> There, where thou seest the cairn at top, dwelt in his cave of stone
> Their hermit Domangart, ten years; the tempests from the sea
> On one side dashed him, and on one the wet west blanched him."[2]

We have already suggested that these desert hermitages were most often places of retreat for a certain period of time; thus, in this instance, Domangart's period of seclusion lasts ten years; the hermit at the summit of Slieve League in Donegal is said to have remained there for seven years; and Adamnan relates that when Libranus Arundineti confessed his great sin to Columba and sought from him a way of expiation, the latter answered him thus: "You must do penance for seven years in Tiree; you and I, with God's blessing, shall survive that period;" and he adds: "After the end of seven years, as I said, you will come to me during the Lent, and you will approach the altar and partake of the Eucharist on the great Easter festival."[3]

---

[1] Three kinds of boat appear to have been used by these sailor monks:—canoes, probably made by hollowing trees, such as have been found in bogs and the bottoms of lakes; currachs, made of skins stretched over a wicker framework; and small sailing vessels, thus described by Adamnan: "The sailors having raised the sail yards in the form of a cross, and having spread the sails upon them, we put to sea." Twelve such vessels, he states, were employed to convey oak trees by sea from the mainland, which were necessary for the repair of the monastery on Iona. See Reeves' Adamnan, lib. ii. cap. 45, p. 176.

[2] Congal, a poem by S. Ferguson, p. 7. Bishop Cedd, A.D. 659, complying with the desire of King Ethelwald that he should build a monastery within his territory, chose himself a place "among craggy and distant mountains, which looked more like lurking places for robbers and retreats for wild beasts than habitations for men, to the end that, according to the prophecy of Isaiah, 'In the habitations where before dragons dwelt might be grass with reeds and rushes.'"

[3] See Reeves' Adamnan, lib. ii. cap. 39, pp. 157, 158. "Cui sanctus, Surge, ait, et reside. Tum deinde residentem sic compellat, Septennem debebis in Ethica pœnitentiam explere terra. Ego et tu usquequo numerum expleas septennalium annorum, Deo donante, victuri sumus. . . . . Iisdemque diebus ad monasterium Campi missus Lunge, ibidem plene expletis in pœnitentia septem annis, ad Sanctum, diebus quadragesimæ juxta ejus priorem propheticam jussionem, revertitur." Campus Lunge was a penitential station in the island of Tiree, where a small chapel stood, and the place is now marked by a very ancient cross and some curious sepulchral slabs. See page 59, ibid.

When contemplating the monastic cells upon these islands, the impression conveyed to many minds that they were once tenanted by some mournful hermit, some Irish Christian fakir, whose whole existence was passed in fanatic absorption of mind and physical inertness, seems to be entirely false. These buildings, rude yet permanent as the rocks on which they stand, were inhabited by men whose character is sufficiently striking to give them an interest in our eyes. With all capacities of love and gentleness, they are but wild and rugged seamen—courageous, ardent, vindictive, and passionately devoted to adventure and travel—yet, when in exile, "with heart untravelled," their love of home is never seen to die. Columba and Brendan stand prominently forth, the first among these original and pathetic forms of men who gave their lives for an ideal cause. Much may be learnt of the capacity for resolute devotion which lies in man as the eye follows their little ships, or still smaller canoes, specks on the wild waste of waters, in which they bore the sacred seed to Iceland and the Faroe Islands, and even, as is believed by Dahlmann, to the coast of America itself.[1]

The first missionaries in Ireland seem to have aimed at conciliating pagan superstition, and they endeavoured to engraft their own faith upon the ancient objects of heathen veneration, dedicating to a saint the pillar stone, or sacred fountain, and claiming for their own sacred books and reliquaries the same virtues which the Druids, by their incantations, pretended to give to rings and stones and talismans.[2] In like manner the bardic order, as we learn from Dr. Todd, was not regarded as essentially hostile to Christianity. The bards on their side appear to have inherited many of the offices and to have assumed several of the pretended powers of the ancient pagan Druids. Dubhtach, chief bard of Ireland, was one of the first of the converts to Christianity, and Benen, Fiacc, and even Columba himself are the authors of bardic compositions.

Such engrafting and interweaving of one system of religion upon another, of which we have so many examples in the early growth of Christianity in Italy, bears fruit of deep and solemn interest when

---

[1] "The accurate, learned, and unwearied Dahlmann," as he is called by Thomas Carlyle. See J. G. Dahlmann, Geschichte von Dännemark, 3 vols. 8vo. Hamburg, 1840-3. See also Carlyle's Early Kings of Norway, pp. 2, 54, where these passages occur: "White Man's Land, called also *Great Ireland*, is supposed to mean the two Carolinas, down to the Southern Cape of Florida. In Dahlmann's opinion, the Irish themselves might even pretend to have probably been the first discoverers of America; they had evidently got to Iceland itself before the Norse exiles found it out."

[2] Todd, Life of St. Patrick, p. 127.

symbolized in the art and architecture which belong to the same period. It now remains for us to establish by a close examination of these ruins, that a corresponding link between pagan and Christian forms of building is to be found in the early monuments of Ireland.

Our inquiry commences with that long line of forts which guards our western shores.[1] There are many points about these remains which should make us hesitate to associate them with the very first races who peopled these islands. They could scarcely have been the work of a nomadic tribe; their builders must have meant them to endure for generations to come. Earlier races have left us their mighty pyramids, but they were for the dead; these are places of shelter and defence for the living. Rude as they are, they still seem many degrees in advance of what we have learned of the first efforts of man either for habitation or defence. The earliest defensive works appear to have been mere banks of earth and stone, enclosing a certain space for the acommodation of the tribe and of their cattle. M. Viollet-le-Duc[2] has shown that the primitive rampart in Gaul consisted of coarse gravel mixed with earth, bonded together with trunks of trees raised in layers to a height of five feet and surrounding an area of 200 feet in diameter, while access was gained to the top by an inclined plane and the entrances were mere notches in the embankment. In districts where wood and earth are scarce, it is, of course, natural that stone should be the material selected, but stone embankments may be thrown up with little evidence of the forethought, systematic labour, and constructive skill that are clearly discoverable in these great Irish forts. For a period so rude and primitive as that of the Pagan Gaels, when cemented and tool-dressed masonry was unknown, the construction of these walls is marvellously fine. Without mortar of any kind, they are raised in such compact and close-fitting masses that they have been enabled to endure the wind and rain of many centuries. Built of stones varying in size according to the districts in which they are found,[3] each wall consists of a central

---

[1] See Notes on Irish Architecture, Plates I. to XV. vol. i. Lord Dunraven examined twenty-four such forts on the west coast of Ireland, seven of which were in the Islands of Aran. They are almost always placed in isolated and commanding situations. The writer refrains from offering any further opinion as to the date of such buildings. All that can be done as yet is, by following various lines of investigation, to diminish the wide area of time over which they have been spread by drawing them within a gradually narrowing space.

[2] Annals of a Fortress, p. 13.

[3] These stones are often of great size, from 5 ft. 7 in. long by 3 ft. deep, to 9 ft. long by 3 ft. deep.

core of rough rubble, faced on both sides by stones, carefully chosen and laid so as to produce an even surface. Three such structures, thus composed of a rubble centre and faced in dry walling, form a triple compact mass, usually 18 ft. in thickness and 20 ft. in height. In many cases vertical jointings are observable in these walls,[1] a circumstance that suggests the idea of the work having been portioned out in lots to the labourers. It seems as if the wall had been built in short lengths, each completed independently of the other, and such a method would resemble that which the French term building in "parcs." We observe that in some very few instances, such as the Dubh Cathair,[2] Kilfenora, Cahir Dún Fergus, and the Cashel Bán, the masonry betrays haste and comparative want of care, but in other cases great attention has been paid to the construction. The stones which are fixed as headers are tilted downwards towards the face of the wall, a device adopted to keep the water out of the joints by letting the moisture drain off the surface, such as is seen in mason's work in the North of England. Mr. Wilkinson, who has paid great attention to our early architecture, is of opinion that the large blocks were quarried, and that tools[3] were employed in that process; but however this may be, it is certain that no marks of masons' implements have been detected upon the stones in position; nothing like the rude mortice and tenon joints in the Stonehenge trilithons.

The existence of regularly formed doorways, such as that of Staigue Fort or Dún Aengus, at once stamps these buildings with an architectural character, and seems to point, however faintly, to the germ of that intelligence which afterwards bore fruit in the finely proportioned portals of Banagher and Maghera. "The evidence of regular design at once raises these forts to the rank of 'buildings,' and places them far above the ordinary camps and strongholds of the Britons,"[4] the entrances to which are but gaps in the bank. In these

---

[1] See Notes on Irish Architecture, vol. i. Plates IV. and XIII.

[2] *Op. cit.*, Plate VI.

[3] This is the opinion of the author of a short but practical and sensible essay on the Ancient Architecture of Ireland, Mr. George Wilkinson, who remarks at p. 59 of his work, "That tools were known and used as far as necessary there can be little doubt, for the raising such a mass of materials required more than a collection of surface stones, and they show every appearance of being quarried or properly broken from larger blocks." M. Viollet-le-Duc considers that the first implements used for quarrying were strong levers of wood hardened by fire, with which the stones partially below the level of the ground were forced up. Such primitive tools must have been superseded by iron when the stones were quarried for these Irish forts.

[4] The editor has to thank Mr. George Clark of Dowlais for most of these observations on the forts of Ireland.

doorways, which are all formed with inclined sides and horizontal lintel, we see, as at Staigue and Dún Aengus, that the weight of the superstructure is thrown off the lintel by means of a still wider stone placed a layer or two above it (fig. 1), and at Dún Aengus a vertical line formed by a projection of the portion of the wall around the doorway seems to have been intended to follow and mark out its outline, as did the architrave in apertures of a later date. These entrances vary in depth from 16 to 27 ft., according to the thickness of the wall, and are roofed by a series of stone slabs from 6 to 8 ft. in length. In some cases a reveal in the centre of the passage shows that it was occasionally furnished with double doors, which were also fastened with bolts, or rather bars of wood, the holes for the reception of which may still be seen. These fastenings are mentioned in the life of St. Columba, where it is said that when he knocked at the gate of King Brude's fortress the doors instantly flew open, the bolts having been driven back suddenly with great force. The door is sometimes approached by a passage between two walls formed of long stones set upright—a feature which is afterwards seen repeated in the entrance to St. Brendan's oratory. Platforms, offsets, or banquettes ran along the inner sides of the walls, to which four, and sometimes even ten, independent flights of steps gave access (figs. 2, 3). Passages and dome-roofed chambers occur in the thickness of the walls, and in the inner area of the fortress little round huts with conical roofs, or long ones of the form of upturned boats, are found constructed in clusters.

The dome formed by the projection of one stone beyond another till the walls meet in one flag at the apex, and the horizontal lintels of the doorways, are forms universally adopted by early races in all periods of the history of man and in various portions of the globe before the knowledge of the principle of the arch had reached them, while the resemblances in masonry which have caused our antiquaries hitherto to style it Cyclopean and Pelasgic appear to arise entirely from the condition of the builder's knowledge and a certain similarity in the geological formation of the country. It is a remarkable fact, that neither in Greece nor in Italy is this so-called Cyclopean or polygonal style of construction ever found except where the hard limestone that forms the framework of both countries supplied the materials close at hand.[1]

---

[1] Among the earliest architectural remains found at Hissarlik by Schliemann, the walls, though of massive construction, so far as their thickness and solidity are concerned, have no resemblance to Cyclopean structures, but are composed of stones of

These stone forts are found on the western shores of the counties of Kerry, Clare, Galway, Sligo, while occasional examples of them also occur in Mayo, Donegal, and Antrim. Eighteen of these monuments have been described and illustrated by Lord Dunraven, nine of which are in the islands of Aran off Galway Bay, and three in Kerry.

---

moderate size, with the interstices filled with clay. This difference may be accounted for by the fact that the soft tertiary limestone of the hill of Hissarlik is totally unsuited to such massive work; and so in Ireland it may be questioned whether the art of stone building in certain districts throughout the country did not occasionally arise from the abundance of stone and scarcity of earth, while in other places, where stones were not available without quarrying, we find earthen forts, raths, and embankments.

CHAPTER II.

Early Christian Monasteries.

And watching, as a patient, sleepless eremite,
The moving waters at their priest-like task
Of pure ablution round earth's human shore.

AT a distance of about twelve miles from the westernmost point of the coast of Kerry, stand the two islands of the Greater and Lesser Skellig. The first of these is a rock dedicated to St. Michael, which, like the spire of some great cathedral, raises its graceful and majestic form, steadfast and unchanging, above the swelling waters of the wide Atlantic ocean. The Church of St. Michael, with its group of monastic cells, is built upon its northern summit, where the rounded form of the hill is tinged with delicate green and roseate colour from the sea plants that grow upon its bosom; while to the south, the bare pointed rock which forms its highest peak, shoots upwards towards the sky. Seen at a distance of some miles from the sea, veiled in summer mist and sunlight, nothing is more lovely than this island; but, as the vessel gradually approaches, the character of the scene is changed, and the cliffs which form its precipitous sides reveal their dark forms, and the great black masses of slate rock grow terrible in their aspect when seen to rise above and overhang the little boat as it approaches the landing-place. This is a narrow cove, where the surrounding cliffs rise vertically to the full height of the island, and at the end of the gully a cave "more black than the blackness" yawns to the wave, which, swelling in slow majestic motion, sinks and engulfs itself within its mouth.[1]

---

[1] Notes on Irish Architecture, vol. i. Plate XVI.

A narrow road, cut on the face of the precipice, and winding in and out, as it follows the outline of the projecting cliffs, ascends gradually to the lower lighthouse. It is defended by a strong parapet wall on the sea side, which, when viewed from a distance, shows like a white waving thread along the dark overhanging rock. About midway it passes along the sides of another chasm, like that at the landing-place, which also ends in a cave, where the wave falls with a deep wild boom. Nothing can be more wonderful than the breaking of the sea upon the cliff as seen from this parapet all along. The clear waters, meeting and commingling, swell and fall far below, and, as they fall, they break into all shades of green, blue, violet and white against the dark grey rock, while, as the wave subsides, its roar is succeeded by the hissing sound of the cataracts of water it has left behind, pouring from the crevices in a thousand streams.

Looking upward and beyond the lower lighthouse, which stands about 140 ft. above the sea, this zigzag road with its whitened parapet may still be seen winding as a white line among the black cliffs overhead. Above, the rock towers higher and higher, and is split into fantastic forms, like the opened leaves of a book set upright, with narrow strips of bright green running between them, or fringing the horizontal blocks of the strata at their feet. When the sunlit mists or vapours sweep in driving clouds above them, the effect is in the highest degree mysterious and beautiful; but, when at one moment these mists rise so as entirely to conceal the heights, and at the next they vanish as if at the touch of some unseen hand, and the cliff again stands revealed against the blue unfathomed sky, it seems as if the whole scene were called up to the eye by some strange magician's wand.

The ancient approach to the monastery from the landing-place was on the north-east side. There are 620 steps from a point of the cliff, which is about 120 ft. above the level of the sea, up to the monastery. The rest of this flight of steps is broken away, and a new approach has been cut by the lighthouse workmen. The old stairs run in a varying line; the steps, which grow broader towards the upper half of the ascent, are lined with tufts and long cushions of the sea-pink, and at each turn the ocean is seen breaking in silver foam hundreds of feet below. The first resting-place is the flagstaff station, from which the descent into the sea is almost perpendicular. It is crowned by an upright rock, which seems to be the last portion of one of those great leaves into which, by its natural cleavage, the rock is separated. It has all the effect of a monument; now like the statue of an archer, and again, when viewed from another point, rising black and rugged somewhat in the form of a rude and time-worn cross.

This island has been the scene of annual pilgrimages for many centuries, and the service of the Way of the Cross is still celebrated here, though with some perfectly traditional forms of prayer and customs, such as are now only found to exist among the islanders along the west coast of Ireland. From the last place mentioned a long flight of steps reaches to " Christ's Saddle," or the Garden of the Passion. Here the pilgrim rests before commencing his final ascent to the Oratory. This valley is a narrow saddle-shaped strip of land between the two extreme heights of the island, either side being perpendicular to the sea. It is covered with a soft green sod. Standing at that side which faces the western horizon, the whole of the great Spit, as the highest point of the island is called, may be seen rising from the sea—a sheer precipice from summit to base. It runs up like a Gothic tower, girt with buttresses and pinnacles, all in a glory of colours. The black rock at its foundation contrasts with the deep blue of the sea, and above it is variegated with tufts of lichen and sea-pink, fern and moss, which, when lit up by the evening sun, shine out in every shade of green. Towards the summit the rock becomes lighter in tone and less thickly clothed with vegetation, until it ends in a sharp point glittering in the sunlight.

Having rested in this valley, the pilgrim, feet and head uncovered, pursues his way upward on the pathway that marks the " Way of the Cross." Turning the corner, he reaches the third station, called " The Stone of Pain," where is commemorated the moment when Christ, bowed under the weight of the cross, sank for the first time to the ground. Here he finds himself on the edge of a precipice many hundred feet above the sea (fig. 8). From the side strange pointed rocks project like the finials of a spire, and, looking downwards, the eye rests on one of these rocks below, which has, first by nature and then by man, been rudely hewn into the form of a cross, which lays its " dark arms" across the sea. This station is named " The Rock of Woman's Wailing," and here it is that the scene in the walk to Calvary is recalled when Christ turns and says, " Daughters of Jerusalem, weep not for me, but weep for yourselves and for your children ; for behold, the days are coming, in the which they shall say, Blessed are the barren, and the wombs that never bare, and the paps which never gave suck. Then shall they begin to say to the mountains, fall on us, and to the hills, cover us."

Looking upwards, the first glimpse of the cashel or enclosing wall of the monastery is seen ; when the wall is reached, the path leads along a level way through the entrance into the Garden of the Monks; then there is a low covered passage, emerging from which and ascending a few more steps, the platform is reached on which stand the ruins of the Church of St. Michael, and the beehive-shaped cells in which the monks dwelt. The scene is one so solemn and so sad that none should enter here but the pilgrim and the penitent. The sense of solitude, the vast heaven above and sublime monotonous motion of the sea beneath, would but oppress the spirit, were not that spirit brought into harmony with all that is most sacred and most grand in nature, by the depth and even by the bitterness of its own experience.

The buildings which form the monastery occupy a plateau near the northern summit of the rock, about 180 ft. in length by from 80 to 100 ft. in width. They consist of the Church of St. Michael, two smaller oratories, and six anchorite cells or dwelling-houses; there are besides two holy wells, five leachta or burial-places, and several rude crosses. This group of buildings was enclosed on one side by the rock against which they were partly built, and on the other by the cashel or enclosing wall which ran along the edge of the precipice. "The masonry of this ancient wall," writes Lord Dunraven,[1] "is beautiful, and worthy of the builders of Staigue Fort, whose work it strongly resembles. There is the same curve or batter in the outline of the wall, the stones are laid as headers, and fixed in horizontal layers, although they follow the batter. It is astonishing to conceive the courage and skill of the builders of this fine wall, placed as it is on the very edge of the precipice, at a vast height above the sea, with no possible standing ground outside the wall from which the builders could have worked; yet the face is as perfect as that of Staigue Fort, the interstices of the greater stones filled in with smaller ones, all fitted as compactly and with as marvellous firmness and skill. There are projecting stones placed at intervals in the face of this wall, and it has been suggested that they may have been used by the builders to stand on, but it is difficult to conceive men working in such a position at a height of 700 or 800 ft. above the sea. They may, however, have supported a rude scaffolding.

The resemblance between the pagan and ecclesiastical fort is so strong and so significant of the same primitive condition of knowledge in the builders, that some comparative study of both monuments is required before we discover those points of difference which should prevent us from falling into the error of supposing that all the monastic forts were originally pagan and afterwards converted to Christian uses. This was the case doubtless, in some instances, as at Kilbannon

---

[1] Notes on Irish Architecture, vol. i. p. 30.

and Kilmurvey,[1] but in others the monuments themselves bear witness to a difference in original intention and design. In the first place, the pagan fortress is composed of two and sometimes three areas or wards, the interior, or fort proper, being either an oval, a circle, or half an ellipse, but with no sign of variation in the ground-plan which would suggest that it was meant to enclose structures already in existence; whereas the Christian fort deviates from the regular oval or circular form so as to take in the oratories and other buildings it is meant to protect. Again, while the inner area of the military fort varies in extent from 227 ft. to 60 ft., that of the cashels remains about 140 ft. in diameter, being in accordance with the measurement said in the old legends to have been adopted by St. Patrick in the monastery built under his direction at Ferta, near Armagh, as well as in other cases.[2] While the masonry of these walls is exactly similar to that of the forts, there are differences in their construction which can only be accounted for by the differing requirements of their builders. The military defences were in general triple, or at least double compacted walls, and it was Lord Dunraven's opinion that this style of building was simply chosen as the easiest method of erecting a wall of very great thickness. The cashels of the monasteries were single walls somewhat less broad and massive, and there appears to have been a corresponding inferiority in their height, which, if we may take that of Inismurray as a standard, did not exceed 13 ft. The inner face of the military wall is furnished with platforms and flights of steps by which the defenders could reach the parapet in times of attack; the doorways, though similar in form, are always smaller by about 1 ft. 6 in. each way in the monastic buildings. The outwork, resembling the *chevaux de frise* of a modern fortification, by which the approach to the fort is rendered difficult, has never been observed outside the ecclesiastical cashel. May it not be held that all such differences arise from this, that the original and paramount purpose of one was defence in time of war, and of the other was seclusion?[3]

---

[1] St. Fursey's monastery in Suffolk was built in a *castrum*. See Bede, Ecc. Hist., chap. xix. p. 139, Bohn Ed.

[2] "The way in which Patrick made *Ferta* was this: Seven score feet in the Fort, and seven and twenty feet in the Great House; and 17 feet in the Kitchen, and 7 ft. in the Oratory. And it is thus the houses of the Churches were built always." (Todd, St. Patrick, Apostle of Ireland, p. 477.)

[3] The erection of the cashel of St. Cuthbert on the island of Lindisfarne is thus described by Bede. "He had there, after expelling the enemies, with the assistance of the brethren, built himself a small dwelling, with a trench about it, and the necessary

All peculiarities of masonry that are observable in these buildings of the pagan period are also found to exist in the cashels and cells of the Christian monasteries, but the latter in their turn exhibit certain changes indicative of advance ; the stones of which they are formed are sometimes rounded by tools, the oratory is always rectangular and an east window is introduced, while the symbol of the cross impresses the buildings with an ecclesiastical character. The east window is extremely rude, either square or round-headed ; if the latter, the arch is merely scooped out of a single stone. There is always a broad internal splay and the aperture is generally on the face of the outside wall, but in some instances the window is set in the thickness of the walls and expands both outside and inside.

It is not easy to determine how such windows were closed ; we learn from Bede (Vit. Cuth. ch. xlvi.) that they were in some instances filled with straw, and in others that skins were nailed against them. Eadbert of Lindisfarne is said to have covered them entirely with lead (Id. liii. ch. 25).

The oratories that are found in the group of monastic buildings within these enclosures, nine of which were examined and illustrated by Lord Dunraven, seem to form a link between the round beehive-shaped cell common to both pagan and Christian forts, and such more finished buildings as that of Gallarus. The roof is in the form of an upturned boat.[1] They are angular, oblong structures, with walls either sloping in a curve towards the roof or built in steps, as that on the Magharees (fig. 9) and Bishop's Island. It may be a question worthy the consideration of authors more competent to deal with these subjects than the writer, how far in these rude oratories we may trace the germs of what in after times were developed into marked features in the churches of a more advanced style. Is it possible that the plinth, from which both tower and church are seen to rise, may have originated in the retention of this first step which forms the wide foundation of the rude oratory ; also that the projections, evidently intended for shelter to the doors, formed by two rows of upright stones, may have given rise to the deep pilasters at the corners which serve as shelter

---

cells, and an oratory. . . . when he had here served God in solitude many years, the mound which encompassed his habitation being so high that he could from thence see nothing but heaven, to which he so ardently aspired." Bede, Eccl. Hist., chap. xxviii. p. 227, Bohn Ed. "It was built of sods and stones so large that five men could hardly lift them, and was nearly round, being four or five perches in diameter, and the wall inside was higher than outside." Bede, Vita S. Cuthberti, cap. 19, sec. 30.

[1] Ceterum adhuc ædificia Numidarum agrestium, quæ mapalia illi vocant, oblonga, *incurvis lateribus tecta, quasi navium carinæ sunt.* Sallustius, Bell. Jugurth.

to the east and west walls? May not the projecting stones seen in the corners and the roofs of the monastic cells, which some have thought to represent the handles of the ark, have been originally meant as

PILASTER.

supports for scaffolding or pegs by means of which a covering of sods or thatch was tied down on the roof, and afterwards retained as ornamental features like gargoyles at the corners of the buildings?

There is, however, one especial feature in many of these oratories and cells for which no mechanical or utilitarian object can be suggested, which nevertheless at once conveys their story and marks the dawn of Christian decorative art. Over the doorway five or seven quartz stones, rounded and waterworn, whose whiteness tells in strong contrast to the dark slate of which the walls are often built, are set in the form of a cross (fig. 10). There is a deep interest in the picture this calls up to the mind, of the early church-builder going down to search on the wild Atlantic shore for these large white stones, and carrying them up, one by one, to set them in his wall, so as in this utterly simple way to stamp his dwelling with the symbol of his faith.

The belief that the early churches of Ireland were generally of wood is much shaken by the evidence of the monuments themselves as well as by the testimony of the oldest Irish writers. The Virgin Crumtheris[1] is described as living in a stone-built oratory near Armagh in the fifth century, and we find stone buildings mentioned as erected in parts of the country where wood must have been quite as easily attainable as stone, if not more so—for instance, in the Martyrology of Donegal (p. 95) St. Becan is described as building a cashel at

---

[1] See Colgan, Trias Thaum., p. 163. Annals of Ulster, A.D. 788. O'Conor, Rer. Hib. Script., tom. iv. p. 113. Petrie, Eccl. Arch., p. 347.

Emlagh in East Meath (Imlech-Fiach in Fera-cul-Breagh), for which stone was evidently the material chosen. The story is as follows:—

"When Columcille and the king of Erinn, Diarmait, son of Fergus, ... came to where Becan was, they found him erecting a fort and a wet cloak about him, and he praying. Concerning which is said:—

> "Making a wall, praying,
> Kneeling, pure prayer,
> His tears flowing without unwillingness,
> Were the virtues of Becan without fault.
>
> "Hand on a stone, hand lifted up,
> Knee bent to set a rock,
> Eyes shedding tears, other lamentation,
> And mouth praying."

It is true that in the description given in the Annals of the Four Masters of the destruction of the church of Armagh by the Norsemen in the year 890, the following lines occur:—

> "Pity, O, Patrick, that thy prayers did not stay
> The foreigners with their axes when striking thy oratory."

And "the allusion here," as Dr. O'Donovan observes,[1] "to the axes might suggest that the oratory at Armagh was of wood, unless it be

DOORWAY OF ST. FINAN'S ORATORY.

understood that the axes were used to break open the door." In like manner the numerous instances recorded of the burning of the churches by the Norsemen have been taken as proof that these buildings were altogether composed of an inflammable material, although we know that the Cloicctech or belfry, which was always

---

[1] Annals of the Four Masters, vol. i. p. 546, note b.

of stone, is also frequently described as "burnt" by the same marauders. All that is necessarily meant to be conveyed in such passages is that whatever was combustible in these buildings, such as the floors, roofs, etc., was burnt, just as in the present day we speak of houses as liable to be burnt, the walls of which are of stone or brick.

It may be suggested also that those passages so often quoted from Bede and William of Malmesbury, in which it is said that most of the oratories of the Scotic saints were formed of wattles of wood and clay, may be merely applicable to the erections of the first Irish teachers in Scotland and the north of England. Their buildings, like the tent of the nomad, or the temporary shed of the foreign missionary at the present day, might naturally have been of some less permanent material than they would use for that church in their native land, near which they might hope to spend their life and await their death. However this may be, we have, at all events, sufficient evidence that, even in the very earliest time, wood was not the only material employed.

The most interesting point about these oratories is their form. It is found that they were invariably small and angular, and this plan, which was very generally adopted both in England and Scotland, was followed as a rule in the Irish Church so long as its architecture preserved a native character. When Christianity spread, and larger churches were built and a chancel was added to the building, the square end was always retained. It is possible that at the time immediately preceding the introduction of Christianity into Ireland this simple form may have been in use elsewhere for Christian churches. Three churches on the Continent are described as showing examples of this type: the Churches of Sitten in Switzerland and San Giovanni e Paolo at Ravenna, have square east ends instead of apses, and the Chapel of Mouxi in the south of the Duchy of Chablais is described by Kugler as a simple oblong containing a later, but also oblong, altar compartment.[1] The Roman type, so far as we are familiar with it, does not agree with that found in Ireland, it is cha-

---

[1] The two buildings first mentioned have high and slender towers, one square, the other round and detached, like so many of our Irish round towers, and in the third the west doorway has a horizontal lintel surmounted by a round arch. The cruciform shape which has since been usually given to churches in England was seldom adopted even there till after the tenth century. The first instance of the kind is generally supposed to have been the church at Ramsay, built in 969 (Gale, Hist. Ram., c. 20). In an ancient Anglo-Saxon poem (Ethelwulf de Abbat. Lindis., c. 22), mention is made of a church built in the shape of a cross. In general, however, the Anglo-Saxon churches approached the form of a square (Ibid. c. 20. Bede, l. ii. 14). A square-ended chancel may be seen at Headbourn Worthy Church, near Winchester.

racterized—not by its square end, but by its rounded apse at the east end. However, the adoption of this basilican form dates not from the period when Christianity was first introduced into Rome, but from the time when it was adopted by the emperors, and when the basilica was converted into a Christian temple. May it not then be supposed that in the centuries before this there was a type, now lost in Italy, but which reached these islands in the fourth and fifth centuries? This is suggested by Mr. Freeman in a letter to Lord Dunraven, where he says, speaking of these angular oratories, that they possibly "represented the earliest churches of all before the basilicas were christianized, and therefore before the apsidal form was introduced."

If we contemplate the condition of the Church at the period in which Christianity first penetrated into Ireland, it seems possible that we may find a clue to the origin of this angular and narrow type. The first meeting-houses of the early Christians were the "large upper room" and the subterranean vaults of the catacombs. The memory—not of the gorgeous basilica of the church of the emperors,—but of such modest chambers, was the tradition borne to Ireland by the first missionaries from the Continent.

In the representation of the Temple of Jerusalem as it was conceived by the Scribe of the Book of Kells in the seventh century we have doubtless a faithful image of this early type as it appeared externally—an oblong, rectangular building with a high-pitched roof and finials on the gables such as still are found in parts of Ireland near the buildings from the roofs of which they have fallen. It is the old traditional form of the Ark—that building in which the Church was rescued from the Flood—of the shrine in early Christian art, in which were entombed the relics of some form that "once had been the Temple of the Spirit," and it is the form of the Tomb and mortuary chapel which was preserved in Ireland even after the establishment of Romanesque architecture.[1]

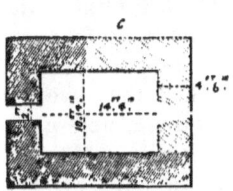

GROUND PLAN OF TEMPUL GEL.

The association of the church and the shrine with the tomb in

---

[1] It may be here noted that in such places as Clonmacnois, most of the small churches grouped together within the cemetery were mortuary chapels, such as Temple Kelly, Temple McLaughin, and others belonging to the kings of Hy Many, Moylurg, and North and South Munster, etc. The circular churches of Romanesque architecture are, according to Mr. Fergusson, derived from the Roman tomb, such as that of Cecilia Metella or Helena; and besides the circular type, there was another class of tombs in Rome, or columbaria, generally oblong or square rooms. Hist. of Architecture, vol. i. pp. 319, 381.

the minds of these early Christians is not to be held as indicative of gloom in their forms and mode of worship; on the contrary, it is rather the result of that happier condition of mind which led them when speaking of the grave to term it "the place of resurrection;" the gloom of the tomb is dispelled. These things are illustrated in various passages in the lives of the early saints connected with the founding of churches. They sought the knowledge of the place in which they should be buried from some holy man gifted with the spirit of prophecy, that in that spot they might erect their church and cells. Thus in the life of St. Moedoc we read: "Another day some good men prayed God to show them the place of their resurrection, wishing to serve God near it. Then the Angel of the Lord said unto them, 'Go ye to St. Moedoc, and he will show unto you the place of your resurrection.' When they had come to him the Saint said unto them, 'Did ye hear the voice of a bell when ye were coming hither?' They answered, 'We did not hear it.' The Saint said unto them, 'Come with me, and I will show you the place in which ye shall rise again.' They went together, and the Saint of God showed unto them the place of their resurrection, and there those wonder-working men remained during their life and till their death."

This rectangular type is, as we have already remarked, found in all the oratories of the first monasteries, and there seems no reason to doubt that they belonged to a period ranging from the fifth to the seventh century and are the very buildings erected by those founders with whose names they are connected, such as Mochua, Brendan, Finan, Senan, Fechin, and others. The dates at which they lived or died, as given either by the annalists or martyrologists, enable us to form an approximate idea of the age of these monasteries. Mochua, founder of Nendrum, is said to have died in 497; Brendan of Inisglora, died 577. Finan of Lough Curraun, who is said also to have founded the Church of St. Michael on the Skellig, lived at the close of the sixth century; Muredach, from whom the island of Inis-murray (Inis Muiredach) is held to have been named, was a contemporary of St. Patrick; and Molaise, after whom the present church is called, died in the year 560; while Fechin of High Island, and Molaga of Leaba Molaga, died in 665. A comparison between the buildings of Brendan (fig. 12) and Finan and those of Fechin and Molaga bears testimony to the slow and gradual improvement which was taking place from the sixth to the seventh century.[1] The stones in the latter instances are sometimes cut, and the cross or a rude architrave is seen carved on the doorways, and cement is first introduced in a very sparing

---

[1] See Notes on Irish Architecture, vol. i. Plates XXIII. XXX. XXXV.

manner. That these monasteries and cells remained in use to a comparatively late period, seems also certain from the notices in the Annals of the Abbots in the monasteries on the Skellig and the island of Inis-murray, which occur as late as the ninth and eleventh centuries. In Scotland such island hermitages were in use at a still later period, and a tradition is recorded in the "Scoti Chronicon" (lib. v. cap. 37) that in the year 1123 Alexander I. lived three days on the island of Inchcolm, where he was driven by a storm and " where at that time lived an islander hermit who, belonging to the service of St. Columba, devoted himself sedulously to his duties at a certain little chapel, there content with such poor food as the milk of one cow and the shell and small sea fishes which he could collect."

CHAPTER III.

STONE CHURCHES WITH CEMENT.

HE tendency of writers on the History and Antiquities of Ireland to exaggerate the age of her monuments and to antedate the period of her intellectual growth by attributing to the sixth century what really belongs to the ninth and tenth, has led to much misapprehension as to the causes of her rise and fall. Nothing can exceed the rudeness of those relics of the early Christian teachers that have been preserved for us through the care of their relic-loving successors in the eleventh and twelfth centuries. We read of bells, but we find them to have been as inferior to the bronze bell of the tenth century as the uncemented stone oratory is to the Romanesque church of the twelfth, for the actual seventh century bell remains to speak for itself within the shrine that was made to preserve it some centuries later; and we read of crosiers, but find them to have been the oaken staff of the itinerant bishop which is still visible through the chinks and openings of the metal case in which it was afterwards enshrined. But, perhaps, nothing helps the mind more vividly to realize the simple practices of these early Christians than the sight and touch of the rude stone chalices, such as have been preserved to the present date in a few of our most remote churches. We are rather led to conclude that the period between the sixth and ninth centuries in Ireland was one of steady progress both politically and intellectually from a very rude beginning. Her borders were enlarged by the colonization of a great portion of the south of Scotland[1]

---

[1] Fergus, son of Erc, lord of Dalriada, sailed from Ulster into Scotland, and in A.D. 503 founded a Dalriadan kingdom there. He also visited Man and the Hebrides, and about A.D. 580, Baeden, king of Uladh (or Ulidia) cleared Man of the foreigners, and received tribute from Munster, Connaught, Skye, and Man. From this time it is said that the island belonged to Ulster. Ogygia, pp. 323, 466; Ussher, Brit. Eccl. Antiq. vols. v. and vi. Reeves's Adamnan, pp. 433, 437.

and the conquest of the Isle of Man,[1] and her sphere of intellectual and moral usefulness was extended to Germany, Flanders, Switzerland, and Gaul, while her missionaries first bore the Christian religion to the heathens of Northumbria, Scotland, Iceland, and the Faroe Islands. It would be well if we could learn more of the life at the centre of that star that sent its rays so far. It was about the beginning of the sixth century that a colony of the Irish, then termed Scoti, part possessors of Dalriada, or the northern half of the county of Antrim, passed over to the nearest part of Argyleshire, where they permanently settled, and founded the kingdom of British Scotia or Dalriada, Cantyre, and Knapdale, being the first lands thus colonized. It was not till nearly a century had elapsed that the Dalriadan rulers exchanged the rank of lord for that of king; and in the ninth century the final conquest of the south of Scotland was effected by the Irish. In the year 590 a council was convened at Drumcheatt (Drumkeat), on the river Roe, in Londonderry, which was attended by Columba—where Aedan, lord of the British Dalriadans, obtained a formal recognition of his independence, and was proclaimed king. It was at this council also that the alliance of the regal and ecclesiastical power of Ireland was first cemented. This event was followed by the battle of Moyra, which proved the expiring effort of the Pagan and Bardic party in Ireland against the newly consolidated power of Church and Crown.[2]

---

[1] While the Romans were in Britain Man was an Irish island, and it will be seen that a connection long existed between them. See Rolt's Hist. of the Isle of Man, p. 3, Lond. 1773.

[2] The most ancient, as well as one of the most interesting monuments of Celtic literature, called St. Patrick's Hymn to the Holy Trinity, is certainly prior to the sixth century; the hymn of Broccán and Ultán may be attributed respectively to the middle of the seventh century; but the actual remains of this early date are excessively few. Columbanus, born at this period, was the author of an Exposition of the Psalms; Epistles to Pope Gregory the Great and Boniface the IVth on the Eastern question; a Treatise against Arianism, along with many other treatises, as well as being the founder of a monastic rule, described by Ussher as equal in importance to the Benedictine. It is not till we approach the end of the eighth and the beginning of the ninth century that we have existing proofs in any number of the intellectual capacity of the Irish at this time, but the very condition of the language in the ninth century points to the pre-existence of intellectual power in its possessors. The most copious specimens of old Irish prose yet discovered are comprised in Tirechan's Annotations, contained in the Book of Armagh, which date from 704, in the handwriting of Ferdomnach, who died in Armagh in the year 844. The St. Gall MSS. Leyden copy of Priscian, written by Dubthach about the year 838, and the Irish glosses in the Berne codici, as well as the Book of Deir, may also be enumerated as belonging to this period. It was about this time that the Culdee order was founded by Aengus, and Johannes Scotus Erigena, and Dicuil the geographer, also lived and wrote. See Letronne, Recherches Geogr. sur Dicuil (par. 1814); Reeves, Adamnan, p. 169, note i.

The next event, and one which marks a third epoch in the history of the Irish Church, which therefore would naturally lead to a fresh development in her church architecture, was that recorded in the reign of Aed Oirnidhe, when the clergy were exempted from attending the chieftains in military expeditions. The influence of this change will be traced in a subsequent chapter, when the church architecture of Ireland showed a clearly defensive or protective character.

The buildings which come next in order of development were probably erected after the Council of Drumcheat, when the Church of Ireland first attained a stable position; and it seems likely that the transition from the dry wall and undressed masonry to the cemented walls and dressed stones of the later buildings, in which picked and chiselled work is visible, took place in the sixth, seventh, and eighth centuries. Chancels, with a regular radiating arch, have been added to many of these buildings afterwards; but where a knowledge of the true arch is manifested, it seems more likely that they belong to the period of the erection of the first detached belfries, that is, as we have already said, to the ninth and tenth centuries. The transition from the false to the true arch seems to be marked by such buildings as the church on Friar's Island, near Killaloe, and St. Columba's house at Kells. In the first, the vault of the chancel is formed of overlapping stones, while the chancel arch is built on the radiating principle; in the second, the vault is formed in the primitive manner, half way up, while towards the top the arch is keyed.[1] The building we hold to have been erected in the year 807. (See Chronicon Scotorum, p. 125.) The annalists record the foundations of great numbers of churches in the sixth and seventh centuries, but we have already seen what was the rude and primitive style of building then in use. They also record the erection of many churches in the eleventh and twelfth centuries, but the existing remains of these buildings prove that an ornate Irish Romanesque was the style then practised. It seems fair to assume that these intermediate buildings belong to an intermediate date, and that the reason why their erection is not noticed by the annalists is that they were not new foundations, but merely rebuildings, on a better principle, of the rude oratory—often, perhaps, of wood—of the first Christian missionary. The house of Columba at Kells and the west end of Tuaim Greine[2] are the first examples for the date of which there is historic evidence. The latter with its belfry was erected by the Bishop of Clonmacnois and Tuaim

---

[1] See Introd. p. 9.   [2] See Notes on Irish Architecture, Plate LXIV. vol. i.

Greine, Cormac Ua Cillen, of whom it is said, "Sapiens et Senex, et Episcopus equievit in Christo, A.D. 964." He also built Temple Cillen at Clonmacnois. In the doorway, with horizontal lintel and inclined sides, in the massive polygonal masonry and square pilasters at the corners, we have the Irish church of the beginning of the tenth century, immediately before the transition to Romanesque, which seems to have begun in the reign of Brian Borumha.

The third period in Irish architecture is marked by the introduction of cement, and embraces those churches in which there are but slight traces of mortar, down to those of a later period in which the stones were regularly bedded in this material. The cement of the earliest builders on the sea-coast often largely contained shells and sea-sand, while inland a compound of mud and gravel was used. In many cases the walls appear to have been first dry-built, and then this composition was poured in a liquid state to filtrate through from the top; later on, the wall was well built with two faces and a rubble core grouted in a similar manner; while in the time of Cormac O'Cillen we have the stones well bedded in good mortar. The archaic and so-called Cyclopean character of this masonry, especially in the limestone districts, is very striking, even though cement be used. The great stones varying from ten and even seventeen feet to eight and six feet in length, are often found dovetailed and fitted into one another, as the great stones above the lion's gate at Mycenæ; and polygonal masonry often appears in company with ashlar, while ashlar is seen occasionally superimposed by rubble and wide-jointed, irregular courses of stone. That masonry so archaic in character should occasionally be seen in company with sectional and surface mouldings as in Temple Martin, Temple Cronan, and St. Dervila's Church,[1] is a phenomenon which could only occur in a country where the chisel had been long in use, and the progress of sculpture, with still ruder tools, from its first beginnings in the works of the primitive tomb builders, had been uninterrupted. The use of the chisel seems to have been introduced into this country, not only before the Anglo-Norman invasion of the twelfth century, but even before the advent of the Christian missionaries of the fifth; and in the sculptured sepulchral slabs, as well as in the terminal crosses of Ireland, there is ample evidence of the gradual development of skill, from the mere shallow surface work of the primitive stone-cutter to the deeper undercutting with chisel and hammer by which groups of small figures or intricate designs are thrown up in relief. That such raised work

---

[1] *Op. cit.*, see vol. i. pp. 105, 106, 108.

is seen on the slabs at Clonmacnois belonging to the dates 887, 899, 914,[1] 994, as well as on the slab of St. Berichtir,[2] who died A.D. 839, and the High Cross of Muredach of Monasterboice, before 923, proves that there was sufficient skill existing in the country at these dates for the execution of any simple work, such as the chevron or pellet mouldings—which whether incised or in relief are in themselves but forms of ornamental design common in all archaic art.

The features which give these churches a distinctive character are the doorways, east window, plinth, pilasters, and corner-stones, and their forms seem all to be developments from the architecture of a primitive period. The doorways with inclined sides and horizontal lintel have grown in height and dignity of proportion, and are decorated with the architrave, sometimes double, but generally single, like that on the doorway of the Treasury of Atreus, or those of the Etruscan tombs. The doors of the little churches on the islands of Inismain (figs. 17 and 20) and MacDara (fig. 16) in the County of Galway, as well as that of Kilfrauchan in the same county, and Kilcrony, in the county of Wicklow, are good examples of the plain, square-headed door, while the architrave is clearly defined in that of Temple Martin, in the county of Kerry (fig. 32). In many instances a reveal on the inside may be seen with stone sockets above or in the lintel, which were appliances for the shutter that served the purpose of a door. The only window in these single-chambered churches was above the altar in the east wall, and this is almost invariably round-headed, the arch being scooped out of the stone while the sides incline, as we see in the churches of MacDara (fig. 14), Kilmore Moy (fig. 21), and Altannin (fig. 27). In some instances, as in the east window of Kill Enda (fig. 15), the south windows of St. Caimin's Church in Inismain, and Trinity Church, Glendalough (figs. 18 and 19), the arch is pointed; formed of two stones, laid in such a manner as to make two sides of an equilateral triangle. The aperture rarely exceeds 9 in., but there is a wide internal splay; punched work is seen on the stones of many of these windows, as at Kill Enda. In the churches of the Four Beauties, Temple Assurnidhe and Kilgobnet, the ancient stone altar is still standing beneath these simple little windows, and garlanded with woodbine, ivy, and the thorny bramble, seems to speak of the sacred customs and symbolic rites of the early builders of these oratories.

---

[1] *Op. cit.*, see Plates LXXI. and XCI.
[2] See Ulster Journal of Arch., paper by Dr. Reeves, vol. vi. pp. 267, 275; Christian Inscriptions of Ireland, vol. ii. p. 54.

The plinth we have already met with in the oratory of Gallarus and in some of the monastic cells. It is a square, plain, projecting face at the bottom of a wall immediately above the ground. In classical buildings the plinth is sometimes divided into two or more steps, and in Gothic buildings it is generally in two stages, the tops of which are either splayed or finished with a moulding. The next feature appears to be more common, and bears a rude similarity to a pilaster, which it must be termed for want of a better word. In classical architecture the pilaster[1] is a square column, generally attached to the wall, from which it projects from a third to a sixth of its breadth; in Saxon architecture such columns are found running up vertically in rows on the face of the wall as well as on the corners; but in Ireland they are seen only at the angles, and are simply prolongations of the side walls in the primitive churches, and are sometimes continued all along the gable, as in Inis-mac-Dara, or along a portion of it, as at Kilmalkedar.[2]

The projections, like brackets or gargoyles, alluded to above, which are placed at the four corners of these churches, at the angles of the gable, are among the most peculiar features of these churches, and are found in the oldest and rudest buildings,[3] as well as in others of a later date, as for example in the primitive church of St. Colman Mac Duach in Aranmór, and in the Cathedral of Clonmacnois, rebuilt in the year 1089.

In the older churches of Ireland, marked by the doorway with horizontal lintel and inclined sides, we find that the chancel is not bonded into the nave, and in four instances, viz., our Lady's Church and Trinity Church at Glendalough, St. Brecan's in Aranmór, and Banagher Church, the two portions of the buildings are contemporaneous, and afford evidence of the retention of the horizontal lintel after the knowledge of the arch had been attained. A very striking example of this is seen in the interior of the doorway of Banagher,[4] (figs. 33, 34), where a relieving arch is thrown over the lintel, as also appears in the doorway of St. Kevin's Church (fig. 30), and the cathedral at Glendalough.

---

[1] The gradation in the forms of such pilaster buttresses is well illustrated by the following instances:—Leabha Molaga, Notes on Irish Architecture, Plate XXXV.; at the Church of St. Colman Mac Duach, Plate XXXIX.; Kill Enda, Plate XLI.; Dulane, Plate XLVII.; Clonamery, Plate LIX., and Tomgraney, Plate LXIV.

[2] *Op. cit.*, Plate XCIII.

[3] Compare the examples of these brackets in Plates XXXVII., XLIX., LII., LIV., Notes on Irish Architecture, vol. ii.

[4] *Op. cit.*, Plate LXI.

Stone Churches with Cement.

No fixed plan seems to have been adopted in these buildings, as to the relative proportions of the two parts of the building. In Tomgraney the chancel was originally the same length as the nave as well as the same width; it is now 10 ft. longer. There is a difference of only 4 ft. in the nave and chancel of Trinity Church at Glendalough, and from this the difference varies 5 ft. 6 in., 6 ft. 6 in., 11 ft. 4 in., 15 ft., to 23 ft. 6 in., the chancel of Glendalough Cathedral being just half the size of the nave. At first the chancel does not appear to have been better or even as well lighted as the nave, and it is impossible to decide now whether there was any difference in the roof. The earliest arches appear to have been semicircular, and spring from jambs which incline like the sides of the doorways.

The earliest form of these arches, as that of Trinity Church, Glendalough,[1] is without imposts. They consist of a single sweep or soffit only, no sub-arch and no moulding or even chamfer; but the voussoirs are dressed and fitted with skill. Then the arch of Oughtmama[2] in Clare springs from imposts with a chamfered edge about 6 in. high and projecting only two inches, and the voussoirs are but 4 in. thick and uncut. The chancel arch of Glendalough Cathedral was probably not more elaborate, to judge from portions of its jambs still existing, which are without mouldings. The size of these arches varied from 9 to 10 ft. in width and 12 to 13 ft in. height. In some cases the arch is set back from the jambs from which it springs in this manner, a peculiarity which is represented in the arch in the Book of Kells, beneath which the figure of Christ is standing.

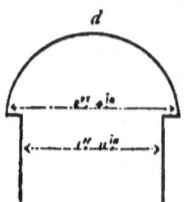

Such an arch may also be seen in the church of Weir on the island of the same name in the Orkneys.[3] At first no impost is seen; then a rude impost formed of an unsquared block of stone is introduced, as at Kilmacduach in Aran,[4] and then appears the chamfered impost, as at Oughtmama. Where the chancel is not bonded into the nave, and where the masonry is different in character from that of the latter, it may be presumed that the chancel is an addition of a later date, and the arch being in general built on the radiating principle would support this theory; for the knowledge of the true arch does not seem to have reached Ireland till some time after they built stone churches with cement. With the addition of the chancel arose the necessity of

---

[1] Plate L., ib. [2] Plate LIII., ib.
[3] See Orkneyinga Saga, Introd. p. xcvi.
[4] Plate XI., Notes on Irish Architecture, vol. ii.

lighting the nave, and windows were introduced into the side walls, often square or triangular, always inferior in construction to the east window; a little window is sometimes introduced in the east end of the south wall, the purpose of which appears to have been to cast additional light on the altar.

These buildings were in some instances roofed with shingles, but a sufficient number of examples remain to show that solid stone roofs were not uncommon. Such roofs were built on the same principle as those of the uncemented oratories, until the period of transition from the false to the true arch, which is marked by such a building as St. Columba's house, described in the Introduction to this work.[1] This structure appears to have been erected at the beginning of the ninth century, as we read:—"A.D. 807. Building of the new establishment of Colum Cille at Cenannus (Chron. Scot.). A.D. 614. Cealach Abbas Iae finita constructione templi Cenindsa reliquit principatum." (Ann. Ult.)

Before passing on to the study of the later and richer style, it may be well to pause and contemplate the long series of primitive remains already illustrated, and dwell upon the history they disclose and the wider interest connected with them, following the guidance of Mr. Freeman, and working by the light shed on the subject by his singular insight. Such study may bring the whole history of "the Church and her material fabrics before us in a new garb," and her estate may be vividly realized by these examples, when "her temples were but the damp cave, or the rude hut; when she dwelt not as yet in the halls of the patrician and the palace of the emperor." "These buildings, themselves of the most venerable antiquity, the earliest existing Christian temples in northern Europe, are the representatives of others more venerable still; they derived not their origin from the gorgeous basilicas of Constantine and Theodosius, but in them we behold the direct offspring of the lowly temples of the days of persecution,—the humble shrines where Cyprian bent in worship and which Valerian and Diocletian swept from off the earth."[2]

In the second part of Lord Dunraven's work photographs are given of a large number of these little churches, whose style belongs to that of the entablature and not the arch, all the doorways having horizontal lintels and inclined jambs. The strikingly archaic aspect which we have already noticed in the masonry of these buildings is

---

[1] Notes on Irish Architecture, vol. i. Introd. p. 9.
[2] See History of Architecture, p. 196; Works of Walter Moyle, vol. i. pp. 376 to 396. London: 1726.

only increased by the character of their apertures, and it may be well to remember that the air of great antiquity which hangs round many of them is likely to lead to misconceptions as to their date. Built, as they were, of the materials found nearest to hand, the massive, so-called Cyclopean, character of their masonry may be due to the geological formation of the places in which they are principally found, and for this reason consideration should be given to the nature and general aspect of the country in which they stand. These districts are in the counties of Clare and Galway, and in the Islands of Aran, which lie at the entrance of Galway Bay, and which are, geologically, a portion of the county of Clare.

The greater part of these districts is entirely composed of limestone, lying in horizontal strata, sometimes slightly curved, and occasionally traversed by veins of black, green, and white marble, fit for architectural or ornamental purposes. There is something very singular in the aspect of the country, which often stretches to the horizon like one continuous quarry, the stone lying on the level face of the plain, from which blocks of almost any length may be obtained, some of the beds being unbroken for upwards of 50 ft.

The hills in the Aran Islands are low, rounded, and gray, in no part rising to a greater elevation than from 400 ft. to 500 ft. There are no rivers in these islands, and the absence of even a running mountain brook tends to give peculiar value to the springs which are scattered through these districts. Thus many of the wells are here held sacred to this day. These fountains, with their equally sacred trees, covered with votive offerings of propitiation or gratitude to the spirit of the place, form studies of the deepest interest, particularly where, amid the wild scenery which generally surrounds them, groups of worshippers, in the rich colours of their national costume, add to the solemn character and poetry of the scene. In Aran Môr, or the Greater Island of Aran, there are two lakes, Lough Dearg and Portowen, which are formed by the entrance of the sea through subterranean channels. Landward the shore slopes gradually to the water's edge, while seaward the islands slowly rise to their greatest height, then break into those precipices which seem to form a link in the great chain of majestic cliffs that all along the west coast of Ireland stand, like a gigantic wall, facing the Atlantic waves.

The aspect of these islands has been admirably described by Dr. Conroy, in his "Visit to Aran," in the following passage :—" Having gained the low hill that commands the village, we halted to contemplate the weird landscape that surrounded us. It was a scene peculiar to Aran. The island falls from the south-west, facing east and north, and from the vantage ground on which we stood the eye traversed fields upon fields of bare, dark-gray rocks, which now rose into hills, now sank into valleys, according to the action of the force that had originally upheaved the island itself. The ground was covered with rocks, not scattered and disjointed, as they occur elsewhere, but spreading into immense sheets and tables of stone, sometimes 60 ft. broad, as smooth as polished marble, and giving out beneath the tread a sonorous metallic ring. In some places these slabs rise tier upon tier, stone overlapping stone, with a precise regularity of mass and form which reminded you of masonry cunningly piled by giant hands. Winding in and out in a thousand mazes, a thread of fresh green herbage could, on closer inspection, be traced along the hillside, up-springing where the natural cleavage of the rocks had left deep fissures, now and then widening into a patch of verdure, in which wild flowers of every hue bloomed in luxuriance against the gray crag. Frequent enclosures of stone crossed each other in and out, in almost countless ridges, until it seemed as if both rocks and verdure were covered with iron network of the most irregular pattern."[1]

It is impossible while gazing on such a scene not to be reminded of the word-pictures that Eastern travellers have given us of that great limestone district of Syria, which extends from Lebanon through Palestine, and reaches to Arabia. True, this Irish scene may want the height and extent of the Eastern, especially as found in the Sinaitic district. The hills of the west are not as "the Alps unclothed,"[2] but, when we read of the long, monotonous ranges of mountain enclosing the desert of the "Tih," or the Wanderings, and picture to ourselves their long horizontal lines, and the wide undulating pebbly plain that lies beneath them, the scene still seems to bear upon its face the same aspect of desolation, the same calm grandeur which is to be found here; and the likeness becomes still more striking in what we learn of Palestine from the description of Dean Stanley:—

Rounded hills, chiefly of a gray colour, gray partly from the limestone of which they are all formed, partly from the tufts of gray shrub with which their sides are thinly clothed, and from the prevalence of the olive; their sides formed into concentric rings of rock, which must have served in ancient times as supports to the terraces, of which there are still traces, to their very summits; valleys, or rather the meetings of these gray slopes with the beds of dry watercourses at their feet; long sheets of bare rock laid like flagstones, side by side, along the soil; these are the chief features of the greater part of the scenery of the historical parts of Palestine. . . . .

These rounded hills, occasionally stretching into long undulating ranges, are for the

---

[1] "Visit to Aran." The Rev. Dr. Conroy, Bishop of Ardagh and Clonmacnois.
[2] See Sir Frederic Wenneker's "Notes of a Visit to Egypt," p. 214.

most part bare of wood, forest and large timber (with a few exceptions hereafter to be mentioned) are not known. Cornfields and (in the neighbourhood of the Christian populations, as at Bethlehem) vineyards creep along the ancient terraces. In the spring, the hills and valleys are covered with thin grass, and the aromatic shrubs which clothe more or less almost the whole of Syria and Arabia. But they also glow with what is peculiar to Palestine, a profusion of wild flowers, daisies, the white flower called the Star of Bethlehem, but especially with a blaze of scarlet flowers of all kinds, chiefly anemones, wild tulips, and poppies. Of all the ordinary aspects of the country, this blaze of scarlet colour is perhaps the most peculiar, and to those who first enter the Holy Land it is no wonder that it has suggested the touching and significant name of the Saviour's blood-drops."[1]

It has been already observed that the Islands of Aran are geologically a portion of the limestone district of the county of Clare, and the nearest point of the mainland to them is at the foot of Black Head. This mountain, crowned by Cahir Dún Fergus, forms a noble termination to the north-western part of Clare. While in some places the headland descends abruptly to the sea, in others the shore stretches out from its foot in low, flat ridges of black rock, intensely black as seen against the dazzling whiteness of the waves. Here, even in calm weather, the Atlantic rollers advance in slow procession, and heave their volumes of clear green water, transparent as liquid emerald, while the breeze which catches the snow-white crest of the wave casts the foam around it and above it in a veil of unimaginable purity and beauty.

This rocky coast, which gradually rises to the cliffs of Moher on the south, remains low and monotonous along the north of Clare; but, passing inland, the limestone hills increase in beauty and grandeur, rising to a much greater height than they had attained in Aran. Even where their height is inconsiderable, the forms in which their rocks are broken are full of majestic beauty. In the valleys at their feet, great masses of rock, built of squared blocks of limestone, rise like citadels, while the mountains lie in terraces of stone marked by flowing curves, line following line in slow succession, till they seem to rise by giant steps to their smooth and rounded summits. At their base the land stretches out in flat, horizontal lines of flagstone, which give all the repose of still water to the landscape, and when at early dawn far on the horizon the level lines of the gray and desert plain are met by level lines of crimson light and bars of purple cloud in heaven, nothing can exceed the solemnity of the picture. The view becomes less mournful and desolate in character as the road approaches the country round the Lake of Inchiquin, which is the very

---

[1] Stanley, "Sinai and Palestine," p. 138.

heart of Clare. Here "the bareness of the rocks upon her border" is softened with exquisite luxuriance of verdure and fulness of colour, and fringed with the delicate fronds of the maidenhair fern; in the nooks and dells among the rocks are spots "unutterably green," harmonizing with the peculiar warm and rich gray of the limestone rocks that rise above them, while the wild flowers that gem these corners and little nests, glow with a colouring only the more vivid as contrasting with the quiet hue of the rest of the landscape. The purple foxglove, heather, geranium, and wild thyme, with the golden leaf of the variegated ivy, the crimson berries of the orchis, and red fruit of the wild strawberry, all forming rich contrast with the pure delicate hue of the harebell and forget-me-not and speed-well, "which make a blueness there as of the sky when it is deepened in the water."[1] Here the sides of the hills are often wooded, principally with wild ash and oak, and at their feet lie rocks covered with velvety moss of a golden-bronze colour, ferns, and ivy. It is as if Nature, like a tender mother, had but reserved all her richest gifts for this, her least happy child, and flung around the barren surface such a veil of graceful foliage, and so garlanded the stones with wreaths of creeping plants, that all sense of desolation, or even want, is lost. Standing on the higher ground other thoughts fill the mind—the ruined church and tower—the castle—forts and tombs of a prehistoric age strike the eye at every turn, and in the far distance rise the pale desolate hills, like echoes from the Holy Land, speaking to the mind of sacred memories and truths where no change is.

---

[1] Felix Holt, vol. ii. pp. 56, 57.

CHAPTER IV.

Ecclesiastical Towers.

THE hope of defining the steps which mark the ascent of architecture in Ireland, we have striven to indicate by her monuments that gradual progress, from the first rude style that seems to have prevailed at the time of the introduction of Christianity into the country, to that of the close of the ninth century, when the use of cement and the hammer was known to Irish builders, but when the horizontal lintel had not yet been superseded by the arch. At this point we arrive at a class of buildings which forms a striking innovation in the hitherto humble character of Irish church architecture, that is, the lofty pillar tower. In the beginning of this century the existence of 118 of these circular ecclesiastical towers in Ireland was asserted, and a complete list of them will be given in the Appendix to this work. The latest researches have led to the conviction that the type was not peculiar to Ireland before the eleventh century; and twenty-two foreign examples of similar towers may now be added to those of Ireland, making in all 140 of these remarkable structures. The present chapter will be devoted solely to an examination of such as have been found in Ireland, while in the next some further suggestions as to their probable age and origin will be offered.[1]

---

[1] In 1792 Dr. D. A. Beaufort published a list comprising fifty-six of these buildings in his work entitled Memoir of a Map of Ireland. Among the posthumous papers of Dr. Petrie and the letters of Dr. O'Donovan, when engaged on the Ordnance Survey, more or less information is supplied as to seventy-six of these structures in Ireland. Mr. George Wilkinson, in his valuable work on the Practical Geology and Architecture of Ireland, has given useful notes on twenty-five of these towers. The Rev. Dr. Reeves also gives careful descriptions of many of them, which may be found scattered throughout his various works. Guided by the information gathered from such sources, Lord

It becomes evident that when the seventy-six remaining towers of Ireland are compared, a certain development of knowledge and skill in the art of building may be traced in these various examples, and that such changes are analogous to those which took place in the church architecture of Ireland after the eighth century. A rough classification is attempted in the following table, showing the gradation in masonry and the corresponding change in the character of the apertures observable in these towers.

First Style.	Second Style.	Third Style.	Fourth Style.
Rough field-stones untouched by hammer or chisel, not rounded, but fitted by their length to the curve of the wall, roughly coursed, wide-jointed, with spalds or small stones fitted into the interstices. Mortar, of coarse, unsifted sand or gravel.	Stones roughly hammer-dressed, rounded to the curve of the wall, decidedly though somewhat irregularly coursed. Spalds, but often badly bonded together. Mortar freely used.	Stones laid in horizontal courses, well-dressed and carefully worked to the round and batter, the whole cemented in strong plain mortar of lime and sand.	Strong, rough but excellent ashlar masonry, rather open-jointed, and therefore closely analogous to the English-Norman masonry of the first half of the twelfth century; or, in some instances, finest possible examples of well-dressed ashlar. Sandstone in squared courses.

BROAD CLASSIFICATION OF THE TOWERS ACCORDING TO THE AVERAGE STYLES OF THEIR MASONRY AND APERTURES.

Names of Towers. N.B. Exceptional towers marked in italics, perfect towers in small capitals.	Masonry.	Dimensions of Perfect Towers.	Doorways.	Windows.
LUSK, CLONDALKIN, TEACHDOE,[1] Drumboe, Swords, Drumcliff, *Castledermot*,[2] *Scattery*,[3] *Antrim*,[4] Oran, *Turlough*,[5] *Trummery*,[6] Drumcleeve, Rathmichael, Fertagh.	First Style of masonry.	Lusk, 100 ft. high by 43 ft. circum.; Clondalkin, 85 ft. by 43; Scattery, 125 ft. by 52 ft.; Antrim, 92 ft. by 50 ft.; Turlough, 70 ft. by 57 ft.	Of same material as the rest of the building, sometimes stones roughly dressed; square-headed with inclined sides 5 ft. 6 high by 2 ft. wide. 8 ft. to 13 ft. above ground.	Same material as the rest of the building; narrow apertures, square-headed or triangular, with inclined sides, near level of floors within tower.

[1] *Teachdoe.* Figure of Christ in rude relief over the doorway.

[2] *Castledermot.* The doorway does not correspond with masonry of the rest of the building. It is arched and moulded.

[3] *Scattery.* The doorway is on the ground floor; probably being on a small island the additional precaution of raising the door was not thought requisite.

[4] *Antrim.* The doorway has a cross carved in relief upon it, and the whole tower has more the appearance of having been hastily erected than that of great age.

[5] *Turlough.* The form of this tower—low and wide—suggests that it may belong to a totally different type.   [6] *Trummery.* This tower is attached to a church.

Dunraven selected sixteen for illustration, which might be taken as typical examples of these buildings, but among them there is unfortunately no good example of the first and apparently earliest style. The notes on these, added to the information above mentioned, assist the effort now made to classify and arrange them according to the development of architectural skill shown in their construction.

Ecclesiastical Towers.

NAMES OF TOWERS. N.B. Exceptional towers marked in italics, perfect towers in small capitals.	MASONRY.	DIMENSIONS OF PERFECT TOWERS.	DOORWAYS.	WINDOWS.
Iniscaltra, Clones, MEELICK, Aghavuller, *Donoughmore*,[1] *Roscrea*,[2] *Kildare*,[3] Kilree, Kilmacduach, Kilcullen, Aughagower, Kilbennan, CASHEL,[4] MONASTERBOICE,[5] Aranmor, Tullaherin.	Second Style.	Meelick, 70 feet high by 42 ft. circum. Cashel, 80 ft. by 42 ft. Monasterboice, 110 ft. by 51 ft.	First idea of arch, curve scooped out of three or five stones. Architrave occasionally occurs: stones of same material as tower, but roughly worked to the round.	Same material as rest of building; sometimes roughly cut and squared. Same form and size as before.
DEVENISH,[6] Glendalough, KILLALA, Kinneth, Cloyne, Armoy, Rattoo, Ballagh, Disert-Aengus,[7] *Dromiskin*, Kilkenny, Drumlane.	Third Style.	Devenish, 76 ft. high by 43 ft. circum. Killala, 84 ft. high by 51 ft. circum.	First idea of arch, curve scooped out of three stones: stones of some finer material than the wall of the tower, generally sandstones or some free-working stone; pellet and roll mouldings occasionally introduced.	Same form as before, but of finer material than the rest of the tower, and the windows generally better proportioned than the earlier ones.
TIMAHOE,[8] Annadown, Aghadoe, TEMPLE FINAN, Kells,[9] O'Rorke's Tower, ARDMORE,[10] Disert O'Dea.	Fourth Style.	Timahoe, 96 ft. by 60 ft. Temple Finan, 56 ft. by 49 ft. Ardmore, 98 ft. by 52 ft.	Regular radiating round arch of six or more stones, with architrave, or fine examples of the decorated Irish Romanesque of the 12th century.	Same form as before, of sandstone cut and squared.

Conclusions to be drawn from the above table:—

I. That these towers were built after the Irish became acquainted with the use of cement and the hammer.

II. That the towers were built at or about the period of transition from the Entablature style of the early Irish period to the round arched decorated Irish Romanesque style.

III. That the largest number of these towers were built before

---

[1] *Donoughmore*. The doorway of this tower is of finer material than the tower; has architrave heads at the springing of the arch, and Crucifixion sculptured in relief.

[2] *Roscrea*. A ship and an interlaced ornament incised on this doorway.

[3] *Kildare*. Inserted Romanesque doorway.

[4] *Cashel*. Door ornamented with incised architrave.

[5] *Monasterboice*. Double architrave runs round doorway; moulding in relief.

[6] *Devenish*. A rich cornice moulding runs round the top, and the doorway is ornamented with architrave.

[7] *Disert-Aengus*. Doorway ornamented with roll and pellet mouldings; architrave in triple band.

[8] *Timahoe*. Doorway richly sculptured Irish Romanesque.

[9] *Kells* is rubble work, chiefly sandstone, but some limestone used; carved heads on doorway, and five windows on upper story.

[10] *Ardmore*. Roll mouldings round doorway and external bands to mark stories and moulded heads as brackets inside.

this transition had been established and while the Irish builders were feeling their way to the arch.

IV. That as this transition took place between the time of Cormac O'Killen and Brian Boruma, i.e. between 900 and 1000, the first groups of towers belong to the first date.

Any effort to classify them according to such changes is replete with difficulty. There are three towers, each of which exhibits the extreme styles, ashlar and rubble masonry occurring simultaneously in their walls—Kells (fig. 68), Drumlane, and O'Rorke's tower at Clonmacnois; and it cannot be said that here the rudest masonry is the oldest, for in two instances the ashlar masonry is at the lower part of the tower and the rubble above it; but such cases are exceptional and very rare. In Devenish (fig. 63), which is carefully and strongly built of cut stone, but little cement is used. In most instances the stones, though more or less roughly worked, are laid in horizontal courses.[1] The towers of Killossy, Dysart O'Dea, and Ardmore (fig. 71) are the only ones existing which show string courses outside marking the stories inside. The average height of these buildings is from 100 to 120 ft., and the circumference 50 ft. Two towers, those of Turlough and Dromiskin, are therefore exceptional in character, and though of rude masonry are probably of a late date. Here the walls are 5 ft. thick, and there is only 13 ft. difference between the circumference and the height of Turlough, while Dromiskin is 66 ft. in circumference and only 35 ft. in height (see figs. 77, 78).

The average thickness of wall at the basement in the whole 72 towers is from 3 ft. 6 in. to 4 feet, there being 40 towers out of the 72 which have walls of this thickness, and the others only vary a few inches more or less. The average diameter at the level of the doorway is from 7 to 9 ft. internally. Some are unusually broad, as Oran, which is 11 ft. across, Dysert O'Dea 10 ft. 2 in., and Kildare 9 ft. 3 in. These towers taper and the walls diminish in thickness towards the top. All their apertures have inclined sides, being on an average 2 in. wider at the base than at the top. The doorways of the earliest towers have horizontal lintels, and vary in size from 4 ft. 8 in. high by 1 ft. 11 in. wide,—6 ft. by 2 ft. 2 in.,—5 ft. 2 in. by 1 ft. 10 in.,—5 ft. 6 in. by 2 ft.,—5 ft. 10 in. by 1 ft. 8 in. The highest doorway, that of Lusk, (fig. 42) is also the narrowest, so there appears to have been no very regular proportion observed between the width and the height of the doorway. The height of these apertures from the level of the ground

---

[1] See the History, Architecture, and Antiquities of the Cathedral Church of St. Canice, Kilkenny, by the Revd. James Graves, and J. G. A. Prim, pp. 114 to 122.

is generally 13 ft. That of Scattery (fig. 36) is on the ground level, Lusk 8 ft. above, and the others 8 ft., 11 ft., and 13 ft. above. The doorways always face the entrance of the church to which they belong, unless in those instances where the church is evidently much later in date than the tower.

In the doorway of the tower on Scattery Island we see the false arch carried half way up and then surmounted by the horizontal lintel. In the doorways of Killree (fig. 46) and Kilmacduach belfries, the arch is cut out of one stone, in that of Meelick (fig. 51) the arch is scooped out of five stones, while that of Aghavuller (fig. 44) is a good instance of the first approximation to the radiating arch with the architrave. The number of windows varied according to the number of stories in the tower. There are almost always four placed at opposite sides in the top story, and generally so as to face the four cardinal points of the compass.[1] In form these were long and narrow, either triangular-headed, or with horizontal lintel and inclined sides, measuring 2 ft. high by 1 ft. broad. In very few instances are they round-headed. One of these apertures are found in each story, and they are rude or finished, in accordance with the general style of the building in which they occur. The most curious point about the windows in the other stories is that they were invariably within one or two feet of the floors. Sculptured ornament is found on the apertures or on the walls of fifteen of these towers, the most common decoration being, as is the case with the early churches, the architrave band, such as is seen at Aghavuller (fig. 45), Donoughmore, Drumcleeve, Cashel (fig. 55), Monasterboice, Disert Aengus (fig. 59), Devenish and Kells (fig. 66); the Crucifixion is rudely sculptured over the doorway of the tower of Teachdoe, and in some cases, as at Kells and Donoughmore, heads are carved at the springing of the arch in the rounded doorway. The cross within the circle is sculptured in relief over the doorway of Antrim tower, while the corbels which support the floors are carved at Roscrea and Ardmore (fig. 69), and a string course runs round under the conical roof of Devenish tower, decorated with pellets, human heads, and scrolls, while the doorways of Timahoe and Kildare towers are rich examples of Irish ornamented Romanesque.

It will be observed that those towers which merely exhibit a simple incised architrave line or cross belong to the two first styles, and that all sculpture in relief and undercut is confined to those buildings of

---

[1] There are only two in the top of Temple Finghin belfry, which also differs from the others in being only 56 ft. in height, and there are five in the upper story of Kells and six in that of Kilkenny.

the finer masonry of the third and fourth style. Incised ornament is common on the pillar stones and sepulchral slabs of Ireland in the ninth century, but it is difficult to prove the existence of the third and fourth style even on sepulchral monuments till the period ranging from A.D. 923 to 1200.

Internally these towers were divided into six or seven stories; the floors, which were of wood, were supported in one of three different methods. The beams either rested on projecting abutments in the walls, or there were holes for the joists; or, thirdly, corbels or brackets supported the floors, sometimes richly decorated, as at Ardmore. Stone floors may be seen in the lower stories of Meelick and Kinneth. That of Meelick is a very flat arch resting on the first offset in the wall; that of Kinneth is quite level and ingeniously constructed of slate flags; both floors have a well-hole in the centre. The section of the tower of Devenish, fig. 61 of this volume, shows the interior arrangements of such buildings.

In the third or middle story of many of these towers, stones are seen to project like brackets from the wall, and one such in Lusk is in the form of a large rude hook. These appliances were probably meant for hanging book-satchels or other valuables of the monastery from, and the chamber in which they occur may have been that specially devoted to the safe-keeping of the church valuables in troublous times.

The position of these towers was almost invariably about 20 ft. to the north-west end of the church, and they were so placed as to command the entrance to the church.[1]

One of the most important discoveries achieved since Dr. Petrie published his investigations is that described by the Rev. James Graves, as the result of the excavation made by him and the Dean of Ossory, in the year 1847, at the base of the round tower of Kilkenny. From the facts then observed, it can be clearly proved that the belfry was erected on a piece of ground that had been used as a

---

[1] Referring to the position of these towers, Lingard remarks: "If I may be allowed a conjecture on a subject which has exercised the ingenuity of many writers, I conceive such towers to have been originally built at a short distance from the church, that the walls might not be endangered by their weight; and that they were not considered merely as an ornament, but used as beacons to direct the traveller towards the church or monastery." Lights were kept burning in them during the night—at least, such was the fact with respect to the new tower at Winchester, which we learn from Wolstan consisted of five stories, in each of which were four windows, illuminated every night, looking towards the four cardinal points. Lingard, Anglo-Saxon Churches, vol. ii. p. 379.

Christian cemetery for a period of time long preceding that of the foundation of the tower. The first or upper stratum, which was 2 ft. 8 in. in thickness, consisted of matter formed from the accumulation of rubbish that had fallen from the top, or been thrown from time to time into the tower. The second, which was about 18 in. thick, was composed of calcined clay containing fragments of burned human and other bones, and of charcoal in large masses and scattered pieces; the lower part of the stratum was made up of rich loam, mixed with some calcined clay, small portions of burned and unburned bones and charcoal—these things all bearing evidence of some great fire at a period nearer to that of the erection of the tower. The third stratum, 1 ft. 7 in. in thickness, was composed of rich black earth with fragments of

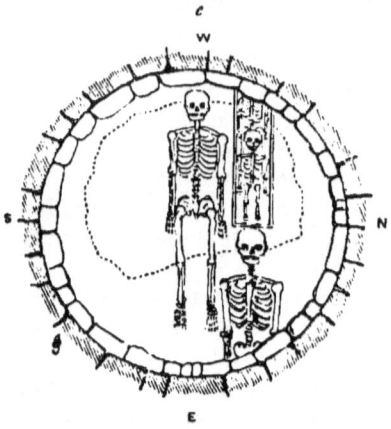

human and animal bones, and spalds of the dolomite partially used in the construction of the tower. When this last deposit was cleared away, a pavement was reached on a level with the external base course. The pavement, which is marked in the annexed diagram by dotted lines, did not form a complete floor to the tower. On raising it and continuing the excavation carefully, the group of skeletons as represented in the diagram was found, with the remains of the timber coffin in which the children's bodies had been laid. All these bodies lay beneath the level of the foundation of the tower, and portions of the coffin and of the two other bodies extended beyond the circle of the building, which had evidently been raised above the ground which covered them, and without knowledge or thought of the forms that lay below. That these were the forms of Christians is rendered probable by the position of the skeletons, lying east and west, for it is held that the

Pagan Irish on their conversion to Christianity made a change in their mode of burial, as it is said in the Lebar na huidre, Cormac Mac Art, monarch of Ireland, "the third person who had believed, in Erin, before the arrival of St. Patrick," told his people to bury him *with his face to the east.*

The church of St. Canice, originally founded in the seventh century, was probably the nucleus of a cemetery which, like Clonmacnois, remained from that period in constant use, and the tower cannot have belonged to this very early period, inasmuch as several centuries must have elapsed before the soil of the cemetery could assume the character it presented beneath the foundation of the building, of a soil "that had for ages been made fat by fresh accessions of the mortal remains of poor humanity."

In the year 1085 we read that "Ceall-Cainnigh was for the most part burned." Mr. Graves suggests that the edifice then partially destroyed may have been a timber structure, and that it was soon rebuilt, as appears by the record of a second conflagration seventy-one years later. It is very probable that on the rebuilding of the church this protecting tower was erected, and that the conflagration, signs of which were discovered in the excavations, was that fire recorded by the annalists in 1114, when its timber floors, together with the human beings then within its walls, were consumed.

Another fact which ought not to be passed over with regard to this tower is, that it, along with Monasterboice and Kilmacduach, bears evidence that the builders were not careful to secure a firm foundation for the ponderous mass they were about to erect; and just at that point where the lower extremities of one of the skeletons are concealed by the foundation of the tower, the summit of the structure overhangs its base about two inches. This proves a considerable subsidence, as Mr. Graves remarks, "when a wall originally built to a batter of twenty-six inches leans over its base even to the small extent of two inches." The tower built over a cemetery subsided at the point of least resistance afforded by the substratum, *i.e.*, over the spot left vacant by the natural decay of the human form beneath.

The fact that most if not all of these towers were erected in cemeteries which had been previously used for Christian interments, and in places where Christianity had been already established, seems borne out by much collateral evidence of the same nature.[1] The tower does

---

[1] When the tower of Down was thrown to the ground and cleared away to its foundation, the vestiges of a more ancient building, probably the original church, were found beneath it, running directly across its site, so that the tower was evidently not

not always appear to have been built by the same hands as the church. The churches and little oratories in Aran bear marks of much greater antiquity than the stump of the round tower near Killenda, built in

ROUND TOWER, KILLENDA.

regular courses of well-rounded stones. The Christian epitaphs which may be held to be contemporaneous with the architecture of the primitive period, such as are found in Kerry, partly in Ogham and partly

CHURCH ON IRELAND'S EYE.

in a rude Roman character, all witness to an earlier and ruder Christian period than that in which such towers could be erected. Fourthly, the

---

coeval with the first Christian edifice. It should be noted that this primitive building was of stone, not wood.

tower is placed to the north or north-west of the church, from respect to the wish which is even now generally entertained by the Irish to be buried to the east or south. The cases of the three leaning towers of Ireland, Monasterboice, Kilmacduach, and Kilkenny, may point to another inference besides that of their erection in a soil long softened by interments. It appears almost incredible that masons so skilful as those who raised these particular towers should have been so ignorant as to base their ponderous mass on such an insecure foundation. May it not be explained by the fact that they were not in this instance working with that forethought which is the offspring of experience and the slow growth of native effort, but that tower-building was a new art to them?

Whatever doubt may still linger in some minds regarding the connection between the *detached* towers and the church, we hardly think

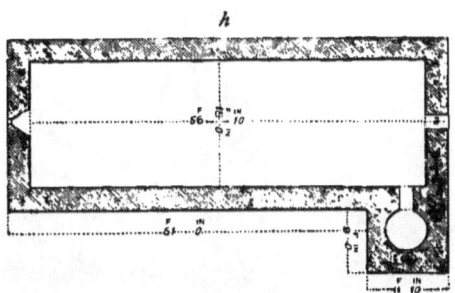

GROUND PLAN OF TAMLAGHT FINLAGEN.

they will still deny an ecclesiastical character to those which are attached to and evidently coeval with these buildings. The date of such towers was held by Dr. Petrie to be little anterior to the twelfth century. Nine of these structures have been found in Ireland, and two in the Orkneys. Of the history of the erection of these buildings nothing is known, excepting of the two last, which, to judge from the architectural features of the two churches to which they belong, certainly appear also to be the two latest. Their names are given in the following list in the chronological order which we imagine they should assume:—

1. St. Kevin's, Glendalough, Co. Wicklow.[1]
2. Trinity Church, Glendalough, Co. Wicklow.[2]

---

[1] See Notes on Irish Architecture, vol. i. Plate LXXXVIII.
[2] Ib., vol. i. p. 99.

Ecclesiastical Towers. 63

3. Church on Ireland's Eye, Howth, Co. Dublin.
4. Tamlaght Finlagen, Newtown Limavady, Co. Londonderry.
5. Temple Finan, 1100, Clonmacnois, King's County.[1]
6. Dungiven, 1100, Keenaght, Co. Londonderry.
7. Killossy, near Naas, Co. Kildare.
8. Trummery, Co. Antrim.
9. St. Michael le Pole, Dublin.

The belfry appears to be coeval with its church in every instance. In two instances, the first and last on our list, the tower springs from the roof of the church. In the other cases it rises from a square base about 15 ft. in height. In the church on Ireland's Eye, it was placed

KILLOSSY.

at the east end of the building, and the square basement story formed the little chancel of the church. It was 42 ft. in circumference, and probably 60 ft. high. The tower of Trummery church was also at the east end, and was entered from the corner of the church through a low narrow archway. The tower of Temple Finan at Clonmacnois was also entered from the chancel. The other three towers on our list are at the south-west corner, or west end of the church. Dressed stone and Romanesque ornament are found in the apertures of the other structures, and even the oldest of these, that of St. Kevin's at Glendalough, was built after the introduction of the regular arch, an example of which may be seen over the west doorway of the church.

---

[1] Notes on Irish Architecture, vol. ii. Plates LXXXIX. and XC.

The date of Temple Finan at Clonmacnois is still uncertain, but the church of Dungiven appears to have been founded by O'Cahan in the beginning of the twelfth century, as we learn from the following entry in the History of Irish Monastic Foundations by Allemande, an Augustinian friar, quoted by Archdall (Monast. p. 92):—

"A.D. 1100. O'Cahan, Prince of the country, founded a priory here for canons regular following the rule of St. Augustin."

There can be no doubt of the tower and church being coeval, and we may believe their age to be that which is assigned to them by our Annals, that of 1110; the beauty of the masonry, the way in which every stone of the edifice is squared with the chisel, the general form of

ST. MICHAEL LE POLE.

the structure, the small round-headed Romanesque doorway, the choir arch, and the narrow angular-headed windows of the choir all belong to that age. The larger windows of the nave are a more modern introduction, their style being that of the thirteenth or fourteenth century. They were probably built in 1397, when the church, having been polluted by the effusion of Christian blood, was solemnly restored by the Archbishop of Armagh.

A number of towers which bear more or less resemblance to those of this country still exist, or are known to have existed, in other places besides Ireland. They are high, slender, and circular, with pointed roofs, and occasionally built of brick. The examples of such on the Continent which may be here mentioned are, the tower of Dinkelsbühl in Bavaria, the belfries of San Nicolo at Pisa, San Paternian at

Ecclesiastical Towers. 65

Venice, six belfries at Ravenna, one at Scheness in Switzerland, two at the church of St. Thomas in Strasburg, two at Gernrode in the Hartz, two at Nivelles, one at St. Maurice Epinal, one at St. Germain des Prés, one at Worms in Hesse Darmstadt, St. Gertrude Nivelles, Uzes in Department of Gard, and two at Notre Dame de Maestricht in Belgium. In Scotland such round belfries occur at Brechin, at St. Brigid's church at Abernethy, St. Magnus's in Egilsha; and till a late period two such towers were standing at Deerness in the Orkneys, and three in the Shetland Isles; St. Lawrence's church in West Burra, St. Magnus's at Tingwall, and another at Ireland Head; while one has been described in Stremoe, one of the Faroe Islands, and

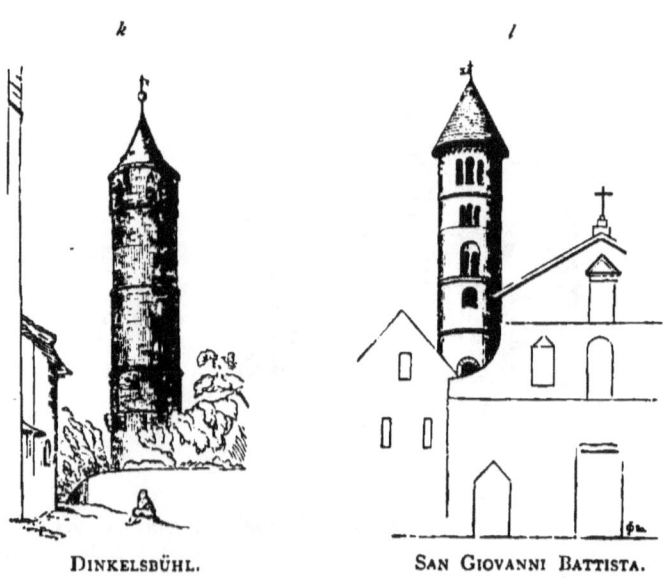

DINKELSBÜHL.   SAN GIOVANNI BATTISTA.

the tower near St. Patrick's church in the Isle of Man is another. The first on this list of fifteen foreign round towers is not ecclesiastical. It has been described by Mr. F. W. Burton in a letter to Dr. Petrie as one of several round towers which with some square turrets strengthen the walls of Dinkelsbühl. This tower is about 120 ft. in height, and divided into four stories, the lower springing from a plinth which now rises 4 or 5 ft. from the ground. The original doorway is 20 or 25 ft. above the ground. The upper story appears to be more modern than the remainder of the tower. Other towers of a similar character may be seen along the Main, and such examples are valuable, as showing the earliest type of defensive or protective tower in Europe.

In the library of St. Gall,[1] near Lake Constance in Switzerland, a plan on parchment is still preserved of this monastery, where the two circular towers of St. Michael and St. Gabriel are represented standing at the west end of the church, and equi-distant from the semicircular atrium; and Professor Willis, quoting from the inscriptions on this ancient plan, held to be the work of Eginhard, observes that the "ascent to the summit of the towers and to their chapels was (as is also shown in the drawing) by a winding[2] staircase, and that the whole building could be overlooked from them, '*ascensus per cocleam, ad universa super inspicienda.*' Campaniles or bell-towers, as is known, had not been brought into frequent use in the construction of churches very long before this plan was made—perhaps first under the reign of Charlemagne."[3] The same writer alludes to a floral ornament in the plan, which is also often seen in manuscripts of the ninth century, and which Lord Dunraven suggests may indicate the ornamental finial of the conical roof. Referring to the circular belfries which he examined at Ravenna, Lord Dunraven relates that he there observed six round campanili belonging to churches founded in the fifth and sixth centuries, one of which, that of San Giovanni Battista, is here illustrated. "It is attached to the north-west corner of the aisle, which is, however, of a much later date than the tower. There are four windows in each tier. The internal diameter at the bottom is 10 ft., and the height of the tower by estimation about 100 ft. The base is hidden in the sketch by the modern façade of the church. This church is said to have been built by the Empress Galla Placidia in the year 438, and consecrated by S. Peter Chrysologus. The conical roof is of shingles. The campanile of S. Apollinare in Classis is the finest at Ravenna. It stands on the north-east side of the church, from which it is 26 ft. distant. The wall is 6 ft. 6 in. thick, and the internal diameter of the tower 19 ft. Its height I should judge by estimation to be from 140 to 150 ft.

"Circular campaniles are said to exist in the northern parts of Lombardy, among the secluded Alpine valleys, but I was not fortunate enough to find any of them."[3] "Several of the Italian campanili

---

[1] Bauriss des Klosters St. Gallen vom Jahr 820, Ferdinand Keller, Zürich, 1844.

[2] According to Ferdinand Keller, these towers were divided into stories. A separate stair or ladder probably led to each story.—ED.

[3] Archæological Journal, vol. v. p. 85.

offer peculiarities of shape. The one attached to the church of S. Giovanni e Paolo, at Ravenna, is rectangular in the lower half, and round in the upper. The internal diameter of the rectangular part is 5 ft. by 3 ft. 9 in.; of the circular part 5 ft. 1 in. The height by estimation may be between 70 and 75 ft. At Venice I found, connected with the church of S. Paternian, a very curious campanile, externally an irregular hexagon, internally round; the internal diameter is about 8 ft. The campanile of the Benedictine abbey of S. Nicolo, at Pisa, of the thirteenth century, has the lower story circular, the next two octagonal, and the fourth or upper story hexagonal."[1]

CHURCH OF NOTRE DAME, MAESTRICHT.

Two brick towers of St. Thomas's church at Strasburg rise at each side of the apse, which itself resembles a lofty polygonal tower; one is merely a stair turret,[2] and still contains the spiral stone staircase, but in the other no trace of a staircase can be seen. At the church

---

[1] See Memorials of Adare, by the Earl of Dunraven, p. 222. Dictionary of Architecture, E. J. Anson, issued by the Architectural Publication Society, art. Campanile. Statique monumentale de Paris, A. Lenoir, Plate VII. Mellin, Monuments française, vol. v. p. 57.

[2] At the ancient church of Hythe in Kent there is a stair turret very similar in form to the Irish round tower, though of smaller dimensions. See Ulster Journal of Archæology, vol. iii. p. 27.

of Notre Dame in Maestricht and at Gernrode the circular towers are at the corners of the west end, and the latter building is said to have been founded A.D. 960.¹ The tower of St. Gertrude, at Nivelles, stands at the south-west end of the church, founded at the beginning of the eleventh century and dedicated in 1045, the Emperor Henry IV. assisting at the ceremony.² The stories of this tower are marked by external bands, as at that of Ardmore.

ST. MAURICE, EPINAL.

The tower of Epinal, represented in the accompanying woodcut, taken from a sketch made by Samuel Ferguson, Esq., is attached to the church of St. Maurice, at Epinal, in Lorraine. The details of this interesting church and tower have been described in a letter to Mr. Ferguson from Monsieur Carro, and another from Mr. Parker of Oxford to Lord Dunraven.³ The nave and transepts date from the tenth century. At the end of each transept is a circular tower, that on the north side partly ruined. It is built of small stones with wide joints of mortar, with probably only about one-half of its original height standing; it is 10 ft. in internal diameter, and the walls are

---

¹ See Hist. of Architecture, Ferguson, vol. i. p. 569. ² Ibid., p. 539.
³ See Memorials of Adare, pp. 222, 225.

about 3 ft. thick. The southern, which was rebuilt in the thirteenth century, is about 112 ft. in height, and nearly 7 ft. in internal diameter,

WEST END OF CHURCH AT GERNRODE IN THE HARTZ.

ST. GERTRUDE AT NIVELLES.

the walls being 3 ft. 6 in. in thickness.[1] It is formed of large squared stones of regular masonry, and is built up against the end wall of the transept. A winding staircase extends to the height of about 50 ft.

---

[1] See Memorials of Adare, pp. 222, 225.

In the old tower the stairs appear to have reached higher. The windows of the southern towers are square-headed and small. The door is on the level of the ground, the entrance being from the transept.

St. Geneviève.

In the eleventh century we find a great effort was made to rebuild the monasteries in France; preserving the church only as a consecrated place, they raised new cloisters, etc., and monastic architecture began to assume a more civil than ecclesiastical character. At this period the abbey of St. Geneviève was rebuilt. The choir belongs to the earliest years of the twelfth century, and the round tower stood at the south-west corner.[1]

The author of "The Characteristics of Old Church Architecture in Scotland" describes the towers in the following words :—
"In spite of its few plain features, flatness, and hardness of outline, there is much of picturesque character in the Scoto-Romanesque church tower. In general expression, however, it conveys the idea of a fortification—which, in some cases, it probably was—rather than that of a campanile." The prevailing type, we are informed by the same writer, is that of a square building, rising to about 100 ft., tall and narrow, and ending in a steep saddle-backed roof. This description exactly corresponds with the ancient square belfry of the church on Iniscloran, in Lough Ree, County of Galway, and with that of Mungret; but there are four examples of the cylindrical detached tower, with conical roof, perfectly similar to the Irish belfries. Two are on the mainland—Brechin, in Forfarshire, and Abernethy, in Perthshire. They are perfectly Irish in form, dimensions, and internal arrangements.

---

[1] Nothing now remains of this tower except the base. See Viollet-le-Duc, Dictionnaire de l'Architecture française, vol. i. p. 283, note 2. See Statique monumentale de Paris. Atlas, Tome Premier. Époque Chrétienne, Abbaye de Sainte Geneviève, pl. vii. In plate ii. fig. viii., representing sarcophagi found in this abbey, a fragment of interlaced moulding may be seen with that peculiar horseshoe pattern which is seen on

Ecclesiastical Towers. 71

The masonry of the basement of Brechin resembles that of the belfries of Kilmacduach and Killala, while above it is spawled like that of Cloyne. All the apertures are perfectly Irish in character, except the doorway, which, though round-headed and with inclined sides, yet varies from the Irish decorated Romanesque doorways in many important points. It does not consist of several orders, as the doorways of Timahoe and Kildare belfries, but all the ornament, formed of raised figures and

MUNGRET.

pellet mouldings, is external, and on the face of the wall.[1] This tower[2] was used as a belfry in the year 1776, when Pennant describes the "two handsome bells" then hanging in it. The belfry at Aber-

---

the roof of the temple as represented in the Book of Kells. Again, an interlaced band runs along the abacus of one of the capitals in the choir, see pl. xiii. In the plan of the abbey of St. Germain des Prés made in the middle of the sixteenth century, such circular towers with conical roofs and square or triangular-headed apertures are represented (Lenoir, vol. i.). This abbey was rebuilt early in the eleventh century, preserving the nave; a new monastery was constructed by a lay architect, Pierre de Montereau.

[1] See Stuart's Sculptured Stones of Scotland, vol. ii. Plate I.

[2] The following note is extracted from some memoranda found among Dr. Petrie's papers:—"Henry de Lichton, Vicar of Tethnot, had delivered to Patrick, Bishop of Brechin (1354-84), a large white horse, and had also given a cart and horse to carry stones to the building of the belfry of the church of Brechin, in the time of Bishop Patrick, and which cart was brought by Elias Wright, then residing at Finhaven."

nethy belonged to the church founded by St. Nechtan, and dedicated to the memory of St. Bridget. This building appears to be of two dates, the upper story being late Norman, while below the character of the masonry and apertures seems to be that of a much ruder period. The doorway is round-headed, the arch being scooped out of a single stone, and its sides incline.

DEERNESS.

The church of Deerness, in Orkney, had two cylindrical towers, as represented in the accompanying woodcut. The church was divided into nave and chancel, the latter being vaulted, A doorway opened

ST. MAGNUS.

from the chancel on a spiral staircase, leading to a small apartment between the towers on the second story, from which was the entrance to the second tower. Tradition states that bells were hung in these towers, but is silent as to the name or date of the builder or founder of the church.[1]

---

[1] Dr. Hibbert remarks, in a letter to Dr. Petrie :—" I was grievously disappointed to find, on visiting Deerness, A.D. 1832, that the proprietor of the land had levelled the

The church of St. Magnus in Egilsha is dedicated to and was in all probability founded by St. Magnus, who first visited this island in the year 1098. He is said[1] to have been murdered by the followers of his cousin, Haco, and buried in this church first, about the year 1136, then afterwards his bones were removed by his mother, Thora, to Birsa, and finally to Kirkwall. We may conclude that the date of the erection of this building is somewhere between the years 1098 and 1136. This church has a belfry attached to it, and belongs to that class of which eleven examples have been described as existing in Ireland, although only four now remain in good preservation, and the church to which it is attached appears to bear a strong resemblance to St. Kevin's church, at Glendalough, with no regularly built radiating chancel arch, but a little barrel-vaulted chancel, roofed with stone externally.

The belfry of St. Patrick's church, in the Isle of Man,[2] is also a

St. Patrick's Church, Isle of Man.

tower of the same type as the Irish detached round tower, although its character is now altered by a modern castellated top, which replaces the conical roof, and a flight of stone stairs leading up to the

---

whole of the ancient structure to the ground, and thus no memorial remains but the drawing in my possession; and the length of the foundation of the church (from W. to E.), as far as the steeples, appeared to me about 13 yards long. The breadth across at the east end, including the diameters of the two towers, appeared to be about 18 yards (paces), the space intermediate to the two towers not being above 2 yards wide, but these measurements were made with difficulty. The natives described the church as once having had a thatched roof upon it. It was built of very hard lime. I estimated the inside diameter of one of the towers at about 6 feet."

[1] See Hibbert's Shetland. See The Orkneyinga Saga, J. Anderson, Ed. Introd. p. c. Low's Tour through Orkney and Zetland. MS. in possession of David Laing. Article on The Twin-Towered Churches of Denmark, by J. Kornerup, in the Aarböger for Nordisk Oldkindighed, for 1869, p. 13. Orkneyinga Saga Torpeus. Barry's Orkney, p. 151. Pennant's Tour in Scotland, Plate II. p. 161. Proceedings Soc. Antiqs. Scotland, vol. iv. p. 188. Black's History of Brechin. Characteristics of Scottish Architecture, p. 24.

[2] See Architectural Journal, 1848. Petit.

doorway. It is situated opposite the west end of the church of St. Patrick, whose door looks towards it. This church is nearly destroyed, although parts of the side walls stand. There are no remains of doors or windows; some of the courses of masonry in the walls are herring-bone.[1]

At the first glance it may seem that the examples of foreign towers brought forward in this chapter do not sufficiently resemble those of Ireland to justify the idea of there being any connection in style between the two. These foreign towers are tall and slender. To the eye accustomed to consider the mere aspect of the solitary Irish bell-house there seems to be nothing in Italy, in England, or even in Germany, to compare with the height and slenderness of the Irish towers. This is quite true, but only as regards the aspect of these buildings. Place the towers of Ravenna, or that of S. Maurice at Epinal, in a country where the average height of the churches is from twenty-five to thirty feet, and set the towers to stand, not against, but apart from, such buildings, and their aspect will be much the same. It is not in its size or form that the Irish tower is so singular, but in its isolation. The continental towers here spoken of are all of an early date. The oldest—those at Ravenna—are all, in Mr. Freeman's opinion,[2] later than the time of Charlemagne. The others belong to a period close upon the Carlovingian era, and are among the very few examples still left of French and German architecture before the eleventh century. May not such scattered in-

---

[1] There are ecclesiastical round towers in parts of England, such as that of the church of Tasburgh, and at Keswick, and South Ockenden, but they are not of a similar type to those of Ireland. See Mr. Hudson Gurney, English Round Towers. Lingard, speaking of the first belfries in England, remarks:—" I conceive that originally the towers were distinct from the churches, like the celebrated round towers that are still remaining in Ireland. Thus a tower had been erected before the western entrance of the old church at Winchester, as we learn from Wolstan :—

" Turris erat rostrata tholis quia maxima quædam
Illius ante sacri pulcherrima limina templi," etc.
Act. SS. Ben. vol. ii., Pl. 70.

[2] There seems to be no evidence that the churches now standing at Ravenna are the original work of this early period. Mr. Freeman observes: "'The Ravenna towers have a rougher and earlier look than the square towers, but this may partly be owing to their shape, partly to the practice of blocking up most of their windows. Their date is uncertain; *but they are later than the days of Charles the Great.* The local writer Agnellus, writing soon after his time, describes the churches of Ravenna nearly as they still are; but he says not a word about bell towers." See Historical and Architectural Sketches, p. 51.

stances still standing on the Continent—may not such towers as those of Ravenna, Uzes, Worms, Strasburg, Belgium, and Lorraine—be held to mark the path by which the form found its way to Ireland after the year 800?

KELLETSTOWN.

CHAPTER V.

Origin and Use of Irish Church Towers.

BEFORE entering into the question of the probable origin and date of these Irish towers, it was thought desirable to offer the foregoing sketch of such examples as still exist of similar buildings in other countries, and it is now most necessary to arrive at some decision as to the primary purpose for which they were built—whatever may have been the uses to which they were afterwards applied, whether in Ireland or on the Continent. The nobility of a building depends on "its special fitness for its own purposes."[1] The ordinary Romanesque campanile—the main object of which is to lift a sonorous signal on high, in order that it may be heard afar, is a simple shaft, and when the necessary height is reached the belfry is left open at the sides, with a roof supported by pillars and arches, and an unbroken winding staircase inside leading up to the place in which the bells were hung. The ecclesiastical round towers of Ravenna and Ireland varied from such in one or two important points, which gives them a defensive character. They were divided into a series of chambers or stories—as in the case of the military towers of Dinkelsbühl, and the apertures at the top were barely large enough to supply free egress to the sound of a good-sized bell. Viewed as simple belfries, and no more, they would appear as poor conceptions and failures in design; but the dignity of their aspect forbids the suspicion of incompetency in their builders. It has been well said that the tower "is in its origin a building for strength of defence and faithfulness of watch rather than splendour of aspect; its true expression is of just so much diminution of weight upwards as may be necessary to its fully balanced strength."

With that insight which is alone the defining mark of genius the

---

[1] Stones of Venice, vol. i. pp. 194, 199.

writer of this passage perceives and declares the original meaning and intention of the first lofty towers of Europe, and the ecclesiastical towers of Ireland preserve an early type of such,[1] almost extinct elsewhere—in the same way as her angular churches preserve the memory of some type anterior to the basilica.[2] The first intention of the Irish tower was for "strength of defence and faithfulness of watch." Bells, small as those which are left to us still, were deposited in them, and they were termed bell-houses, or places for the housing of bells. Then, when after the twelfth century, bells of greater size and deeper tone were founded, the art of building belfries in Italy and France was developed also. The bell to be heard afar should be hung on high, and the chamber at the summit of the tower in which it was placed should be open at each side; thus the noble campanile of Venice, or that of Pisa, was developed. Such development was checked in the twelfth century in Ireland. The central tower of the Cistercian or Franciscan church, introduced while this early type was still the custom of the country, was a second, new, and foreign importation, never stamped by a native Irish school, which soon after ceased to exist.

The name by which these towers are usually distinguished by the annalists is Cloicethech, signifying bell-house, with its cognate Welsh *clochdy*. The English word belfry, the old French *berfroi*, and this from the Middle High German *bercvrit*, meant a movable tower, and was applied to a piece of carpentry destined for military uses; these terms have not always been confined to bell-towers in France or elsewhere. It is stated by M. Viollet-le-Duc, that "Les tours roulantes de bois destinées à l'attaque des places fortes pendant le moyen âge, et jusqu'à l'emploi de l'artillerie à feu, sont aussi nommées *beffrois* ou bretêches."[3]

The origin, half-military, half-ecclesiastic, of our round towers, seems to be conveyed in this word belfry. It is difficult to believe

---

[1] "Turres vocatæ, quod teretes sint et longæ: teres enim est aliquid rotundum cum proceritate, ut columnæ."—Isidor. Orig. lib. xv. ch. 2.

[2] Mr. Fergusson, speaking of the ground plan of the Monastery of St. Gall, published by Mabillon, and held by him to have been the work of Eginhard, in the reign of Charlemagne, draws attention to the fact that in the text which accompanies it no mention is made of bells in connection with the towers which stand at either side of the entrance to the church, but rather that the writer intimates that the towers were designed for watch-towers.—See Hist. of Architecture, vol. i. p. 564.

[3] *Bretêche*, s. f. On désignait ainsi, au moyen âge, un ouvrage de bois à plusieurs étages, crénelé, dont on se servait pour attaquer et défendre les places fortes. Quand il s'agit de l'attaque, la bretêche diffère du beffroi en ce qu'elle est immobile, tandis que le beffroi est mobile.—Dict., vol. ii. p. 186.

that the first great towers near the churches of Ravenna and Ireland were merely, or even primarily, intended for hanging bells at their summits. Even could the existence of very large bells at so early a period as the Carlovingian era be proved, the towers themselves of Ravenna and Epinal, as well as those in Ireland, are not so constructed as to show that their primary object was for the emission of sound, or its transmission over a very wide tract of country. The apertures at the top are much too small. But the bells of the eleventh century, both on the Continent and in Ireland, were generally small, and light.

CAPITAL IN CHURCH OF ST. GEORGE DE BOCHERVILLE.

Only after the year 1200 did they begin to make them of any great size; yet, notwithstanding the diminutive nature of the bells from the tenth to the thirteenth centuries, it appears that the belfries were quite equal, both in height and diameter, to those of a later period, and their purpose must have been independent of the use of a sonorous signal, however they may have served for the safe-keeping of those objects always held among the most sacred treasures of the churches, and preserved with the crosier and the shrine in these keeps of the monastery.[1]

---

[1] " Græci multò recentiùs à Veneto acceperunt, qui (ut tradit Sabellicus) Ænnead.

Irish Church Towers.

The especial sacredness attached to bells was not peculiar to Ireland.[1] They were set apart from all secular uses, and blessed or consecrated, and that the custom even of baptizing bells existed in

KING DAVID IN MS. PSALTER.

FEMALE BELL RINGER IN ILLUMINATED MS.

9 lib. 1 circa AN. DOM. 874. Basilio Imperatori duodenas magni ponderis, artificiique non vulgaris dono misit campanas; suntque Venatorum munere tum primum Græci campano ære usi."—Spelman, Glossar., p. 98. When the Abbot Agilulfus rebuilt the church of St. Columbanus, at Bobbio, between the years 883 and 905, he is described as placing bells in the tower: " Ipsam denique eamdem Ecclesiam venerabilis Abbas Agilulfus ex lapidibus struxit, turrimque super eam ædificavit, et campanas in ea fecit pendere, sicut nunc cernitur."—Fleming, Collectanea Sacra, p. 245.—Messingham, Florilegium, p. 240.

[1] Mr. Brereton, writing in the year 1763, states that Bishop Pocock had seen a large trumpet of iron, which was dug from the bottom of one of these towers, and adds that "several such have been found in Ireland, near these buildings; some of them are exhibited in one of the plates published by this Society, and others are now extant in the Royal Museum." If this statement be correct, this would point to their occasional use as watch-towers, but the editor has not yet succeeded in finding any confirmation of this statement.—See Archælogia, vol. ii. p. 82. In the pontificate of Stephen, A.D. 754, Christian congregations are said to have been collected by the sound of trumpets :—

" Ære tubas fuso attollit, quibus agmina plebis,
Admoneat laudes, et vota referre tonanti."—Flodoard in Stephen II.

However, his successor, Stephen III., about 780, erected a tower on the church of St. Peter at Rome, and placed in it three bells; and in 850 Leo IV. built a belfry, and set in it a bell with a golden hammer.—Anastasius in Steph. III., and Leon. IV. " Fecit etiam ibi ipsum campanile, et posuit campanam cum malleo aureo."—Spelman, Glossar., p. 98.

the eighth century is proved by the fact that Charlemagne issued an express injunction against it,[1] or against some superstitious practice regarding the blessing or consecrating of bells.

BELL-RINGER AND PLAYER ON THE ROTE IN ILLUMINATED MS.

Bell-ringing in the tenth century appears to have been practised in two different ways, one being the mere use of the signal bell of the handbell-ringer; the other, the art of the carillon player, which

---

[1] "Etsi Capitularia Caroli Magni anno 780 edita n. 18, jubent *ut cloccæ non baptizentur*, antiquus tamen usus ecclesiæ obtinuit, ut signorum seu campanarum benedictio baptismi nomine indigitetur. (Martene, Antiq. Eccl. Rit., tom. ii. p. 296 *b*.) The distinction marked in this passage between cloccæ and campanæ, while it must point to a difference in size, need not convey that any bell so large as those we now associate with belfries was intended, but only such variety as the examples which remain to us of these early bells show to have prevailed.

implied a knowledge of music, and the exercise of the player's talent on a series of bells tuned to different notes, which could form an harmonious accompaniment to the harp or rote.

In illustration of this usage, a representation may be seen on the capital of a column in the church of St. George de Bocherville, Normandy, founded by William the Conqueror[1] (fig. *w*), and in fig. *x*, taken from an ancient psalter in the British Museum,[2] King David is represented playing on five bells with a hammer in each hand, while in fig. *y*, taken from a MS. in the Royal Library at Brussels, a female figure is seen seated, and striking four bells in a like manner.[3]

The bells preserved in the Irish belfries, like those referred to in the tower of Armagh at the date 1020, may have been a group of such objects slung in a row from a bar in the upper chamber of the tower, in a manner similar to that in the above illustrations from illuminated MSS. of the ninth and tenth centuries. Thus in fig. *z*, taken from a MS. of St. Blaise, A.D. 800 to 900, five of these bells are suspended in a row and struck by a hammer[4] held in the hand; the bar is placed across a round arch springing from shafts crowned by a capital of an early Romanesque type, and the little tower, which, though in ignorance of perspective, is drawn as if rising on the capital, was most probably meant to represent the belfry in the background where the bells were kept. These slender towers, with small apertures and conical roofs surmounted by a cross, quite correspond with the Irish cloicethech. A type of small belfry placed on the roof of the church, more fitted for the emission of sound, and not built with military or defensive purpose, may have also been in use at this early period. In fig. *a* such a belfry with four bells is represented, and is very different in character from the Irish tower. Here the chamber walls are not merely pierced by narrow slits, such as the apertures in the tops of the defensive ecclesiastical

---

[1] See Turner's Tour in Normandy, vol. ii. p. 13.
[2] In King's Library, British Museum, 20, B. xi.
[3] See Ellacombe's Church Bells of Devon, p. 306. On the west side of the south-east cross of Monasterboice, a figure is seen bending, as if to strike a bell with a hammer.—O'Neil, Irish Crosses, Pl. 19. And in one compartment of an ancient sculptured cross at Kilcullen, which stands to the north of the round tower, the figure of an ecclesiastic may be seen raising a hammer to strike the bell which hangs before him.
[4] De Cantu et musica sacra a Prima Ecclesiæ ætate usque ad Præseus Tempus auctore Martino Gerberto Monasterii et Cong. S. Blasii in Silva Nigra Abbate.—Fig.

towers, but the belfry is open to the air. This representation of what appears to have been a small structure placed on the roof of the church is found in the Benedictional of S. Æthelwold, executed at Hyde Abbey about the year 980.[1]

The office of bellringer in Ireland was associated with that of porter, and the Irish word for bell-ringer, *aistire*, is, as Dr. Petrie remarks, obviously formed from the Latin *ostiarius*. Le Blant, in his work on Christian Inscriptions, tells us "L'office d'ostiarius est souvent mentionné dans les textes antiques; c'est le plus humble degré des fonctions de l'Eglise. L'ostiarius était le gardien du Saint lieu; il en défendait l'entrée aux indignes et annonçait le jour et la nuit les heures de la prière;"[2] and the same writer adduces evidence of the existence of such an office in the year 551. In Ireland, at a later date, the work of the *aistire* is divided into two classes. "Noble his work when the bell is that of the cloicthech, humble his work when it is a hand-bell."[3] This passage can hardly be taken as evidence that the tower-bell was larger than the hand-bell, since, even were such the case, the task of pulling a large bell with a rope cannot be deemed nobler than that of swinging a hand-bell, but it may point to such a difference as exists between the carillon bell-ringer and the mere servant who swings a hand-bell.

The same progress and development may be traced in bell-making as is perceivable in other forms of art in Ireland, and there is as great a difference between the rude iron square bell of St. Patrick in the fifth century (fig. *b*) and that of Cumascach, son of Ailill, in the tenth (fig. *c*), as there is between the oratories of the founders of Christianity and the churches of Cormac O'Cillen.[4] Yet no bell that we have

---

iii. tab. 26. The editor is indebted to Mr. Wm. Chappell for this interesting illustration.

[1] Æthelwold, Bishop of Winchester, in A.D. 963, died 984. The scribe who executed this work, Godemann, was abbot of Thorny between the years 963 and 984. In this, the last miniature in the volume, the bishop is represented giving his blessing. On the little tower of the church a cock is placed—for vigilance.

[2] Le Blant gives the following references to the word Ostiarius:—Du Cange, tome iv. Ostiarius, H. Vo.; Cancellieri, *De Secretariis*, p. 474; l'Abbé Greppo, *Revue du Lyonnais*, tom. xiii. p. 190; Ce mot se trouve cinq fois, Orthographie comme sur le Marbre de Trèves, dans les souscriptions d'un acte de vente de l'an 551 (Marini, Pap. Dipl. p. 183); Une double prière du *Missale Francorum* est intitulée, "Benedictio Usteanii" (Thomasius, Codices Sacramentorum, p. 398); S. Greg. *Opp.*, ed. Bened. tom. iii. pars. 1, col. 220 et 489.

[3] This passage is found in a tract of the Brehon laws, Seanchus beag, preserved in the Book of Lecan.

[4] See Notes on Irish Architecture, vol. i. Pl. LXIV. text, p. 125.

heard of has been found in Ireland to exceed 13 in. in height. They are generally without ornament, but Lord Dunraven in his work on Adare,[1] has described one which is enriched with a border and a cross. It is of fine bronze, and measures 12 in. high, 9 in. wide, and 9½ in. deep. This bell was found at Cashel in the year 1849.

If we adopt the idea that the cloictige were not only, as their original name proves, places where bells were housed, but also where carillons were played, we need not disconnect the towers from bells,

BELL OF ST. PATRICK.

CLOG BEANNAIGHTHE.

or sever them from the beautiful associations with their sound which still linger in the traditions of the peasantry, and which their name conveys. Thus the memory of a bell which once hung in the bell-house of Aughagower, in the county of Mayo, is still preserved in the neighbourhood, where the people say that it was buried for concealment in a bog close by, and that of a quiet evening its sound, "like silver," can be heard across the waste; the same story is told of the bells of Ferta, hidden in a neighbouring swamp; and Dr. Petrie relates, that at Rattoo a silver bell of wonderful sweetness is said to have hung in the upper story of the tower, but during the "troubles" it was thrown into the River Brick. It cannot now be found, though its melancholy tones used occasionally to be heard rising from the water.[2]

---

[1] Memorials of Adare, p. 152.
[2] The writer carried an ordinary dinner-bell to the top of Clondalkin round tower, and observed that the sound seemed much greater when heard within the topmost

If we examine the statements regarding these buildings in the annals we find that the bell or bells of the monastery are generally enumerated among the ecclesiastical treasures destroyed in the attack upon the church tower. Besides the relics and the crosier of the patron saint of Slane, which had been removed for safety into the cloicc-thech, "the bell, which was the best of bells," was also burnt when the Norsemen stormed the place. However, there is no evidence to prove that this crosier was anything better than the oak staff

ANCIENT BELLS OF IRELAND.

of St. Erc, who is said to have died in the year 514, and the bell, than the hand-bell of the altar. The same authorities allude to the destruction of the *bells* of Armagh. And Cashel was traditionally called Cashel of the Bells; but we have no reason to believe that these were more than small bells similar to those that have been found in such numbers in Ireland.

---

chamber of the tower than in an ordinary hall, and a friend standing at a distance of 100 ft. from the building, said the tone was quite as loud as when rung beside her down on the level of the ground. This bell, being of good bell-metal, the composition of which does not appear to have been known before the thirteenth century, would, of course, yield a much greater volume of sound than the thin bronze or iron

Dr. Lynch, writing in the reign of Queen Elizabeth, has also alluded to these towers in a manner which shows, not only his conviction of their ecclesiastical purpose, but also of their comparatively late date. " None of them," he says, "are ever found in Ireland, except in cemeteries of cathedral churches or of the most celebrated abbeys." And again he remarks (vol. ii. p. 191), referring to the progress of the art of building after the time of St. Columba : " In later ages those slender, high, and round pillar towers, which still stand near most of the cathedral churches of Ireland, began to be erected of stone and used as belfries, after the invasions of the Danes." Then, in allusion to their purpose, he observes :[1] " In course of time the custom was introduced of hanging bells in the top of

---

of the tenth-century bells. Nevertheless, we may believe that the small bells of an early period may have been as audible from the top of these towers as at their base or within their churches. Although such bells never could have sufficed for sonorous signals by which the inhabitants of the wide tracts of country visible from the summits of these towers could be summoned either to prayer or arms, yet it may be held that five small bells tuned to the five notes which composed our ancient scale, and played with a metal hammer while slung on a bar of wood or iron, might produce a delightful effect within the tower, and also be quite audible to the inhabitants of the monastic buildings that clustered round its base. In this manner we may account for the bars of iron or of oak said to have been observed at Ballagh, Trummery, Ardmore, and Clondalkin. The first allusion made to these towers is where the legend is related by Giraldus Cambrensis of the city buried in Lough Neagh, whose church towers could be seen, in calm weather, through the water; and as the belief was that this lake had its origin in a flood that had occurred in the first century of the Christian era, it is held that Giraldus must have considered such submerged buildings as pre-Christian. But at most he does but compare them to the church towers built after the fashion of the country, and the legend belongs only to a whole cycle of such stories of buried cities or churches found in the British islands and off the coast of France, as well as on the shores of the Dead Sea, where Chateaubriand and Lamartine met with the same legend. In England, the idea is generally to be found in mining districts, where the miners say, that not only the bells of these buried churches may be heard from the bowels of the earth, but men's voices also chanting hymns and anthems. In mountainous districts the peasants collect in the fields or valleys to hear the bells, which are sure to sound out for joy on Christmas eve, from beneath their feet. In Germany, the legend is of a lost church in a thick dark forest, which has suggested some beautiful lines to the poet Uhland; and there are many which speak of submerged cities, as in one of the lakes at Crossmere in Shropshire, where a chapel is said to have been submerged, and the villagers tell that the bells may constantly be heard ringing beneath the still waters. Much poetry hangs about such legends wherever they occur, relating how, through the silent night— whether to the fisher, or the sailor, or the miner—they speak of a city or a temple that is buried, or a life that has passed away into darkness, yet lives, and with its pure and tender sound calls to us from the deep.

[1] Cambrensis Eversus, with translation by the Rev. Matthew Kelly, vol. iii. p. 343. (Celtic Soc. Dubl. 1851-2.)

them, and using them as belfries, not towering, as at present, over the centre of the church, and resting on arches, but raised to a suitable height from the ground plane of the cemetery."[1] From these observations it must be allowed that we should look to some other use for the church towers of Ireland besides the mere hanging of signal bells; and although we hold that they were used, as their name indicates, as places for the housing of bells, yet that the primary purpose for which they were meant was the accommodation of bells alone, seems a theory which is wholly untenable. We must reconsider some of the material evidence afforded by the structures themselves, if we would learn the original object of the builders. First, it should be remembered that they were altogether closed in; that their small doorways, from 4 to 5 ft. 6 in. in height, were evidently furnished with double doors.[2] "The exterior door," as Mr. Wm. Morrison has remarked, "placed necessarily in an innermost position, was deemed indispensable," while the interior one was hung within the inner face of the wall from projecting brackets of stone. That these double doors were of iron is rendered probable by the fact that one was in existence to a late date in the tower at Iniscaltra. It hung inside the arch, and was remembered by the oldest inhabitants of the neighbouring country at the beginning of this century, and the traces of the hinge fastening on the left side were seen by Dr. O'Donovan, while on the right a piece of the iron holdfast still remains where the bolt entered. In this tower, as well as in those of Roscrea, Rattoo, and Armoy, Ardmore, Fertagh, and Kilkenny, appliances for an inner and permanent door, either a socket, pivot-hole, or projecting stone for receiving bolts, have been observed, along with the bolt-holes and rebate or stop, at both sides, for fastening the outer and removable shutter. These contrivances, along with the fact that the doorways (like those of the circular military towers at Dinkelsbühl) were generally from 10 ft. to 13 ft. above the level of the ground, were certainly means resorted to as protection from forcible entry; and it is evident that, at a subsequent period, those defences have been designedly, and often carefully, removed, owing perhaps to the increased security of the country. A close examination of the other apertures in these buildings leads to the conviction that they were more of the nature of loopholes than apertures either for the admission of light or for the emission of sound. They were placed near the floor, one on each story, and each commanding a different side of

---

[1] Cambrensis Eversus, with translation by the Rev. Matthew Kelly, vol. ii. p. 191.
[2] Eccl. Arch. of Ireland, pp. 370, 374. (Trans. R. I. Academy, vol. xx.)

the tower, one almost always over the door. Weighty missiles could be thus pushed through them and let fall on the besiegers underneath, and in some instances, as at Lusk, the cill slopes downwards externally, as if to afford facility for pushing such missiles outwards through the thickness of the wall.

Dr. Petrie, who held very strongly to the opinion that these towers were used for places of safety and defence, as well as for belfries, quotes a passage in support of this view from an essay by Colonel Montmorency on the subject, where he remarks:[1] "The pillar-tower, as a defensive hold, taking into account the period that produced it, may fairly pass for one of the completest inventions that can well be imagined. Impregnable every way, and proof against fire, it could never be taken by assault. Although the abbey and its dependences blazed around, the tower disregarded the fury of the flames; its extreme height, its isolated position, and diminutive doorway, elevated so many feet above the ground, placed it beyond the reach of the destroyer. The signal once made, announcing the approach of a foe, by those who kept watch on the top, the alarm spread instantaneously, not only among the inmates of the cloister, but the inhabitants were roused to arms in the country many miles around." And it has also been observed by Sir Walter Scott, "These towers might possibly have been contrived for the temporary retreat of the priest, and the means of protecting the holy things from desecration on the occasion of alarm, which in those uncertain times suddenly happened and as suddenly passed away."[2] Consisting of a series of small chambers one above another at a height above ground, they were fitted for places of stowage for the sacred things of the church, places of passive defence for the aged and weak, and could afford temporary shelter for from forty to eighty persons from the attacks of an enemy only armed with bows and arrows and such weapons as we know were in use at the time in the north-west of Europe.

It is also worthy of note, that in the two instances where these towers are mentioned by Giraldus Cambrensis, writing in the year 1187, there is nothing said to support the idea that they were then regarded as built for the purpose of upraising a sonorous signal, although their ecclesiastical character is distinctly asserted. He speaks of the "ecclesiastical towers which, according to the custom of the country, are slender and lofty, and moreover round." He does

---

[1] Eccl. Arch. of Ireland, p. 373.
[2] See Quarterly Review, vol. xli. 1829.

not here allude to the practice of erecting such buildings as being a thing of the past, but expresses himself as if speaking of a custom that existed at the period in which he writes, and implies that the towers he alludes to were such as the Irish were building when he visited the country; and in the story he relates of the falcon of Kildare the incidental allusion to the "church tower" is another instance which conveys that they were held to be ecclesiastical in the twelfth century.[1] This is an important fact to observe, since it is an argument against the theory of the remote prehistoric period of the erection of these buildings, while it is quite compatible with the belief that many of them may belong to the eleventh or twelfth centuries.[2]

When a number of observations, starting from independent sources, are all found to converge on one given point, arguments founded on such, which, if taken separately, might each prove insufficient for the establishment of any theory, must gain almost incontrovertible force if thus endowed with united action. In this instance six various leading courses of observation point to the close of the ninth century for the date of this striking innovation in architecture:—

1. Correspondence of masonry with that of other buildings of this date.

2. Correspondence of architectural style of the first examples with ditto.

3. Condition of iron fittings in harmony with this date.

4. Defensive ecclesiastical buildings not required before this date.

5. Historical notices and traditions of the towers, first associating them with this date.

---

[1] " Turres ecclesiasticas, quæ more patriæ arctæ sunt et altæ, necnon et rotundæ." Topog. Hib. dist. ii. cap. 9 (Opp. vol. v. ed. Dimock, p. 92). "A tempore Brigidæ falco quidam egregius locum istum frequentabat, qui et ecclesiasticæ turris summitati insidere consueverat." Ib. cap. 37 (p. 122).

[2] It is quite impossible that iron exposed to the air in the damp climate of Ireland should last for thousands of years, and yet, as I have been informed by Professor Emerson Reynolds, an iron bar of moderate thickness might last a very considerable time indeed, even when exposed to damp and wind. The first effect of such exposure would be to coat the iron bar with a protecting covering of oxide of iron; and though, of course, this would gradually drop off and expose the underlying metal to the damp and wind, it would take a very long time to eat completely through the bar. If the iron were near the sea, perchloride of iron would be formed, and the process of disintegration would be more rapid. Those towers are all inland where such iron fittings have been found, and these observations lead to the conclusion that, while it is possible for iron to endure eight or nine centuries in such positions, it is not to be believed that they have lasted for eighteen hundred or two thousand years.

6. Existence of analogous buildings on the Continent at or about this time.

The conclusion drawn from all these data being that such towers, though constructed from time to time over a considerable period, and undergoing corresponding changes in detail, were first built at the close of the ninth century, and that a number seem to have been erected simultaneously, it now remains for us to investigate the external causes which led to the introduction of this defensive element in the architecture of the church.

"La marche des arts est lente, conséquente, logique, les grands résultats ne sont que le produit d'efforts considérables, suivis, réguliers, de traditions perpétuées ou reprises, mais dont il est facile de retrouver la trace, pour peu qu'on s'en donne la peine. S'il y a des soubresauts, des revirements brusques en politique, il n'en est jamais ainsi dans les arts, et surtout dans l'art de l'architecture."[1]

To trace out the history of the causes which produced the great effort manifested in the apparently simultaneous erection of many of these buildings forms the next part of our task.

The reluctance still shown by many to part with their faith in the vast antiquity of these "pillar towers," even now, after the conclusive arguments by which Dr. Petrie fixed their Christian origin and use, can only be understood when we realize the visionary charm that such experience robbed them of, which to men of much poetic feeling has seemed to cling around their walls as naturally as the mosses and lichens with which they are clothed.

> "O, mystic Tower! I never gaze on thee,
> Altho' since childhood's scarce remember'd spring
> Thou wert to me a most familiar thing,
> Without an awe, and not from wonder free.
>
>   *   *   *   *
>
> "Oh, structure strange and column-like and high!
> Thy lofty brow is lifted towards the sky,
> And all things human that around thee lie,
> Thou, lonely watcher, here, ere they began,
> Saw'st as they rose around thee."[2]

But truth may clothe these ruins yet with that deeper poetry which belongs to honest labour, and reveals in their worn stones the signs of

---

[1] See Viollet-le-Duc, Entretiens sur l'Architecture, tom. 1ᵉʳ, p. 198.
[2] Hist. and Antiqs. of St. Canice's Cathedral, pp. 124, 126. Sonnets by the Rev James Leckey.

noble effort and of progress in an ideal cause. "Here," says one of our greatest living authors, "undoubtedly lies the chief poetic energy: in the force of imagination that pierces or exalts the solid fact, instead of floating among cloud-pictures."[1]

---

[1] Daniel Deronda, book iv. p. 326.

KILLMALLOCK CHURCH AND TOWER.

CHAPTER VI.

THE NORTHMEN IN IRELAND.

PUGIN has observed in his essay on the Revival of Christian Architecture that "the history of architecture is the history of the world;"[1] therefore in tracing the origin and growth of new forms in this art, we may expect to find a parallel stream in the course of events which mark the career of the race to whom it belongs. Where any decided innovation occurs in the architecture of a country, it seems probable that some revolution in its history may be found to account for the phenomenon. Hitherto the churches of Ireland, in their humble proportions and symmetrical simplicity, were the natural offspring, not only, as Dr. Petrie has beautifully expressed it, "of a religion not made for the rich, but for the poor and lowly;"[2] they were also the result of choice and adherence to a primitive national system. Even after the introduction of the ornamented style termed Irish Romanesque, we find that there was no material departure from the simple ground-plan and small dimensions of the earlier churches of the horizontal lintel. The church system of Ireland continued to be, as it had always been, one that entailed the erection of a number of small buildings, either grouped together, as at Glendalough, or thickly scattered over the face of the country; and at the time of transition to Romanesque there was no corresponding change in the ecclesiastical system of the country.

When the group of humble dwellings which formed the monasteries and schools of Ireland is seen at the foot of the lofty tower whose masonry rarely seems to correspond in date with the buildings

---

[1] Essay on the Revival of Christian Architecture. A. Welby Pugin, p. 4.
[2] Petrie's Eccl. Architecture, p. 190.

that surround it, and which does not, as elsewhere, seem a component and accessory part of the whole pile that formed the feudal abbey, we cannot but feel that some new condition in the history of the Irish Church must have arisen to account for the apparition of these bold and lofty structures; and here we may take up the thread of the history where we left it, at the close of that period of steady progress from the fifth to the end of the eighth century, when the language of Ireland was being developed and her schools were the most frequented in Northern Europe. In the beginning of the ninth century a new state of things was ushered in, and a change took place in the hitherto unmolested condition of the Church. Ireland became the battle-field of the first struggle between Paganism and Christianity in Western Europe;[1] and the result of the effort then made in defence of her faith is marked in the ecclesiastical architecture of the country by the apparently simultaneous erection of a number of lofty towers, rising in strength of "defence and faithfulness of watch" before the doorways of those churches most liable to be attacked. For seven centuries Christianity had steadily advanced in Western Europe. At first silent and unseen, we feel how wondrously it grew,[2] until, in the reign of Charlemagne, it became an instrument in the hands of one whose mission was to strengthen his borders against the heathen, and to establish a Christian monarchy.

Dense as is the obscurity in which the cause of the wanderings and ravages of the Scandinavian Vikings is enveloped, yet the result of the investigations hitherto made upon the subject is, that they were in a great measure consequent on the conquests of Charlemagne in the north of Germany, and on the barrier which he thereby—as well as by the introduction of Christianity—set to their onward march. It can hardly be attributed to accident that with the gradual strengthening of the Frankish dominion the hordes of Northmen descended on the British Islands in ever increasing numbers. The policy of Charlemagne in his invasion of Saxony, A.D. 772, and the energy by which he succeeded in driving his enemies beyond the Elbe and to the German Ocean, were manifestly directed and intensified by religious zeal. The Saxons were still heathens, and the first attack made by the Frankish King was on the fortress of Eresbourg,[3] where stood the temple of Irminsul, the great idol of the nation.

---

[1] See The Story of Burnt Njal. Dasent, vol. i. Introd. p. clxxxix.; also Quarterly Review, No. 283, July, 1876, p. 133.
[2] Works of George Herbert, 2nd ed. vol. ii. p. 127.
[3] Now Stadberg, between Cassel and Paderborn. Gaillard, Histoire de Charlemagne, tome i. p. 344.

We read that he laid waste their temples, and their idols were broken in pieces. " He built monasteries and churches, founded bishoprics, and filled Saxony with priests and missionaries. For some years previously the countries between the Elbe, Upper Saxony, the German Ocean, and the Baltic, had been devastated by the Frankish army, the population flying into Denmark and the North, and the war of Charlemagne," writes Mr. Haliday, " was now a crusade. Its object was alike to conquer and convert. The military and religious habits were united in his camp, which was the scene of martial exercises, solemn processions, and public prayers; and the clergy, who crowded round his standard, participated in the objects and results of his victories." The war thus entered upon leads us to that point in the history of the Western Church when the religion of Christ is first met by a mighty revulsion arising in the mingled grandeur and gloom of all that is great and all that is false in the spirit of ancient heathenism, when the flood, driven backwards into northern seas, first heaved its mighty volume of resistant waters, and broke in a great wave upon the Irish shore.

However it may appear from ancient authorities that for some centuries before the Scandinavians had occasionally infested the southern shores of Europe, yet in the added light that is cast by the Irish annals upon the subject, we perceive that from this date their piratical incursions afford evidence not before met with of preconcerted plan and insistent energy; and these events in the reign of Charlemagne may lead us to discover what was the strong impulse that thus tended in some measure to condense and concentrate their desultory warfare. Impelled by some strong overmastering passion, these hordes of northern warriors held on from year to year their avenging march; and such was the fury of their arms that even now, after a lapse of a thousand years, their deeds are held in appalling remembrance throughout Europe, not only in every city on the sea shore or on the river, but even in the peasant traditions of the smallest inland village. "Wheresoever," says Mr. Laing, "this people from beyond the pale and influence of the old Roman empire and of the later Church empire of Rome, either settled, mingled, or marauded, they have left permanent traces in society of their laws, institutions, character, and spirit. Pagan and barbarian as they were, they seem to have carried with them something more natural, something more suitable to the social wants of man, than the laws and institutions formed under the Roman power."[1]

---

[1] The Heimskringla, or Chron. Kings Norway, translated by S. Laing, Prelim. Dissert. vol. i. pp. 5, 11.

Yet, when all has been said that can be for the invigorating influence of their energy and the enkindling spark they are held to have borne with them of a free social existence, in which men might have a voice in their government and in the enactment of their laws, it must still be borne in mind that at the period when Ireland was the scene of this struggle, and indeed for two centuries later, the faith of these Northmen was idolatry, and there is no proof that they possessed the knowledge of letters. In contemplating the history of a period which left as it did such important traces in the ecclesiastical architecture of North-Western Europe we may pause to consider the two forms of faith that now met face to face in battle. In both these systems we find belief in the immortality of the soul,[1] but the latter is merely based on faith in the potency for good or ill of the embodied forces of nature. "The primary characteristic of this old Northland mythology," says Carlyle, is the "Impersonation" and "earnest simple recognition of the workings of Physical Nature, as a thing wholly miraculous, stupendous, and divine," the recognition of such forces as personal agencies, gods and demons; and in this faith the main result attained was the belief in an inexorable and inflexible destiny which it is useless trying to bend or soften, and that the one thing needful for a man was to be brave. Odin stands the central figure of this Scandinavian religion; Frigga, Freya, and Thor attend with a number of minor deities, and throughout the whole mythology vestiges of an ancient and general tradition are to be found. Oracles, divinations, auspices, presages, and lots formed parts of their system.[2] The Christianity by which this religion was confronted may be also said to have preserved vestiges of ancient heathenism; but if we contemplate it in the only fair way to look at any form of faith, that is, as revealed to us by its representative men and through the medium of their mind, we behold it as the handmaid of original investigation and discovery. The teachers of Ireland from the eighth to the tenth century declared the spherical form of the earth, and the summer solstice in the Northern hemispheres, while her astronomers had well-nigh anticipated the theory of Copernicus.[3]

---

[1] See Carlyle on Heroes, Hero Worship, and the Heroic in History, pp. 15, 17, 28.

[2] Mallet's Northern Antiquities, p. 103.

[3] Ferghil the Geometer, or Virgilius Solivagus, abbot of Aghabo in Ireland, and bishop of Saltzburg in Bavaria, was one of the most distinguished mathematicians of his time. and among the first who asserted that there were antipodes. See Note by Dr. O'Donovan, Ann. Four Masters, vol. i. p. 391. Lanigan, Eccl. Hist. of Ireland, vol. iii. pp. 179 to 206.

We find these ecclesiastics upholding Greek learning and philosophic speculation, asserting the freedom of the will, even at this early date, and still clinging fast to that faith which more than a century before had given to us the Hymn of Patrick with its passionate and absorbing devotion to Christ; while in the fearless denunciations of sin poured forth by Columbanus and Kilian upon the rulers in whose power they lay, we see the courageous faith of men ready to lay down their life in the cause of that moral purity which is involved in our religion.

Soon after the alliance of the Saxon King Witikind with Sigefroi of Denmark and some time before the establishment of the monarchy in Norway under Harald Harfagra, the Danish ships made their first descent upon the coasts of France and the British islands; and the long series of invasions that ensued proves how the flame soon spread to Norway and to Sweden, which for centuries to come poured its lava torrent upon Western Europe. "We have sung the mass of lances," the Northmen would say, in derision; "it began at dawn of morning, and has lasted until night;"[1] while an ancient bard of Ireland sings :—

> "Bitter in sooth is the wind to-night,
> Rousing the wrath of the white-haired sea;
> For smooth sea-sailing hath no delight
> To Noroway's sons so bold and free."[2]

Ireland, which hitherto had been the "workshop of men famous for learning and sanctity," was now to become the fortaliced outpost of the Western Church.

In the year 794 we read[3] of the first attack made by these invaders upon Irish shores, when a party of the heathen Vikings,

---

[1] Attum odda messu . . . (Olai Wormii Litteraturæ Runica, p. 208). Scriptores rerum Danicarum, vol. i. p. 374. *Ibid.* vol. iv. 26. (A.D. 787 to 835. See Thierry's Hist. of the Norman Conquest, p. 21.)

[2] This quatrain, translated by W. S., is quoted by Zeuss, 928, from the St. Gall Priscian; the original is as follows :—

> "Is acher in gáith innocht,
> Fufuasna fairgge find-folt;
> Ni ágor reimm mora minn
> Dond laechraid lainn oa Lochlind."
> (See Irish Glosses, Trans. Irish Archæol. Society, 1860.)

[3] Wars of the Gaedhil with the Gaill, edited by Dr. Todd, from three Irish MSS., one of which, preserved in the Book of Leinster, is held to date from about the year 1100. See Introd. pp. xlvii. to lvii.

driven from the coast of Glamorganshire, descend upon the little island of Lambay and plunder its sacred shrine. Their advent is said to have been foretold in numerous prophetic warnings :—[1]

"And the Pagans shall come over the wild wave, by whom shall confusion be brought upon the Gael.
"In the abbacy of every church, the black Gentiles of Dublin.
"There shall be of them an abbot over this my church, who will not attend to Matins.
"Without Pater and without credo, without Irish, but only foreign language."[2]

This verse, taken from a prophetic poem attributed to St. Berchan,[3] of Clonsost in Queen's County, who lived at the close of the seventh century, bears evidence to the fact that a belief existed at an early period in Ireland that this war was something different from a mere struggle against pirates, but rather a special contest between the Christian institutions of the country and the heathenism of the new comers.

Is it not then a question worthy of more consideration than it has yet received, whether the theory propounded by many French historians, and supported by Lappenberg, Todd, and Haliday, that the wars with the Norsemen were, in their origin, a struggle between Paganism and Christianity, be true or not? May we not hold it possible that this, the nobler, may also be the *truer* view to take of the origin of these wars? Such enterprises as these great invasions may, in the beginning, spring from just resentment, and be attended with high resolve and nobler aims than those of mere greed or even love of adventure, although in succeeding centuries, obedient to some mournful law of declension and decay, that seems to rule all human effort, the cause may become degraded, and, as in the case of the Crusades, the first pure impulse that fired the undertaking in its youth sinks into pillage and robbery at its close?

At first these invaders seem to have confined their efforts to the outlying islands on the coast of Ireland, and it was not until about the year 818 that we read of a regularly organized invasion, headed by a Norwegian leader named, by Irish writers, Thorgils (servant of Thor), latinized Turgesius; but whom, antiquaries have suggested, may be identified with Ragnar Lodbrok, whose heroism is sung in

---

[1] The Scandinavians and the Scandinavian Antiqs. of Dublin, by Ch. Haliday, p. 14.
[2] Wars of the Gaedhil with the Gaill, p. 11.
[3] See Martyrology of Donegal, Dec. 4 (327), Intr. xxxii. No. 3; xli. No. 19. O'Curry's Lectures, p. 412.

the famous death-song of the Icelandic Skald.[1] This king seems evidently to have aimed at the establishment of a regular government and the foundation of a permanent colony in Ireland, with the subjugation or extermination of the native princes. For this purpose the forces under his command were skilfully posted on Loch Ree, at Limerick, Dundalk Bay, Carlingford, Lough Neagh, and Dublin. He appears also to have attempted, and in part achieved, the establishment of the national heathenism of his own country in the place of the Christianity which he found in Ireland. In the year 839, we read: "Moreover Ardmacha (Armagh) was plundered three times in the same month by them, and Turgeis himself usurped the abbacy of Ardmacha and Farannan." In this passage we learn that he usurped the abbacy, that is to say, the full authority and jurisdiction, in Armagh and the north of Ireland. And the full significance of these renewed assaults upon this church and his final establishment in this place will be perceived when it is remembered that Armagh was the principal ecclesiastical city of the north of Ireland. Thorgils reigned here for four years, while Forannan, the real abbot, or bishop and chief successor of Patrick, was driven out and fled to Munster. Not satisfied with the full supremacy he had acquired in the north, this Pagan achieved the conquest of the other ecclesiastical city of Ireland, Clonmacnois. For this purpose he took command of a fleet he had stationed in Loch Ree, from which place he plundered all the great ecclesiastical establishments upon its shores and the neighbouring banks of the Shannon, as far as Iniscaltra and Lorrha; and, having seized Clonmacnois and burnt its oratories, he appears to have left his wife as sovereign there. The manner in which her office is described is very significant, and seems to bear out the theory that his object was to supplant the national religion by heathenism, to suppress the ecclesiastical as well as the civil authorities of the country, and to destroy the Christian Church. One authority states,

---

[1] This is not the place for any lengthened discussion on a question of this nature, even had the writer knowledge sufficient to cope with it; nevertheless, it would be well that students of Scandinavian literature should remember that much light may be thrown on their subject by a comparison with that of Ireland, that while we are still in the region of myth and heroic legend in Scandinavia, we have more or less attained a period of historic fact in Irish records. And the oldest Sagas—first committed to writing in the 11th century—may possibly be imitations of the historic poems, such as the battle of Moyra, which they had met with in Ireland a century before. "Many such productions," says Dr. Todd, "of undoubted antiquity, are still extant in the Irish language." The first Saga writer in the Norse language, Are Hinn Frode, is said to have been born in Iceland in 1067, and lived to 1148 or 1158. (See Wars of the Gaedhil with the Gaill, p. xxviii. note 2.)

"Cluainmicnois was taken by his wife. It was on the altar of the great church she used to give her answers. Otta was the name of the wife of Torgeis."[1] Another says, "The place where Ota, the wife of Turgeis, used to give her audience was upon the altar of Cluain-mic-Nois."[2] Duald Mac Firbis states, in his Account of Danish Families in Ireland, that "Turgeis took possession of, and held his residence at, Clonmacnois, and that his wife was wont to issue her orders to the people from the high altar of the cathedral church there." The statement in the first of these quotations, that the Queen "delivered her answers" from the altar of Clonmacnois cathedral, seems to point to the establishment of heathen rites in the churches of Ireland, and to suggest that oracles were uttered by her, and it is perhaps in allusion to some such practices that the writer of the Annals of Clonmacnois refers when, describing the ravages of the Northmen, he says, "the churches, abbeys, and other religious places were by them quite razed and debased, or otherwise turned to vile, base, servile, and abominable uses."[3]

The condition of Ireland during the reign of this heathen ruler is thus graphically described by Keatinge, p. 508 :—" It was not allowed to give instruction in letters, nor to live in religious communities, for the Lochlannaigh[4] dwelt in the temples and in the duns : no scholars, no clerics, no books, no holy relics were left in church or monastery through dread of them ; neither bard nor philosopher nor musician pursued their wonted professions in the land. . . . The result of the heavy oppression of this thraldom of the Gaels under the Lochlannaigh was, that great weariness thereof came upon the men of Ireland and the few of the clergy that survived had fled for safety to the forests and wildernesses, where they lived in misery."[5]

---

[1] See Fragment in the Book of Leinster of the Wars of the Gaedhil with the Gaill, edited by Dr. Todd, p. 226.

[2] See Wars of the Gaedhil with the Gaill, p. 13, and Introd., p. xlix.

[3] McGeoghegan's translation of the Annals of Clonmacnois.

[4] The term Lochlann is supposed to signify Lake-land, and may have been applied to Norway. (See Todd, Wars of the Gaedhil with the Gaill, Introd., p. xxxi.)

[5] A curious picture of the barbarous practices of these invaders is given in the following extract from the Irish Annals:—" Now at this time, Maelsechlain of Teamhair (*i.e.*, Malachy of Tara), sent ambassadors to the Danes, and at their arrival the Danes were cooking, and the supports of their cauldrons were heaps of bodies of the Lochlanns, and one end of the spit on which the meat was hung was stuck into the bodies of the Lochlanns . . . . . The ambassadors of Maelsechlain beheld them in this condition, and they reproached the Danes with this savage conduct. The Danes replied, 'This is the way *they* would like to have us.' They had a great wide trench filled with gold and silver to give to St. Patrick, for the Danes were a people who had a

At this period, says the annalist, " the sea seemed to vomit forth floods of invaders, so that there was not a point of Ireland without a fleet." But the victorious career of this "servant of Thor" was soon to receive a check, and in the year 845 the fresh armies of the invader were met with a vigour that equalled their own. "When," says Keatinge, " the chieftains of Ireland saw that Turgesius had brought confusion upon their country, and that he was assuming supreme authority over themselves, and reducing them to thraldom and vassalage, they became inspired with a fortitude of mind and a loftiness of spirit and a hardihood and firmness of purpose that urged them to work in right earnest, and to toil zealously in battle against him and his plundering hordes." He then enumerates nine battles fought in various parts of Ireland, in which the Norsemen were signally defeated; and these victories were followed up by the capture and death of Thorgils.

A period of "rest to the men of Erinn" is said to have now ensued, which endured for forty years, during which time Ireland was regarded as a place of comparative safety; we read in the Annals of Ulster that the shrine of St. Columcille, with his *minna*, or precious things, was removed to Ireland, "to protect them from the foreigners;" and the year before, as the same Annals inform us, Ruaidhri, son of Mervyn, King of Britain or Wales, fled to Ireland to escape the Danes.[1]

During the peace which ensued between the years 875 and 916, the same vigorous efforts were made to restore the churches and monasteries in Ireland that we again read of in the beginning of the eleventh century; and the communication with France, which had existed in the reign of Charlemagne, was continued in the reign of Charles the Bald, at whose court Johannes Scotus Erigena remained for some time. It is stated by Ware that in the year 848 King

---

kind of piety, *i.e.*, they gave up meat and women awhile for piety."—See Fragments of Irish Annals, p. 125. Trans. Irish Archæological Soc. (Dublin, 1860.)

[1] The victories gained over the Norsemen under Malachy the First are not the only proofs afforded by the history of this period of the vigour and courage of the Irish nation in the ninth century. It was in the year 842 that the final subjugation of the south of Scotland was effected by the Albanian Dalriada, whose emigration from Ireland has been already alluded to. We learn from Dr. Reeves that "In the year 838, Keneth Mac Alpin, the thirty-fourth ruler of the Albanian Dalriada, ascended the throne, and in 842 he subdued the Picts of North Britain, thus becoming master of the entire country between Edinburgh and Caithness. From this time the specific name of Dalriada began to fall into disuse, until at length the whole kingdom was called Scotia or Scot-land, after the name of the race which had branched into it from Ireland, and to whose arms it had gradually submitted." (Reeves's Adamnan, p. 433.)

Malachy obtained a signal victory over the Danes; "whereupon he sent ambassadors to Charles the Bald, king of France, with presents, desiring liberty of passage to Rome." And it would seem from the following passage in the Norman Chronicle that the Franks were cognisant of and grateful for the successful resistance made by the Irish to their common enemy. "In the year 848, the Northmen lay waste and burnt Burdegala (*i. e.*, Bordeaux) in Aquitania—captured through the treachery of the Jews. Afterwards Metullus, which hamlet they lay waste and give over to the flames. The Scots, breaking in upon the Northmen, by God's help victorious, drive them forth from their borders. Whereupon the King of the Scots sends, for the sake of peace and friendship, legates to Charles with gifts."[1] Another proof of the existence of such friendly relations between Ireland and France may be found in the epistle of Alcuin to Colchu, lector of Clonmacnois, when the former was resident at the court of Charlemagne.[2] "It was also in the reign of this great king that two learned Irishmen, Clemens and Albinus, were placed at the head of schools, the one in France, the other in Italy."[3] In the ground plan of the Irish monastery of St. Gall, in Switzerland, said to have been drawn by Eginhard, secretary to Charlemagne, we find the detached circular belfries introduced, and standing opposite the west door, such as we hold were afterwards copied in Ireland.[4]

When we study the history of architecture in Gaul during the eighth and ninth centuries we find that little now remains save the mere débris of monuments belonging to this period, and that such fragments are examples of a very rude art, being a sort of compromise between Roman traditions and influences spreading from the East through Ravenna. In the eighth century, Leo the Isaurian, in his Iconoclastic Movement, is said to have caused a great influx of artists into Italy and France.[5] "Painters and sculptors took refuge on the coast of Italy, and spread through the whole country. It was among these emigrants that Charlemagne found the artists who were to assist him in developing the *renaissance* he projected. The round

---

[1] Chronicle of the Deeds of the Normans in France, ap. Andr. Du Chesne. Historiæ Francorum Scriptores, t. ii. p. 524. Lutet. Par. 1636.

[2] This letter is preserved among Archbishop Ussher's Epistolæ Hibernium. Epist. xviii. Works, vol. iv. p. 466.

[3] Hallam's Middle Ages, vol. iii. p. 529. "Karolus magnus Imperator in tantum dilexit locum S. Galli, et ita familiaris, erat fratribus ut eum non aliter nominarent nisi noster Karolus."—Ekkehardus, vit. B. Notkeri, c. 29, G. p. 277.

[4] Bauriss des Klosters St. Gallen vom Jahr 820. Ferdinand Keller. Seite 20.

[5] See Entretiens sur l'Architecture, par M. Viollet-le-Duc, tom. 1er, pp. 196, 258.

towers of San Giovanni Battista and San Apollinare, in Classis, with others of the same character in Ravenna, as well as the town of St. Maurice, at Epinal, Ste. Geneviève, St. Germain des Prés, Aix la Chapelle,[1] may all derive their origin from this influx of Byzantine workmen into the north of Italy and the court of Charlemagne, and the circular tower may be a reminiscence of the Eastern cylindrical pillar. However this may be, we find that it was immediately after this accession of Eastern influence in France, as well as in consequence of certain impulses or necessities not springing from the religious sentiment, that the first ecclesiastical towers were raised. M. Viollet-le-Duc has, as we have before remarked, shown what was this external cause. He attributes it entirely to the necessity felt by the Franks of that time of protecting their churches from the attacks of the heathen Northmen in the valleys of the Loire and Seine and on the north and west coasts of France; remarking that they defended their churches with towers, which were naturally built near the door of the church, as being the point most liable to attack;"[2] and he adds, that it is indeed in those countries which were particularly ravaged by the periodical incursions of the Northmen that we see abbatial, and even parochial churches, preceded by massive towers, "of which, unfortunately," he says, "nothing but the lower stories are now left to us."[3]

Ozanam, speaking of the Irish ecclesiastics of this period, observes, "Une sorte de piété filiale les poussait de préférence vers ces Eglises des Gaules d'où ils avaient reçu l'Evangile." This being so, strengthens the probability that the two churches—simultaneously attacked by the armies of a common foe—did adopt a similar method of protection and defence. But, it may be argued, if the type was originally imported from France, why are such detached church towers not to be seen there still, when they are so common in Ire-

---

[1] The lofty round tower of the cathedral of Uzes near Nîmes, a portion of which is still standing, was divided into seven or eight stories. See L'Architecte, 2ᵉ série, No. 19, pp. 297-300.

[2] "Prope valvas majoris ecclesiæ campanarium erexit."—Du Cange, voce Campana. It was at the close of the ninth century, i.e., between the years 884 and 893, that Ireland was visited by the pilgrim Ananloen, from Jerusalem, who "came to Ireland with the epistle which had been given from Heaven at Jerusalem, with the Sunday Law and good instructions," or as the Ulster annalist has it, "with forfeiture for breaking of the Saboth day, and many more other good instructions." Such a visitant, living nine years in the country, at a time when the work of restoration was being carried on, might naturally introduce some foreign element into the architecture of Ireland. See Annals of the Four Masters, vol. i. pp. 537-551.

[3] Dict. de l'Architecture française, Viollet-le-Duc, vol. iii. pp. 286, 288.

land? The answer to this is, that the continental church towers of the Carlovingian age have been almost wholly destroyed, and generally replaced by towers of a later and more beautiful type, while those of the first type still stand in Ireland. However, we may learn from the few examples of this date remaining in France and Italy, that the first ecclesiastical towers may be divided into two types: the one a development of the cupola, the other tall, slender, pointed; the one a low massive tower which acts as a central lantern, the other that type which rises into the spire. The first is not seen in Ireland at an early date; the second, when round, generally stands alone. On the Continent, the tall church tower, whether round or

CHURCHES AND TOWERS AS REPRESENTED BY FRESCO PAINTERS AND ILLUMINATORS OF THE TENTH AND ELEVENTH CENTURIES.

square, is also occasionally detached, as at Pisa, but is generally at the corner of a lofty church, such as St. Maurice and St. Geneviève. Only the oldest and simplest type of such belfries ever reached Ireland and Scotland. The round tower with conical top was a common form in the earliest periods of Christian architecture, and is often represented in early bas-reliefs, illuminated MSS., and frescoes, and such is the form of the watch-tower of the feudal abbey as well as castle. The circular form seems to be the first chosen in all primitive buildings, and the conical roof is the simplest covering for

---

a, b, i. Peintures à fresque de St. Laurent hors des murs de Rome.
c, d, e. Peintures à fresque du portique de l'église de trois fontaines près de Rome.
f. MS. Grec. bibl. Vatican, VII. siècle.
g. MS. Grec. Vienne, IVe ou Ve siècle. *h.* Miniatures from the bible of St. Paul, Ninth Century. *i, j.* Latin MS. *k.* French MS. Tenth Century. See Histoire de l'Art par les Monuments, par L. G. Seroux d'Agincourt, Tome 5ième, Pl^s. xix., xcviii., xcix.

such that can be erected. The churches of Ireland, being but the size of an ordinary cottage of the present day, never could have supported the weight of a tower of 100 feet in height, and would always have seemed out of proportion to it; but when a watch-tower and keep for the monastery became necessary, when war and rapine called forth the symbol of faith and power in Irish Christian architecture, the lofty stronghold, bearing its cross on high, was erected in the cemetery, and near the doorway of the church.

It has been already observed by Dr. Petrie, that the term *Cloicethech* (bell-house) was used by early Irish writers synonymously with "keep," and did not merely convey the ideas that we now associate with church belfries. Thus, in the following passage from an ancient Irish translation of a life of Charlemagne, preserved in the Book of Lismore, we read, "The earl and his wife fled into the desert valleys and into solitary woods, and made for themselves a cloicethech, in which they slept through fear of the many monsters of the forest." Again, the strong association in the minds of the primitive Irish of the ideas of pride and power with such structures, as well as the interchange of the word cloicethech and tower, is strikingly exemplified in the following passage :[1] "Great indeed was the pride, vanity, and pomp of this sensual king; for it is he who performed an act of pride, such as was never accomplished before, *i. e.*, he erected for himself a tower of bright silver; and great was the size, and breadth, and height of that tower, which was higher than all the other houses of the town, being a bright lofty cloicethech."

The manuscripts from which these passages are taken are all subsequent to the tenth century; and here again it is well to insist upon the fact that the annalists do not record the existence of these buildings, or refer to them in any way before the year 950. In the wars with the Norsemen from 789 to 845, it is said that the "secular and regular clergy, in order to shelter themselves from the fury of the Normans, lay concealed in the woods, where they celebrated the divine mysteries, and spent their days in prayer and fasting;" but in the year 950, and for two centuries later, we read of the cloicethech as a special object of attack to the Norsemen. Slane and Trim are described as "filled with unfortunate people who had fled thither for safety," or as the monastic keep, in which the "distinguished persons, among whom was the lector of the abbey," had concealed themselves. From the table given in the

---

[1] This passage occurs in an ancient tract in the Leabhar Breac, and the king referred to is there named Castroe, king of the Medes and Persians.

Appendix, which contains all the references to these towers that the writer has been able to glean from the Irish Annals, it will appear that the compilers do not mention the word cloiccthech, or bell-house, before the year 950,[1] and that where the uses of these buildings are incidentally alluded to they are invariably spoken of as monastic keeps would be, *i. e.*, as places of protection and refuge. The word occurs, besides, in three ancient manuscripts, the date of which is uncertain: 1st. A poem preserved in the Book of Leinster, which work was compiled by a bishop of Kildare, who died in the year 1160. 2nd. The ancient life of Christ, which is preserved in the Leabhar Breac, a compilation made about the close of the fourteenth century. 3rd. A tract of the Brehon Laws, called " Seanchus beag," preserved in the Book of Lecan, a work compiled in the year 1416 by Gilla Isa Mor. These tracts of course belonged to an earlier period than that of the compilers of the works in which they are found, but their date cannot be fixed in the present state of our knowledge. The first passage alluded to is as follows:—

> " He who commits a theft,
> It will be grievous to thee
> If he obtains his protection
> In the house of a king or of a bell."[2]

This allusion to a bell-house as a place of refuge is found in a poem said to have been composed on the occasion of the inauguration of Aedh Oirdnidhe in the year 799.

The second passage alluded to occurs in an old life of Christ, in relation to the star that guided the Eastern kings to Bethlehem; it is quoted by Dr. Petrie at page 378 of his work:—"[The star] came afterwards a journey of the twelve months in twelve days, and it was higher than a *cloicthech* before us." The third instance where the

---

[1] All the entries regarding these towers which the editor has succeeded in finding are given in a table in the Appendix, so that the reader may see at a glance what amount of light the native records of the country, as yet published, cast upon the question as to the uses and date of these buildings. The oldest transcript that we have of the Annals was made in the year 1416. It is a short tract preserved in the great Book of Lecan, now in the library of the Royal Irish Academy. See O'Curry's Lectures on the MS. Materials of Ancient Irish History, p. 130.

[2] " Cipe do gne in ngait
Bid mor a mela duit,
Mad dia fagba a din
I tiġ riġ no cluic."

This verse is from the poem beginning with " Ceart gach rigo reill " (MS. 23 N. 11, p. 77), Library Trin. Coll., Dublin.

word occurs has been already quoted at page 80 of this volume. Another reference to belfries, in the life of St. Moling, preserved in the Book of Leinster, has been held to prove that such buildings existed in the lifetime of that saint, *i. e.*, in the seventh century;[1] whereas it can only be taken as evidence that the writer of that work, who may have lived in the twelfth century, was familiar with such structures, or at all events that they existed before the date at which the Book of Leinster was compiled.

Till the invasions of the Northmen the Irish ecclesiastic possessed his church and school in comparative peace, and the wall that encircled the groups of cells and oratories which formed his monastery was deemed security enough for him, as for the Egyptian monk in his laura; but in the year 800 all was changed; the attempted colonization of Ireland by a pagan invader, resolved to extirpate[2] the Christianity which he found there, and to establish the national heathenism of his own country, called forth the resistant spirit of the Irish monk, who protected his humble cell by means of the lofty tower.[3] We see then that it was not until those holy places became in themselves an especial object of attack to a heathen invader that their inhabitants, being permitted to remain within their walls, were

---

[1] See Petrie's Eccl. Architecture, p. 393, Trans. R. I. A. vol. xx.
[2] See Wars of the Gaedhil with the Gaill. Introd. p. xlviii.
[3] "The Danes also contributed to keep alive this military feature of Irish monasticism, for although they were too formidable to admit of any organized resistance, they afforded occasional opportunities for desultory retaliation, and after accustoming all classes to deeds of blood, they gradually broke down among the original inhabitants the veneration which was entertained for religious objects and institutions, introducing their sentiments in proportion as they became intermingled with the natives, till it was no uncommon thing for an Irish chieftain to be styled the waster of churches, or for the adventurous population of one province to plunder the churches in another. Amidst all those scenes, the steeples, which we commonly call Round Towers, rendered to the monasteries the most essential service, being places of refuge in the hour of peril, and affording an asylum for a large number, while they presented the least possible surface for assault. In fact, the Round Towers are, in their anomalous proportions, standing memorials of an anomalous church. . . . In succeeding centuries, stone buildings being of rare occurrence, churches were often turned into places of defence, and were frequented not only by those who sought to deprecate the wrath of Heaven, but by those who hoped to escape the rage of man. It was thus that John de Courcy sustained a check from the monastery of Erynagh, when he was mastering Lecale, and afterwards transferred its family to Inch, because it had been 'a fortress against him.' So also when Edward Bruce was spreading desolation throughout the same territory, the church of Brighit, full of men and women, was burned by him."—Note by Dr. Reeves in his Additional Notes to Primate Colton's Visitation, A.D. 1397, pp. 98, 99. Trans. Irish Archl. Society.

driven to erect strong buildings for the housing of their treasures and protection of their aged and infirm brethren.

In the map at the close of this volume an effort has been made to mark out the course of the Norse invasions in Ireland before the tenth century; the red lines mark the course taken by the invaders, and the crosses the churches attacked—many of them persistently and repeatedly—by these heathen warriors. The black circle stands for the round tower, and it would appear that the churches protected by such buildings were those situated in places that had in the first instance proved most liable to attack. They are along the coast and in the valleys of the rivers most infested by the enemy. Before the year 900 the Norsemen had first ravaged the coast and the outlying islands, and then their boats repeatedly were seen on the Boyne, the Liffey, and the Shannon, while the principal lakes in which their fleets were stationed were Loch Foyle, Loch Neagh, Loch Ree, and Loch Derg. In the valleys of these rivers distinct groups of these towers and churches are to be seen that had been for the first seventy years of this war attacked and desecrated with such unparalleled fury. They were also raised in regular lines along the coast from Galway to the Shannon, and from Cape Clear to Waterford.

If we take all those towers which appear to have fallen at an early date, and place them beside those we have classified as apparently first built, it will be found that they belong to the churches first and most persistently attacked by the Northmen in the ninth century. The towers of Ardbrackan, Armagh, Louth, and Slane, were the first to fall, and are the first alluded to in the Annals. Erected possibly by men inexperienced in raising such lofty buildings, their fall was probably due to some imperfection in their construction or insecurity in their foundation. The three last are situated exactly in those places which the Kings Malachy or Flann would have been most likely to fortify in the first instance. We have already alluded to the position held by Armagh as the principal ecclesiastical city of Ireland, and it was probably on this account that it was so persistently ravaged. The church was attacked three times in one month in the year 832 by the Northmen, and the same invaders repeated their acts of desecration in the years 839, 850, 873, 876, 890, 893, 895, 898, 914, 919, 926, 931, 943, 995, 1012, 1016.[1]

When contemplating these dates alone, two impressions are

---

[1] The church of Maghera was also attacked three times in one month, the church of Ardbrackan in the years 886, 949, 992. Clonard, the seat of one of the great schools of Ireland, was invaded in the years 838, 887, 888, 996, 1012, 1016, 1020, and so on.

strongly borne in upon the mind : 1st, that the invader could not in all cases have been actuated by a desire for plunder ; 2nd, that with the defenders some strong motive was at work, which led them so persistently to restore that which their enemies as persistently destroyed. Even supposing the monasteries to have been as rich as those on the Continent of the fourteenth and fifteenth centuries, yet it is not to be believed that the invaders could have found fresh treasures at every attack ; but there is no evidence to prove such wealth, and anything that does remain to us of the goldsmith's art in the early part of the tenth century is not an object to excite the cupidity of an untrained Viking at all so much as the diadem or golden torc or horse trappings he could only hope to find in the forts of chieftains, not in the humble churches of the saints. The ineradicable tenacity with which the defenders held to these little spots of ground, and the persistence with which they restored these places when laid waste, sprang from a deep-seated impulse, perhaps more connected with the cemetery than with the church itself. "The value," says Dr. Petrie, "set upon these cemeteries, is of very early antiquity, and like that attached to Iona, arose out of a belief in the power which the patron saint's intercession would have with the Deity on the last day."[1] Here their founder, the head of their clan, of whom their bishops were the spiritual heirs, had himself reached "his place of resurrection," and in the minds of this simple people he still remained as a chieftain in heaven to lead his clansmen on. This passionate attachment to their graveyards gave rise to the desire of providing them with a strong and permanent protection ; and thus we read that Queen Saba, wife of Donatus, son of Flann Sinna, when in the year 916 she visited Seirkieran, desired to have the church surrounded by a wall, as, she said, was then the case with " each of the most celebrated churches of Ireland." The passage is as follows :—

SECTION OF WALL, SEIRKIERAN.[2]

---

[1] St. Ciaran of Seirkieran, in answer to one of his last prayers for his church, is said to have obtained the promise that the gates of hell should not, after the judgment-day, be closed upon those who were buried in its cemetery. See Hist. of the Cathedral of St. Canice, p. 7.

[2] Except the house of St. Columba at Kells, built in the year 807, this enclosing wall or cashel of Seirkieran, with the base of the church tower, are the only existing

"Afterwards Donatus, son of Flann of the Shannon, was raised to the government of the kingdom. He had for his wife Saba, daughter of Donat, son of Cellach, ruler of Ossory, by whose earnest entreaties he was induced to gird Saighir with a wall; for she bore with difficulty that while each of the most celebrated churches of Ireland was surrounded by a wall, the place where her forefathers were committed to the grave should want defence and ornament. So, therefore, numbers of workmen were sent from Meath, and they carry on the work."[1]

The description given by the annalists of the Norwegian king reigning four years in Armagh, and the striking picture of his wife, both queen and prophetess, delivering her oracles from the high altar of Clonmacnois, are the more impressive when we remember that these places were the two principal ecclesiastical cities of Ireland. The intercourse between the former and the court of Charlemagne has already been alluded to. It is a significant fact, that the first name of a builder of one of these towers, mentioned in the annals in 964, should be that of an abbot of Clonmacnois,[2] Cormac O'Cillen. The next builder named in any authentic history is the good king Brian Boruma (of the Tribute), who succeeded his brother Mahon as king of Munster in 976. He is stated, as Dr. Petrie has already shown, to have erected no less than thirty-two of these structures.

"By him were founded cells and churches and were made stone houses, bell-houses (acus cloictigi), and wood houses in it" [Ireland]. . . . . "It is Brian that gave out seven monasteries, both furniture and cattle and land, and thirty-two bell-houses (acus dá cloicteač tričat)."[3]

Thirdly, another group of these towers is found to belong to the time of Donogh O'Carroll, Prince of Oriel, whose "splendour and magnificence" are extolled by the annalists, and who is said to have bestowed 300 oz. of gold upon clerics and churches. He died A.D. 1170.[4] In his time "churches were founded and temples and bell-houses (cloictigi) were made, and the monasteries of monks and canons and nuns were re-edified."[5]

---

identified specimens we have yet found of masonry, the execution of which is recorded at so early a period as 916.

[1] From an ancient fragment, supposed to be a part of MacLiag's Life of Brian, in library of Trinity College, Dublin.

[2] Annals of Clonmacnois, translated by Macgeoghegan.

[3] MacLiag's Life of Brian.

[4] See Ann. Four Masters, vol. ii. page 1170.

[5] "*Kalend. Januar. . v. feria, x. Anno Domini m.c.lxx.* A prayer for Donnchadh

Thus we find three distinct periods to which these towers may be assigned: first, from A.D. 890 to 927; secondly, from 973 to 1013; thirdly, from 1170 to 1238; and of these three periods the first two were marked by a cessation of hostilities with the Northmen, while the Irish made energetic efforts to repair the mischief caused by the invasions of the heathen. It is clear that these three divisions are distinctly marked by three steps in the progressive ascent of architecture from the primitive form of the entablature to that of the Decorated Romanesque arch. The churches built by Cormac O'Cillen are characterized by the horizontal lintel; the church of King Brian at Iniscaltra, with its still partially developed Romanesque doorway and chancel arch (see figs. 82, 83), while retaining the rude form in its minor apertures, marks a period of transition from the horizontal to the round arched style; and the buildings of Queen Dervorgilla and Turlough O'Connor, with the doorway of Clonfert, show what the latter style became in the lifetime of Donough O'Carroll. If Lusk, Glendalough, Timahoe, and Ardmore are taken as types of this gradation in the towers, we see such signs of progress as lead to the belief that a certain interval of time had intervened between the first and last mentioned of these erections.

There is another point which should not be passed unnoticed—that in the towers belonging to the Romanesque period, such as Ardmore, the apertures at the top are either larger or more numerous than those of the earlier bell-houses, and the walls are decorated

---

O'Carrol, Supreme King of Airgiall, by whom were made the book of Cnoc-na n-Apstal at Louth, and the chief books of the order of the year and the chief books of the mass. It was this great king who founded the entire monastery both [as to] stone and wood, and gave territory and land to it, for the prosperity of his soul, in honor of [SS.] Paul and Peter. By him the Church throughout the land of Airghiall was reformed, and a regular bishoprick was made, and the church was placed under the jurisdiction of the bishop. In his time tithes were received and the marriage ceremony was assented to, and churches were founded, and temples and bell-houses (cloictigi) were made, and monasteries of monks and canons and nuns were re-edified, and nemheds were made. These are especially the works which he performed for the prosperity [of his soul] and reign, in the land of Airghiall, namely, the monastery* of monks on the bank of the Boyne [both as to] stone and wooden furniture, and books, and territory, and land, in which [monastery] there are one hundred monks and three hundred conventuals, and the monastery of canons of Termonn Feichin and the monastery of nuns and the great church of Termonn Feichin, and the church of Lepadh Feichin and the church of . . . ." This entry is found in an ancient Antiphonarium, formerly belonging to the Cathedral Church of Armagh, but now preserved in Ussher's Coll. of MSS. (Class B, Tab. 1, No. 1), Library of Trinity College, Dublin.

---

* Mellifont Abbey. See Ann. Four Mast., 1189.

with bands and mouldings. Such features may suggest that when the attacks of the heathen on our sanctuaries were at an end, although the tower was established as a feature in Irish ecclesiastical architecture, the type had begun to undergo such modifications as, in course of time, might develop into a work of greater beauty. The campanile of Ireland was passing through such transitions as seem to foretell the advent of a type that would have added to its strength and power the loveliness of wisely ordered decoration, and have lightened its blind walls in storied arches, and opened its bell-chamber so that its music, no longer imprisoned, might sound forth,

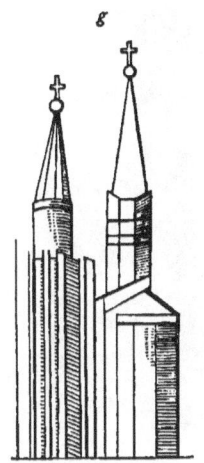

CHURCH OF CHARLEMAGNE AT AIX. ANCIENT SEAL.   CHURCH ON CAPITAL IN ST. SAUVEUR, NEVERS.

and the reserved, self-centred, and resistant tower that had risen in time of persecution, firm in the face of the infidel, might have broken its hard outline into softer forms of varying beauty under the influence of peace.

"There is perhaps no question of early Christian archæology," writes Mr. Fergusson, "involved in so much obscurity as that of the introduction and early use of towers." The difficulty of clearing away such obscurities has arisen chiefly from the want of monuments remaining on the Continent to show what were the earliest types in Western Europe. The light that Ireland might cast upon the subject has not yet made itself felt, because of the uncertainty that has too long lingered about the history of her towers. Dr. Petrie, by his investigations, brought their date down from a pre-Christian time to a period ranging from the sixth to the thirteenth century, and firmly established their ecclesiastical character. Lord Dunraven traced the type from Ireland through France to Ravenna, thereby proving it analogous to that of buildings belonging to an historic period elsewhere. But he felt that the area was far too wide over which Dr. Petrie had extended the practice of erecting these structures, and was gradually arriving at the conclusion that such masonry as they exhibit was not to be found in Ireland before the ninth or tenth centuries, and

TOWER AND CHURCH OF TULLAHERIN, CO. KILKENNY.

that her Decorated Romanesque churches belong to the eleventh and twelfth. Starting from the standpoint of these two archæologists, we may arrive at conclusions which give to these towers their true place in history. From these noble monuments the historian of Christian Art and Architecture may learn something of the works of a time the remains of which have been swept away elsewhere, and it may yet be seen, as in the case of her institutions,[1] customs, faith, and forms in art, so in architecture, Ireland points to origins of noble things.

---

[1] Revue Celtique, vol. iii. No. 9, p. 105.

CHAPTER VII.

OF THE ROMANESQUE OF IRELAND.

OCTOR PETRIE has observed,[1] when treating of the ornamented churches of Ireland, that the "style of architecture variously denominated by antiquaries Romanesque, Tudesque, Lombardic, Saxon, Norman, and Anglo-Norman, belongs to no particular country, but, derived from the corrupted architecture of Greece and Rome, was introduced wherever Christianity had penetrated—assuming various modifications according to the taste, intelligence, and circumstances of different nations," and the same writer adds that it need not "be a matter of wonder that more abundant examples of this style, though on a small scale—such as might be expected in a kingdom composed of many petty and nearly independent lordships—should remain in Ireland, than in those more prosperous and wealthy countries, in which such humble structures would necessarily give place to edifices of greater size and grandeur."

We may learn more fully in the writings of Mr. Freeman[2] how from the primitive Romanesque style, which was common to all Western Christendom, local forms were gradually developed in Italy, Aquitaine, Northern Gaul, Germany, England, and Ireland, "as national speech is developed from the Roman tongue."

Edward the Confessor is recorded to have rebuilt Westminster Abbey in the year 1066.[3] This event marks the introduction of the Romanesque of Normandy into England. Fifty-eight years before,

---

[1] Petrie, Eccl. Arch., Trans. R. I. A., vol. xx. p. 238.
[2] See Hist. of Architecture, chap. ix. p. 195, Historical and Architectural Sketches. Norman Conquest, chapter on Primitive Romanesque, vol. v. p. 602.
[3] Little now remains of the work of this period in the abbey.

the little church of St. Caimin, of Iniscaltra,[1] was built by King Brian Boruma, and this building marks the transition to the enriched round arch style of Ireland. Then it was that the Romanesque wave passed direct from Normandy into Ireland. It appears that at this period in England a primitive Romanesque style already prevailed, which, though it has been termed Anglo-Saxon, was of purely Italian origin. This early style modified the character of that which in the reign of Edward the Confessor came as a fresh importation from Normandy, and to this source may be traced whatever distinctive features separate English Norman from that of Normandy itself. In Ireland, as we learn from such buildings as the churches of Maghera[2] (fig. 35), Banagher[3] (fig. 34), Temple Martin[4] (fig. 32), and Temple Cronan,[5] a distinct style also prevailed at the time in which the Romanesque of Normandy was introduced there. Rude as many of its examples are, this primitive architecture still had sufficient character and vitality to modify the incoming Norman, and to live on, making itself visible in the fresh forms engrafted upon it. The style in Ireland of the eleventh and twelfth centuries is an Irish Romanesque style, and the peculiarities by which it is distinguished are "native traditions handed down from earlier native buildings," such as the primitive erections of the fort builders and early Christian missionaries, characterized by the horizontal lintel or the entablature seen in the first buildings of all countries, and which may be classed as belonging to the architecture of necessity.

It now remains for us to examine what are the points about the Romanesque churches of Ireland which give it this native and distinctive character. They are—

1st. Their simple ground plan and diminutive size.

2nd. Their rich and delicate decoration.

3rd. The lingering of horizontal forms and the incorporation of such in the round arch style.

4th. The retention of the inclined jambs of the primitive doors.

5th. The constant use of certain ornamental designs characteristic of the late Celtic period which had been common to Britain and Ireland before the Roman occupation of Britain.

The reason why the Irish Church persevered in the erection of such small buildings as places of worship may be sought for in the character of the Church system itself. The larger diocesan system,

---

[1] See Notes on Irish Architecture, vol. ii. p. 55, Plates XCVII. and XCVIII.
[2] See *Ib.* vol. i. p. 115.   [3] *Ib.* Plate LX.   [4] *Ib.* p. 105.
[5] *Ib.* Plates LIV. LV. and Plate facing p. 106.

which demanded vast buildings, such as the Norman cathedrals of England, for meetings and ceremonials, did not then prevail in Ireland. The spirit of clanship pervaded the Church, and this spirit, as Dr. Todd has observed, is the key to all Irish history. The Church was composed of small independent families, each honouring its bishop as its chieftain, and holding him to be the spiritual heir and living representative of the founder of the particular church to which they belonged, and the centralization of a less primitive condition was unknown to them. As at the time of transition to Romanesque, there was no corresponding change in the Church system of Ireland, it naturally followed that her ecclesiastics went on erecting buildings, small in size and simple in plan, though rich in decorative detail.

Mr. Freeman observes, in a letter to Lord Dunraven on this subject, that he has noticed in all Romanesque buildings that the larger the scale the plainer the work. "So," he adds, " I should be quite prepared to find very small buildings, like yours in Ireland, much richer than larger ones. Observe that in Ireland, Wales, and Scotland, the fashion of building churches on the enormous scale of Winchester and St. Alban's never came in. The largest buildings, as at Dublin, St. David's, and Glasgow, rank only with the second class in England and France;" and he adds, "and I should expect a greater degree of richness in the Irish buildings simply on the ground of their very small scale. I am convinced that in England, in Romanesque churches, the larger buildings are, the plainer they are—that the main difference introduced by the Norman conquest was a vast increase of scale, and, consequently, a diminution of ornament; in our few Old English buildings we find a sort of barbaric attempt at richness quite unlike the plainness of the early Norman."

Although the mouldings and ornament with which the doorways and other apertures of these Irish churches are enriched resemble Norman work, yet a careful examination of the construction of these buildings will show peculiarities belonging to a system different from that of the Romanesque of England or Normandy. Thus the Norman doorway is composed of round arches, which spring from a series of separate columns forming the sides of the entrance. The arches or orders of the Irish door spring more directly from the sides, inclining towards it from the base. The columns at the sides of the Norman doorway stand forth boldly, each rising from a broad and well defined base, and crowned by its own individual capital. The sides of the Irish doorway are but a transitional stage between the jambs of a square-headed doorway and actual shafts. The angular sides of the three or four orders are rounded off and channelled into groups of bowtels,

Of the Romanesque of Ireland.

with merely slight projections at the feet, scarcely to be termed bases; and, instead of separate capitals to each, a single entablature unites

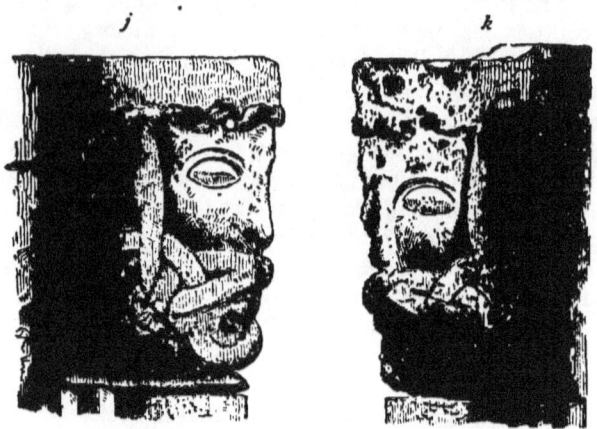

CAPITALS IN THE SAINTS' CHURCH, INCHAGOILE.

the whole, often terminating at the angles with heads of a strikingly archaic character (figs. 91, 92). The doorways of Rahen,[1] Killeshin, Queen Dervorgilla's church, Clonfert, and the chancel arch of Tuam

CAPITALS IN CLONALTIN CHURCH.

afford fine examples of such forms. The archaic character of the entablatures, mouldings, and capitals is shown in the accompanying

---

[1] See piers of chancel arch, Rahen, Notes on Irish Architecture, vol. ii. p. 65, and Plates CII. CIX. CXIII. CXIV. CXVI. CXVII.

drawings of Mr. W. G. Wakeman, from the churches of Clonaltin and Inchagoile, on Lough Corrib. The capitals of this period are always cushion or bell-shaped, and their rounded surfaces are often decorated, as in the example from Banagher Church, with the convolutions of the

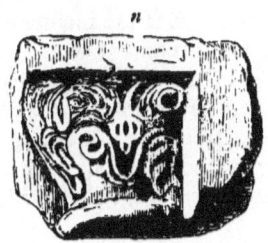

CAPITAL IN BANAGHER CHURCH.

divergent spiral design, and often, as seen in the old church of Trim, assuming the more complex forms resulting " from the division of the bell by recesses into separate lobes or leaves, like those of a rose or

MCCARTHY'S CHURCH, CLONMACNOIS.

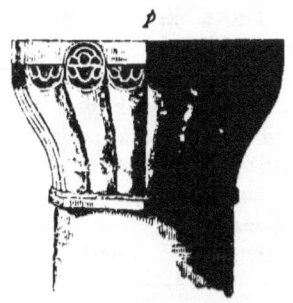

CAPITAL IN CHURCH AT TRIM.

tulip." Fig. *g*, 5, shows a section of one of the capitals in Cormac's Chapel. The bases are remarkably shallow, and, indeed, scarcely deserving of the name where, in some instances, they only serve as a termination for the groups of bowtels which form the jambs. They often consist of two rounds and an intermediate square or hollow, but seldom stand forward on a square projecting pedestal or plinth. Where such do occur, as at Killeshin, Clonmacnois, and Rahen, they show that beautiful feature of leaves connecting the bulbous portions with the square plinths at the angles.[1] (See figs. 103, 104.)

A very peculiar character is given to the round arch doorways of these churches by inclined jambs, and the widening of the doorway at the base.[2] It would seem as if the inclined sides of Maghera doorway (fig. 35), encrusted with ornament so as to resemble a page in one of the illuminated MSS. of the Celtic school carved and wrought in stone, had developed themselves into the jambs of a doorway of the later churches, and these jambs are either angular or channelled into bowtels with their angles rounded off. This singularity must be a traditional form handed down from the earliest and rudest style of

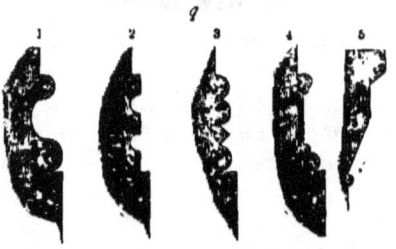

SECTIONS OF BASES, CORMAC'S CHAPEL.

building, when the simple method of forming an aperture was to erect two stones or logs of wood on end, and connect them by a horizontal lintel.

It has been already remarked that an entablature runs along the tops of the semi-columns, from which the arches spring, and this forms a kind of horizontal band connecting them; thus here the expression of horizontal extension is still the lingering idea, and this, we repeat, is the singularity in Irish architecture which stamps it with sufficient individuality to give it a place as a distinct variety of primitive Romanesque.[3] There is a great variety in the appearance of the

---

[1] Ruskin, Stones of Venice, vol. ii. p. 131.

[2] See doorway, Kilmalkedar, figs. 80, 81.

[3] Such clinging to and retention of ancient forms may also be traced in the architecture of Italy, where it is shown by the reluctance men had, boldly to set the arch upon the capital of the column, and their tendency always to thrust in some fragment, as it were, of the entablature which would come between the abacus of the capital and the impost of the arch. In the basilicas of Ravenna there does not seem to be one case where the arch comes down immediately on the Ionic or Corinthian capital; there is always a member thrust in, one which wants a name, and which has been termed stilt. This same tendency to retain the entablature is shown in the side walls and

masonry in these churches, some presenting a much more massive and antique character than others. It must not, therefore, be concluded that they are older, for much depends on the nature and durability of the stone of which they are built, which, except in the case of the Saints' Church in Lough Corrib, is always the stone found in the neighbouring district. Sandstone is the material most commonly used. The free working nature of this stone, rendering it

DOORWAY OF CHURCH, WHITE ISLAND, LOUGH ERNE.

peculiarly suited to buildings which were to be enriched with sculptured ornament, gave it favour in the eyes of Irish as well as Norman builders; but then this stone varies in quality in different districts,

---

doorways of the Church of St. Giles, in Languedoc, built in the year 1116, when, even then, the Provençal architect had not quite cast the entablature aside, but clothed it in a Romanesque form, and made it subordinate to the main design. "All these things," adds Mr. Freeman, "point to an indigenous style, and to a feeling, with regard to classical art, very different from blind imitation or retention. It is an endeavour to retain certain forms which are felt to be graceful, and yet to keep them in their proper relation to others, which it was felt must be predominant." History of Architecture, p. 222.

and while the sandstone found in the neighbourhood of Killaloe, Iniscaltra, and Ardfert, is fine-grained quartzose sandstone of a very durable nature, that used in St. Cronan's Church, at Roscrea (fig. 97), and elsewhere, is coarse-grained, and easily disintegrates when exposed to the action of weather. Again, the primitive character of the

ST. FARANNAN'S CHURCH, DONOUGHMORE.

masonry of Rahen small church is perhaps deceptive, for this church is built in a district where there is no sandstone at hand, but where limestone is the rock which abounds, and the walls are formed of huge boulders and rubble, cemented with ordinary mortar. In some instances there is a combination of rough rubble masonry and ashlar work in the same building, and even in the same wall. At Iniscaltra the difference between the nave, which is built in rough irregular courses, cemented with grouting, and the chancel, which is fine-jointed ashlar, is so striking that it is difficult to believe them to be the work of the same period, but at Tomgraney the lower part of the wall is of fine ashlar, and above it rough rubble work, and stones laid in irregular courses are seen. The oldest masonry in the walls of Aghadoe consists of large blocks of stone, with oblique joints, and not regularly squared. Of herring-bone masonry only four examples have been found, and it is remarkable that they belong to work which is manifestly of widely differing periods, the first observed being in the side-wall of the little oratory in Illauntannig, built of stones fitted without cement; the second in the oldest portion of the church of Killadreenan, in the county of Wicklow, and in the Cashel at Rathmichael; and the last in the round tower of Temple Finghin, Clonmacnois (fig. 53), the roof of which is of herring-bone ashlar. The masonry used by the ancients, and described by Vitruvius as common in the first century of the Christian era, that is, the "opus reticulatum," so called from its net-like appearance, which is formed of squared stones laid diagonally, is never found in Ireland. Long and short work, so often used in England in forming quoins at the angles of churches, has been observed in such a position in the church of Kilnaboy, in Clare, and in the oldest church at Monasterboice, but generally appears in the sides of the doorways and windows.

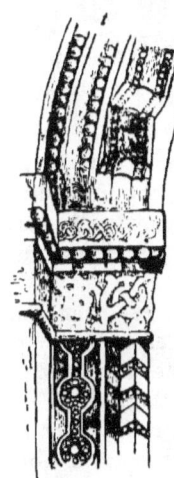

MOULDINGS OF DOORWAY, ST. FARANNAN'S CHURCH.

The bold and lofty system of stone roofing adopted in the churches of St. Flannan, King Cormac (fig. 90), and St. Doulough, was evidently an original conception in Ireland, which the Irish builders were enabled to carry to perfection after the knowledge of the true arch had been introduced. Fourteen buildings may be enumerated which show the gradual progress in this style of roofing, beginning with the oratories of Kilmalkedar, Gallarus, and Inis-mac-Dara, and the well of Tobernadru, near Freshford, in which no knowledge of the true arch is evinced, and the roof is single. The second group includes the church on Friar's Island, St. Kevin's Church, Taghmun, and St. Columba's house, at Kells, where the roof is double, and though the outer pointed arch is still constructed on the primitive system, yet it is supported by a round barrel vault which is formed as a true radiating arch. There is no example of a double-roofed building before this introduction of the knowledge of the arch. The slates of the outer roof are dressed to the rake of the roof outside and inside, and the roofing stones laid at an angle to throw off the moisture. In St. Kevin's Kitchen such roofing is first seen in company with a rough moulding, and an east window with regular voussoirs in the inner arch. In the third and last group the false arch is no longer seen, but the round barrel vault is superimposed by the pointed barrel vault, both built on the regular arch principle; the process of transition to which is seen in the upper

ARCADE, WEST FRONT, ARDMORE.

roof of St. Columba's cell, while St. Mochta's, in Louth, St. Flannan's, St. Farannan's, at Donoughmore, the Sacristy of the Cathedral at Clonmacnois, Cormac's Chapel, St. Saviour's, at Glendalough, and St. Doulough's, all offer examples of this last and most perfect system of stone roofing.

These buildings are invested with a peculiar interest from the fact that they were not only places of worship, but also dwelling-houses, the habitable portion being a chamber over the stone-roofed chancel, to which access was gained from the body of the church by one of three different methods. The first and most primitive, as in St. Kevin's, by a ladder from the body of the church through a hole in the ceiling of the lower story, which hole is afterwards replaced by a doorway over the choir arch, as at Donoughmore, and then a winding staircase, either in the wall, as at St. Saviour's, or in a side tower or turret which leads to the chamber above, as in Cormac's

Chapel. At a later date a small portion of the west of the building has been constructed to answer all the purposes of a dwelling-house, which was evidently separated from the sacred portion of the structure by a wooden partition, or possibly thin wall, and divided by a wooden floor into a basement and upper story. A staircase in the thickness of the wall leads to a doorway opening on the chamber in the upper floor. This peculiarity is to be seen in the church of St. Catherine, in the County of Wexford, and the old church of Castle Gregory, in the County of Kerry, as well as in a fortified church at Clonmines, on

ARDMORE.

the coast of Wexford. The arcades with which the walls of these buildings were in many instances enriched are best illustrated in the churches of Kilmalkedar,[1] King Cormac's Chapel at Cashel (fig. 87), Ardmore, and Ardfert. They consist of a series of round-headed arches supported by columns or piers closed with masonry. No example of an open arcade has been found in an Irish Romanesque church. The three first mentioned form a sequence showing certain points in development. The first consists of six sunken panels divided by rounded semi-columns, with scalloped capitals and moulded bases; in the second the columns are connected, and the panels enclosed by a series of round-headed arches. These arches in the lower story of Cormac's Chapel are enriched with chevron mouldings, and the square piers, carved in diapers and various chequered patterns, are rendered delightful by the effect of alternating light and shade thus

---

[1] See Notes on Irish Architecture, vol. ii. Plate XCVI.

produced. In the third, that on the west wall of Ardmore (p. 118, *supra*), the arches spring from very slender shafts, with capitals and bases, and the panels are no longer blank spaces, but filled in with sculptured figures—either one or two in each panel, carved in low relief. Such arcades are among the most interesting signs of growth in Irish architecture: the walls are no longer blank or silent spaces, but speak of human histories. In the larger semicircular panels the subjects introduced are: a warrior with his shouldered lance in the act of kneeling for the blessing of a bishop who stands above him, " The Judgment of Solomon," the " Dedication of the Temple," and the " Temptation."

Pilaster buttresses are often seen at the corners of the east and west ends of these churches (see fig. 97), but in the most beautifully finished examples, such as the small church at Ardfert, Mona Incha, and the chancel of Tomgraney, these give place to beautifully proportioned columns, on which, in the first case mentioned, an enriched cornice, which crowns the side-walls of the church, is seen to rest (see fig. 108). These quoin shafts are three-quarter columns, with moulded bases and carved capitals, and give a classic character to the building.[1]

The positions afforded for the introduction of ornament in these small buildings are the chancel arches, windows, arcades, quoins, cornices, and doorways, with or without canopies. On these portions of the building all the decorative designs of the native school are lavished. The use of roll and other sectional mouldings is more common in Ireland and in the primitive Romanesque of England than in early Norman work.

The love of incised surface mouldings, giving the face of the stones an effect of delicate and beautiful engraving, is another striking characteristic of Irish architectural decoration, and such ornament is very common throughout the country in the borders and crosses of the sepulchral slabs of the 9th and 10th centuries. Then, as in the windows of Annadown[2] and Rahen, borders of chevron, bead, and even foliate patterns are carved in very low relief, as exquisitely felt in their treatment as they are gracefully conceived. Some mouldings which very rarely occur in England and France are more common in Ireland—such as the battlement, which is also found at Iffley, and the interrupted chevron, which occurs in the church of Grand Mala-

---

[1] The illustrations of this beautiful feature in the Irish church, prepared for this work, were unfortunately mislaid while this volume was in the press. An example is given by Mr. Brash. See Eccl. Arch. pl. xiv. fig. 4.

[2] Notes on Irish Architecture, Plate CXXV.

drerie, near Caen. The occurrence in Ireland of such mouldings as are common to Romanesque architecture in other parts of Western Europe does not deprive her architecture of any of its archaic and national character. The illuminated pages of her sacred writings are, as it were, the precursors of her decorated churches, and all the

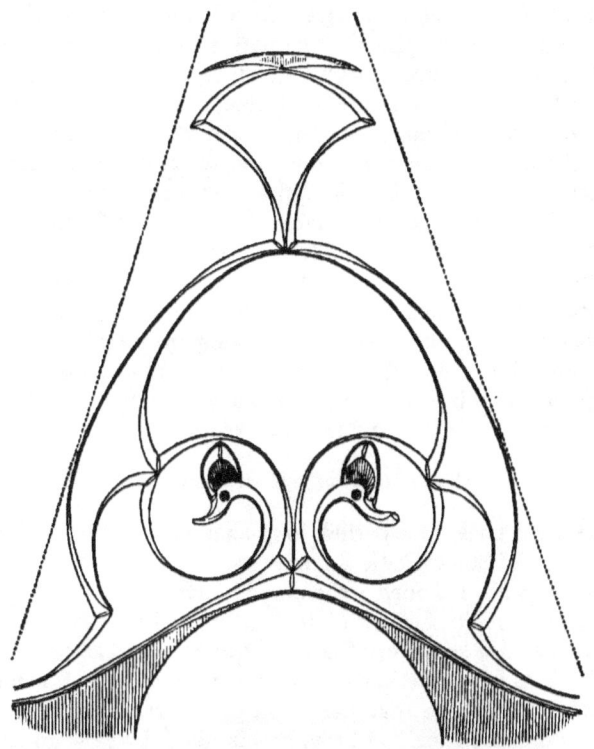

SCROLL ON A BRONZE ORNAMENT IN THE PETRIE MUSEUM.

designs of Celtic art given by the pencil in them are carved by the chisel on her stone monuments. To both may be applied the following remarks, made by Waagen[1] on the work of the Celtic scribes alone:—" The ornamented pages, borders, and initial letters exhibit so correct an architectural feeling in the distribution of the parts, such a rich variety of beautiful and peculiar designs, so

---

[1] German Art Journal, No. 11.

admirable a taste in the arrangement of the colours, and such an uncommon perfection of finish, that one feels absolutely struck with amazement."

All comparative study of national and primitive forms of decorative art seems to show that such distinctive terms as *Runic* and *Celtic* applied to interlaced patterns, knots, and fretwork have been too confidently used. Such designs are found in archaic art in most parts of the world, and still appear in the native work of Japan[1] and India. There are, however, two designs which seem to be specially characteristic of Celtic art; these are a peculiar development of the double spiral line, totally unknown to the Greeks, the Etruscans, and to the nations of the Teutonic race, which is essentially characteristic, not only of the Scoto-Celtic, but the Britanno-Celtic populations of these islands. This is termed the Divergent Spiral or Trumpet pattern, and its appearance in the art of Ireland, from the bronze works of the early Celtic period found in the stone tombs of a pre-historic age to the capitals of Cormac's Chapel, stamps the architecture of Ireland with a distinctive native character. Living on in Ireland when it had died out elsewhere, this design in course of time appears upon her buildings. It is, as it were, the fine and slender thread that binds Irish Christian with Pagan art, and in slow voluminous curves

"Of still expanding, still ascending gyres"

leads the mind back to a period, long ages past, when, perhaps, Britanno-Celtic and Scoto-Celtic art were one.

The appearance of such archaic and native forms in design is not, however, the strongest mark of the individuality of Irish decorative art, since they are seen very frequently in Scotland and the North of England. It is in the delicacy of treatment, and the judgment shown in the use of ornament, that the mind of the Irish artist is revealed. Patience and conscience had brought his hand by slow and toilsome steps to such high skill, that he at last acquired that perfect touch[2] which alone results from a keen sense of perfection in all art; while,

---

[1] See My Circular Notes, J. F. Campbell, vol. i. p. 345. Alluding to the appearance of such designs in Japanese art, Mr. Campbell observes: "Such designs also occur in Icelandic carvings, on certain rare kinds of pottery, in Byzantine churches, and on Persian bronzes;" and adds that, "community of design in basket-work, and in arts derived from baskets, either points to community of origin for Celts and Japanese, or to a common nature in humanity which arrives independently at the same inventions by following the same steps."

[2] See for example the mouldings on the windows of Kilmacduach of Annadown.

in the application of ornament, he never lost sight of the principle that decoration is beautiful only when found in its right place, and when adding to the effect of the form to be adorned. In other words, that it should be held in subordination and subjection to the primary idea, and a noble reserve of power be exercised till the ornament comes forth in the right place, to aid in the expression of the essential elements of the subject, emphasizing its important points, and adding clearness to the beauty of its outline.[1]

The slow and steady progress in such qualities of mind, and the gradual growth from the rude forms of a primitive art to this matured expression of a sense of beauty, may be traced in the progress of art in Ireland from the first centuries of the Christian era to the art of Ireland in the eleventh century. In metal work and sculpture, as in architecture, such change is observable. The workmanship of the silversmith who painfully and faithfully wrought the minute work of the shrines of St. Moedoc and St. Molaise is excelled in freedom and grace by that of the artists of the Ardagh Chalice and the Cross of Cong, where skill at last becomes ancillary to the expression of the sense of beauty.

The period at which this enriched Romanesque style prevailed in Ireland can only be determined by reference to those few examples, the dates of which have been fixed by historical evidence. They are given in a chronological table in the appendix to this work. From this table it will appear that the series commencing with the churches of King Brian Boruma, about the year 1007, closes with that of Queen Dervorgilla, built A.D. 1168, and that the most characteristic examples of this style are the tomb of King Murtough O'Brien, A.D. 1123, Cormac's Chapel, A.D. 1127, the church of Aghadoe, A.D. 1158, the church of Tuam, A.D. 1161, and the church of Clonfert, A.D. 1166. A glance at these dates seems to prove that Ireland was then hardly in advance of Western Europe with respect to her ecclesiastical architecture, however it may establish that she kept alongside of other countries in the path of progress up to the middle of the twelfth century. The history of her arts of metal work and sculpture points to the same conclusion. The series of reliquaries commencing with the shrine of Molaise's gospels, A.D. 1001 to 1025, to that of the Cross of Cong, in 1123, and the series of inscribed and sculptured stones beginning with the Cross of King Flann, son of Malachy, A.D. 914, and ending with that of Turlough O'Conor, at Tuam, in the year

---

[1] See Saturday Review, vol. xli. pp. 302-3. Also Ruskin, Stones of Venice.

1123, prove that not only the art of architecture, but also the arts of metal work and sculpture, reached their highest perfection in the period between the tenth and twelfth centuries, and a comparison of the earlier and later examples of these various arts between the years 914 and 1166 shows that, notwithstanding the disorganized state of the country, there was a steady progress in the arts of Ireland. It is remarkable that the fearful struggle with the Norsemen, which lasted for upwards of 200 years, and ended in the final defeat of these invaders in 1014, does not seem to have materially paralyzed the energies of the Irish nation as regards their native arts. It may be occasionally with nations as with individuals, and in the histories of men we find that some of the greatest works of human genius have been executed under the pressure of pain, or are the results of strong reaction of the brain in a spirit which may be stricken but not broken.

The period is still undecided at which the most wonderful achievement of this school—the Book of Kells—was executed. It was, at all events, previous to the year 1000, when it is first alluded to by the annalists. No effort hitherto made to transcribe any one page of this book has fully conveyed the perfection of execution and rich harmony of colour which belongs to this wonderful work. It is no exaggeration to say that, as with the microscopic works of nature or the delicate framework of a leaf when its skeleton is revealed, the stronger the magnifying power brought to bear upon it, the more is this perfection seen. No single false interlacement or uneven curve in the spirals, no faint trace of a trembling hand or wandering thought can be detected. The intense concentration of mind necessary for the accomplishment of work so minute, where the brain would seem as it were drawn to a needle's point to fulfil its purpose, becomes a pain to contemplate. This is the very passion of labour and devotion, and thus did the Irish scribe work to glorify his sacred book; while the fortress belfries that the warrior monks raised to protect their monasteries, witness to the resolution with which they resisted and drove back the invader.

The history of all these monuments of Irish art, and indeed the inscriptions that many of them bear, give evidence that the cultivation of such arts was not confined to the ecclesiastics alone. In 950 and 964 we read of Fergal O'Rorke, King of Connaught, as builder of the great belfry at Clonmacnois; in 1008 King Brian Boruma (of whom it has been well said, "No other man had been so successful as he had been in combining the whole people in one national object")[1]

---

[1] See Mrs. Ferguson's Irish Before the Conquest, page 282.

seems to have also introduced Irish Romanesque; while King Murtogh O'Brien, and Cormac MacCarthy, and Turlough O'Connor, each laboured in the promotion of art and civilization in Ireland, and their names are connected with, or even engraved upon, the most perfect works of Irish art in existence.

It appears evident that a certain amount of change which is involved in all progress was being wrought in Ireland through the instrumentality of such men, and might have ended in an established monarchy and less local church system. When Lanfranc, in 1074, and Anselm,[1] in 1106, wrote their epistles to King Turlough O'Brien and Gillebert of Limerick, they did so as to friends and fellow-labourers in the cause of law and order. In the hope of extricating the Irish Church from the power of the provincial chieftains, the effort was steadily made to attain unity.[2] This work was supported by Celsus, Archbishop of Armagh, and continued by Malachy, the friend of St. Bernard of Clairvaux. He, with the aid of Malchus, Bishop of Lismore, formerly a monk of Winchester, although a native of Ireland, devoted himself to the study of the customs of the Universal Church, reforming disorders and rebuilding churches. He seems to have striven to widen the merely local and native customs of manner and thought among his countrymen, and to broaden their sympathies from a too passionate clinging to old traditions, and open their minds for the reception of ideas and customs, which would bring them into more perfect harmony with the larger life of Europe.[3]

---

[1] By the advice of Anselm the effort was made to reduce the various liturgies of Ireland under one system.

[2] It seems to have been the aim of each one of these sovereigns to establish a central monarchy in Ireland; and here we may add the following remarks of Sir Henry Maine: "If the country had been left to itself, one of the great Irish tribes would almost certainly have conquered the rest. All the legal ideas which, little conscious as we are of their source, come to us from the existence of a strong central government lending its vigour to the arm of justice, would have made their way into the Brehon Law, and the gap between the alleged civilization of England, and the alleged barbarism of Ireland during much of their history, which is in reality narrower than is commonly supposed, would have almost wholly disappeared."

[3] The friendly relations that existed between England and Ireland in the reign of Muircheartach (Murtogh) O'Brien are witnessed to in the following words of William of Malmesbury in his record of the deeds of Henry I. "Our Henry had such devoted followers in Murcardus, King of the Irish, and in his successors whose names report has not handed down, that they wrote nothing except what flattered him, and they governed in no respect except as he commanded. Although Murcardus is reported, for some reason or other, to have acted during a few days with offensive pride against the English, but soon to have quieted the swelling of his heart, in consideration of the stop put to the navigation and the payment of the seafarers." Chronicle of William of

The changes that gradually appear in the architecture of Ireland from that of her early Church seem to symbolize this new order of things, and in the Romanesque churches, such as Kilmalkedar and Cormac's Chapel, the effect of such efforts becomes visible. Such change as this would have tended not to kill or to crush out the native life, but to harmonize and blend it with that of neighbouring countries; preserving to Irish art the dignity of individuality, with that delicacy of conception and treatment which belongs to her national genius, yet enlarging its forms and multiplying its beauties of detail by the introduction of external and foreign elements.

But such gradual and sure development was suddenly arrested in its course, and again the onward march was stopped by war—a war more fatal in its consequences than the struggle with the Norsemen, because it possessed all the paralyzing effect of domestic strife. The classic pillars and delicately carved arches of Queen Dervorgilla's Church at Clonmacnois lift their mute forms in silent witness to the life as to the death of native art. This church, which seems stamped with the finer grace of woman's hand, was built by the Irish queen, in her last years of penitence, whose tale so mournfully resembles that of Guenevere, not only in her shame and ruin, but in the long chain of disaster in which her country since her fall became involved. " The children born of her were sword and fire." And she too might have dreamt that she beheld her shadow—

"Broadening from her feet,
And blackening, swallow all the land."

It was this queen's lover, Dermot, King of Leinster, who led Fitzstephen and the Anglo-Normans into Ireland to aid him in his war against her husband. Since then the native character of Ireland has best found expression in her music. No work of purely Celtic art, whether in illumination of the sacred writings, or in gold, or bronze, or stone, was wrought by Irish hands after that century. Her language, once so subtle and refined, "seems to lose its grammatical conscience," and her true national life to sink into the sleep of death.

Seated in the nave of the quiet and unpretending church of King Cormac on the rock of Cashel, the mind passes back across the wide space that divides the present from the past, and dwells on the long

---

Malmesbury, Concerning the Deeds of the English Kings, book v. (Of English affairs, after Bede), Henry Saville, p. 51.

chain of monuments, referred to in this essay, as link by link they rise in the clear light of day. First there is the scene in Aran:—

> . . . . . "A promontory of rock
> That compassed round with turbulent sound,
> In middle ocean meets the surging shock,
> Tempest buffeted, citadel crowned."

Grand as is the pagan fort rising here above the wide Atlantic, it is still the grandeur of gloom and solitude, and the mind seizes gratefully each sign of higher life and purer light that may be found in the works of successive centuries, until at last this little church upon the rock is reached, and its round arches close in rest above the head. Deeply impressive as is the message there borne in upon the spirit, it yet should breathe but trust and hope. Here every line seems to be imbued with repose and solemn beauty: the decoration on its walls, so modestly applied and delicately felt that it must be sought through the dim twilight of the nave: the little chancel, once filled with the simple music of old Irish hymns, at the end of which is seen the chamber, suffused with sunlight, holiest of holies, within which stood the table where was echoed back that deed whence all our hope and life must come.

Great as is the interest and even in some cases the beauty of the first system of architecture, that of the entablature, it is clear that the art mounted on other and higher steps when the forms of the round and pointed arch were adopted. While the leading idea of the first is horizontal, and the latter vertical extension, and fatalism and aspiration seem to be the sentiments expressed, that of the round arch is not of extension either way, but of simple rest. And yet it is a rest not without life and motion, but rather the repose of life governed by law.

The suggestiveness of each successive form that marks the steps by which this style arose is felt most clearly if we return to contemplate the doorway of Maghera, work of probably more than a century before. The primitive style of the entablature has not yet passed away, to be succeeded by that of the arch. With horizontal lintel and inclined sides, this doorway stands before us in all the dignity and simplicity of Egyptian architecture, an example—and perhaps the only one—of the entablature style enriched with Christian symbols. The crucifixion, with lance and sponge, the figure of the Saviour draped to the hands and wrists, the three disciples, and the women standing near, are carved upon the lintel, while down the sides the interlacings and the spirals of Celtic art are crowned by the quaint image of a saint " slaying the serpent," a rude image, and yet, such as it is, the utterance of that hope

> " Which dawned in human breasts, a double morn,
> With earliest watchings of the rising light
> Chasing the darkness; and through many an age
> Has raised the vision of a future time
> That stands an Angel with a face all mild
> Spearing the demon." [1]

It is in buildings of such a style as this that we find the early condition of Western Christianity to be symbolized—the gradual emergence from heathen forms and lingering paganism to the things of a fuller and a higher life. Thus far off " in the silver-misty morn " of time this gate may shine with that of Arthur's youthful knight.

> " And there was no gate like it under heaven.
> For barefoot on the keystone, which was lined
> And rippled like an ever-fleeting wave,
> The Lady of the Lake stood: all her dress
> Wept from her sides as water flowing away;
> But like the cross her great and goodly arms
> Stretched under all the cornice and upheld:
> . . . .
> And in the space to left of her and right,
> Were Arthur's wars in weird devices done;
> New things and old co-twisted, as if Time
> Were nothing." [2]

But on the lintel of our Irish door was carved a higher form, beneath whose outspread arms we pass into the sanctuary.

Thoughts such as these arise when the topmost peak of St. Michael's rock is reached, and nothing there is seen but the blue heaven above echoed and deepened in the blue sea beneath. The way of the cross has ended ere this point is reached; every sign of human sorrow, strife, and passion has been left behind; death in life has changed to life in death and peace which is the consummation of all.

It may, indeed, be doubted whether a native life that has left such traces ever can become extinct, and whether it needs but to be truly revealed to win respect. The power of seizing the salient points in national character, and feeling a broad sympathy with the native genius of a foreign race is one possessed by few except the greatest artists and poets; and yet such perception and appreciation of truth

---

[1] Jubal and other Poems, p. 200, George Eliot.
[2] Gareth and Lynette, pp. 15, 16, Alfred Tennyson.

is before all things necessary for early history. Guided by this tender intuition, what seemed weakness is found to be strength, and what seemed false is true. And now, as year by year the secrets of Ireland's past are being unveiled, and truth is added to truth by earnest search and patient labour, it may be hoped that all barriers of evil prejudice which have long divided the children of two kingdoms may be overturned, and that, in the fulness of mutual trust and knowledge, brotherhood may be established. Offspring of a union, whether forced or natural, made long centuries ago, let it be their sacred filial duty to cast out all memories that have hitherto impeded that "marriage of true minds" between the lands that gave them birth, since by such effort peace alone is found. Then "in lone splendour hung aloft the night" that light will be revealed which reigns.

> . . . . . "An ever fixed mark,
> That looks on tempests, and is never shaken;
> And is the star to every wandering bark,
> Whose worth's unknown, although his height be taken."

APPENDICES.

I.—On the Form of the Early Irish Churches.

II.—Ecclesiastical Round Towers on the Continent.

III.—Letters from Mr. Clark, of Dowlais.

IV.—Extracts from Letters—M. Viollet-le-Duc.

V.—Chronological Table of those Examples of Irish Architecture, Sculpture, and Metal-work, the dates of which can be approximately fixed.

VI.—List of Round Towers or Bell-houses of Ireland.

VII.—Table of References to Bell-houses in Seven Books of Irish Annals, from the Tenth to the Thirteenth Centuries.

VIII.—On the Preservation of National Monuments and Ecclesiastical Ruins.

IX.—On the Intercourse which existed between Ireland and France in the reign of Charlemagne.

X.—Map of Ireland illustrative of the Invasion of the Northmen.

XI.—Key to the Map of Ireland.

APPENDICES.

ON THE FORM OF THE EARLY IRISH CHURCHES.

THE idea suggested by Mr. Freeman in this passage, that the form of church preserved in Ireland till the twelfth century points to some original type that seems to have disappeared elsewhere, is one that well deserves future investigation. In Mr. Moyle's letters on the First Churches of the Early Christians, the authorities on this subject which he refers to are:—Sir Henry Spelman's Concilia Britannica, p. 11; Fuller's Miscellanea Sacra; Baronius, Ad Annum, lvii. n. 30; Nicolas Fuller, Miscel. Sacra, l. ii. c. 9; Eusebius, lib. vii. 11, lib. ix. 1, 2; Eusebius, lib. viii. c. 2; Lactant., De Morte Persecut., c. xii.; Gregory Nyssen, in his Life of Gregory Thaumaturgus, speaks of the public oratories of the Christians. Vopiscus, Life of Aurelian, c. xx., sets the "Ecclesia Christianorum" and the "Templum Deorum omnium" in opposition to each other.

It would appear from various passages in these writings, that the apostles and their immediate followers did in the first instance hold their meetings in the upper rooms of their dwellings, but afterwards had regular places of assembly which they termed ecclesia, besides having the practice of meeting in cemeteries, and Mr. Moyle quotes Baronius as alleging that the Christians had little churches, and brings forward other reasons for the belief that the primitive Christians had such small buildings or oratories in Aurelian's time, about the year 270.

The double stone-roofed churches of Ireland form so striking a class of ecclesiastical building that the editor wrote to Mr. James Fergusson, author of the History of Architecture, to inquire whether he had anywhere met with buildings resembling them, and which served at once as churches and dwelling house. She received the following answer to her questions:—

"Your inquiry is, I fear, only too easily answered in the negative. I do not know of any such arrangement as you describe, as existing in Ireland, of a monk living in or over his chapel; but I by no means feel sure that such an arrangement does not, or did not exist in Egypt and the East generally.

"The distinction between a monastery of three or four monks living in cells attached to their chapel and one monk living over it, is very small; still, I cannot help fancying it did not exist in practice: but we know so little of the East that it is difficult to speak with any confidence on such a subject. If such oratories existed they must have been small and insignificant, and while nine-tenths of the larger monasteries are still unknown to us, it is too much to expect the small ones should be described.

"The publication of your book may direct attention to the subject, and when looked for, they may be found; but for the present, I fear, the idea can only be registered as the product of some fertile Irish imagination.

"Regretting I cannot send you a more satisfactory reply,
"I remain, yours, &c.,
"J. FERGUSSON.

"20, Langham Place, *July* 17, 1875."

At the west end of the nave of the Cathedral of Cashel, the pier and angle shafts were a subsequent introduction, with a view to vaulting this end of the church on an intermediate level, so as to utilize the upper portion as an addition to the domestic portion of the building. At Mellifont Abbey, Co. Louth, the church is so divided, the lower portion being ecclesiastical, the upper domestic.

ECCLESIASTICAL ROUND TOWERS ON THE CONTINENT.

an essay written by Ferdinand Keller on the plan of the Monastery of St. Gall, he thus describes the Round Towers therein:—

"At each side of the eastern porch of the monastery stand two towers, which are not only quite out of harmony with the principal building, but, as is the case in most of the old Italian basilicas, are some steps distant and connected with the porch by a covered way. They were apparently divided into stories, and are of a round form, which is singular in campanili. Their height is not stated, and it is not stated whether they were really intended for bells, which was doubtless their chief use. It is also remarked that all the surrounding country can be seen from the top (ad universa super inspicienda) and that at the summit of each there was a chapel containing an altar, one facing the North, dedicated to St. Michael, and another facing the South, dedicated to the Archangel Gabriel. It is also stated, as shown in the plan, that winding stairs lead to the chapels at the top of the towers."

The church of St. Gertrude, at Nivelles, in Belgium, is described by Mr.

Fergusson as having a square east end. He states that it was built in the earliest years of the eleventh century, and was dedicated in 1045, the Emperor Henry IV. assisting at the ceremony. The round tower has unfortunately lost its original, and probably conical top, and the upper story has been replaced by one of much more recent date. Were this tower detached from the buildings around it, its resemblance to that of Ardmore would be very striking indeed.

Letters from Mr. Clark.

The following letter on the Round Towers of Ireland will be read with interest. It was written to the Editor by Mr. Clark, of Dowlais, in answer to some questions as to the age of certain towers in England which had been supposed to have some analogy to those of Ireland.

Dowlais House, Dowlais, Nov. 27, 1876.

"Englishmen are apt to be both positive and wrong when they express opinions upon Irish matters. The latter I may be, but I hope to avoid the former. With this caution, I will endeavour to answer your questions.

"The Irish round towers appear to me to be both Christian and ecclesiastical. Independent of other reasons, this is, I think, shown by their position with respect to many churches founded ecclesiastically at a date which all will allow to be earlier than the earliest of the towers.

"As to their use, my opinion formerly was that they were meant, primarily, to carry a bell; and secondarily, as a place of refuge for the 'persona ecclesiæ,' his assistants, the vessels of the sanctuary, and perhaps such of the very aged or infirm of the people as could not move with rapidity. I am now inclined to consider this latter as their sole original use. They do not appear ever to have contained a frame big enough to carry a large bell, nor is the arrangement such as would give egress to the sound, but would rather tend to stifle it, and that at a height at which large apertures could neither weaken the structure, nor endanger the security of the inmates. Moreover, I do not understand that bells of any considerable size were in early use in Ireland. Those which remain, or of which representations are seen, are small and angular, and fabricated of plates of metal, like a sheep-bell; not cast, and they seem intended to be rung by hand.

"For defence, on the other hand, under certain conditions, these towers are not ill calculated. More than a few persons they could not contain, and no great store of provisions, but they would oppose a stout passive resistance to a sudden and short attack, such as the Norsemen or other piratical marauders would be likely to make upon them. Against such a force, lightly armed as it would be, a tower would be impregnable, unless the enemy had the means of undermining it, or time to collect sufficient wood to roast the garrison, who meanwhile had probably some means of alarming the district. The doorway, small, and ten or twelve feet from the ground, seems to have had double doors, hinged and plated with iron. Even if these were broken in, but a small number of persons could enter, and they would be at an immense disadvantage against those above, who having drawn up the ladder could shoot down arrows, or poke long spears through the rude flooring. Missiles, heavy or hot, I take to have been out of the question, for there could have been no space for storing the one or heating the other.

"Petrie, I think, attributes these towers to all dates between the fifth and thirteenth centuries. If for this opinion there be really sound historical evidence, of which no one is a better judge than yourself, there is no more to be said; but if I may rely upon the material evidence of their workmanship, I do not think them so old, and should be inclined to substitute from the tenth to the thirteenth centuries. However, Irish documentary evidence is, I am aware, copious and correct; it may be that in architecture, as in other of the fine arts, Ireland was before the rest of Christian Europe.

"Your photographs certainly show a great range of masonry in these towers, extending probably over two or even three centuries, but the rudest have no affinity with such structures as the House of Finan, attributed by Petrie to the sixth century. All, even the rudest, are of masonry, that is, of stone bedded in mortar, and not of dry walling like the Scottish brochs, to which the Irish towers are as superior in taste and elegance as they are in constructive style and workmanship. Dry walling indeed is carried to a considerable pitch of perfection in the brochs, as well as in the retaining walls of the chambered barrows of Uley and Stoney Littleton in Gloucester and Somerset, as well as in that very remarkable barrow opened by Mr. Vivian in Gower, all which must be of early date; but the step from this to the rudest cemented work was a great one, and this step the builders of the Irish towers had taken. Still, though all are laid in mortar, the earliest are very rude and the latest very highly finished, and the photographs show a regular series of progressing and improving workmanship until the rubble gave way to ashlar, and the mere rude openings to regularly dressed or ornamented door and window cases.

"Is it not the case that, although there may be early allusions to round towers, the earliest existing tower mentioned in records is not supposed to be earlier than the commencement of the tenth century? As to the analogies of Brunllais, Launceston, Dolbadarn, and Coningsburgh, quoted by Petrie, he could never have seen them, and must have been misled by the exploded volumes of King. Brunllais I visited with the late Lord Dunraven, and it is evidently, as is Launceston, of early English date, one of those towers so common in France and introduced there in the reign of Philip Augustus. Coningsburgh is very late Norman, and Dolbadarn, I should say, of the reign of Henry III. All they have in common with the Irish towers is, that they are circular and have elevated doorways. If they had conical roofs, they were of wood. Pembroke Keep, which is round and domed, had evidently a wooden roof above all, and, as at Coucy, Coningsburgh, and Marten's Tower, at Chepstow, these cones rose not from the outer, but from an inner wall, leaving the battlements open.

"We have not, I believe, in England the detached round tower earlier than the twelfth century. The Pembrokeshire towers, so well described by Mr. Freeman in the Archæologia Cambrensis, are later, and are rectangular. They seem, like your towers, to have been built for defence, though probably rather against the Welsh than against the Norsemen, whose visits were of earlier date, and who gave name to such places as Strumble Head, Skokholm, and Swansea, and indeed to so many others that it seems probable that these marauders became residents, and, I suspect, had as much to do with the English character of the Pembroke peninsula as the far later colony of Flemings. At Bedale in Yorkshire the church tower is fitted up for defence, and has a very curious portcullis, but is of late date.

"As to the word 'Belfry,' I do not suppose it has, etymologically, anything to do with bells. The mediæval 'Belfredus,' 'Berfreit,' or 'Beoffroi,' seems to have been a 'Machina bellica;' a tower of timber on wheels, used to quell the fire of the defenders in a siege, and the name was continued to fixed towers in which look-out men were posted with a bell to alarm the district. 'Bancloches' they were then called.

"I remain, yours, &c.,

"G. T. CLARK."

In another letter Mr. Clark adds:—

"Mr. Freeman, in a noble passage, has spoken of the city of Ravenna as 'a fossil fragment of a world which has passed away, of a world which in some sort had its own being within its walls,' where 'the true life has been kept safe by the abiding death,' the life of the past, unchoked 'as at Aachen by the continued or renewed life of the present.' And this seems to be pre-eminently true of Ireland. Her early life, vigorous in Gospel light, and in arts directed to the adornment of the visible emblems of her faith, was far beyond that of any other northern Christian nation, and far indeed beyond her more powerful and then pagan neighbour. Her wonderful series of Annals are both copious and truthful. Her illuminated manuscripts, the chalices, croziers, and other vessels and ornaments, personal or of the Church, are even at this day prized for their taste and delicacy of execution. No country can point to so complete a series of architectural examples. From the mortarless walls of Dun Aengusa to the Egyptian-like chapels and hermitages of the sixth and succeeding centuries, up to those graceful and elegant round towers, the subjects of so much attention and so much controversy, the series has an unbroken development. Each step displays features peculiarly Irish, until the highest type is reached in a style, the like of which was introduced into England at least a century later from Normandy, but which Irish architecture had anticipated in many of its most characteristic details."

"*Athenæum Club*,
"*London, Nov.* 28, 1876.

"I neglected yesterday to answer some parts of your letter, and now do so on the eve of leaving town. The passage you quote from Freeman is very striking and very characteristic of the writer, but I should have thought that the old life of Ireland had been much encroached upon by Strongbow and his consequences. And, further, that the Anglo-Normans incorporated themselves in many cases with the old Irish is evident from the history of the Fitz Geralds, *plus Hiberniores quam Hibernis*, and the Norman style of architecture which they brought with them must have created a good deal of confusion, seeing that the Irish had a style of their own, full of what we call Norman elements and ornaments.

"The old life of Ireland seems to me to have been largely ecclesiastical, and the arts it fostered were mainly employed upon ecclesiastical objects, and but very little on private and secular life, and probably this is one reason why that old life has mixed so little with a later state of things. Venice has a good deal of this, still under the varnish of modern life retaining much that is old and peculiar. These early and concealed civilizations remind one of the corpse of Charles the Great, dressed in his royal robes, his crown on his head, and seated on his throne in the vault of Aachen, only waiting a touch to be restored to life.

"As to what you say about the circular form, it is the easiest to employ, and the simplest and therefore the earliest, as witness the wigwam or the Scottish brochs. Also, executed in stone, it is the best for *passive* resistance, but for *active* the worst, admitting of no flanking fire.

"The conical roof is the natural termination of the circular tower.

"I remain, yours, &c.,

"G. T. CLARK."

Extract from Letters of M. Viollet-le-Duc.

Monsieur Viollet-le-Duc observes in a letter to the writer:—"Comme il n'existe aucun monument de tour de monastère en France qui soit antérieur au Xième siècle il serait difficile de dire si certains étaient couronnés par des toits coniques. Mais les représentations de ces édifices dans les manuscrits Carlovingiens et dans un grand nombre de bas-reliefs du XI ou XII siècles montrent des tours à toits coniques—ces toits coniques appartiennent à la plus haute antiquité. Cette forme dérivait du système le plus simple de couverture, puisque pour l'établir il suffit d'un arbre central et de chevrons appuyés sur son sommet. . . . Quant aux parties inférieures de ces tours d'églises bâties du VIIIième au Xième siècles, tours évidemment de défense, elles sont carrées, massives, munies d'une seule porte souvent défendues par une porte volant sur gonds. De ces soubassements nous avons des restes à St. Germain des Prés, à Paris, probablement IXième siècle, à la collégiale de Poissy Xième siècle, à l'église de St. Savin près Poitiers (même date), à la petite église de Créteil près Paris (même date). Beaucoup de nos clochers du XII ou XIII siècles sont établis sur des soubassements plus anciens—toujours carrés et fermés.

"A date de Charles le Chauve les monastères durent se mettre en état de défense pour pouvoir résister aux incursions normandes. De ces tours de défenses on fit plus tard des clochers quand l'état pacifié du royaume le permit. Cela n'est pas douteux, puisque, pourtant partout, on trouve au moins les substructions de ces défens et particulièrement dans les églises abbatiales.

"Je crois que la plupart des tours Irlandaises sur les côtes sont des postes de surveillance pour permettre de signaler un débarquement et au besoin de résister quelque temps à une troupe."

In another letter the same writer adds :—Les tours rondes dont vous me parlez, isolées des églises et placées spécialement dans les cimetières sont des tours de lumières, phares ou fanaux, pour annoncer aux voyageurs, la nuit, la présence d'une abbaie ou d'une église. La tour de St. Maurice d'Epinal n'est pas autre classe ; c'est-à-dire, tour fanal et aussi, au besoin, tour de guet, où presque toutes les abbayes avaient des guetteurs, comme les châteaux. J'ai toujours considéré les tours isolées d'Irelande comme ayant été construit pour ces deux fins ; savoir, éclairer ou guetter."

ON THE PRESERVATION OF NATIONAL MONUMENTS AND ECCLESIASTICAL RUINS.[1]

IT is one of the most hopeful signs of the present time that, as a late writer has remarked, "Within the last fifty years a new interest, almost like another sense," has arisen in our ancient monuments of art. While acknowledging this to be the fact, let us also lay to heart the words that follow in warning, lest our enthusiasm, religious, historical, and artistic, should, if not duly restrained, do more for the destruction of these monuments than their preservation.[2] To repair wisely may be a labour incurring a far greater expenditure of time and thought, than to rebuild, or even to restore; yet, when the importance of the work is duly weighed, who will say that such is labour wasted? We never can, indeed, restore the very buildings themselves, the living spirit of which was an inseparable part of the religion, thought, and manners of the past; but is it also true that we cannot revive that spirit? Rather we may hope that it can never wholly die—that it but awaits the term of our long and patient efforts to re-awaken in fresh vigour. Much may be done by loving contemplation of such works as it has once touched with its quickening fire, and therefore we are bound to spare no effort to keep these works among us for centuries to come.

With this single object of preservation in view, we should now turn to the sister island, Ireland, and watch the progress of the works being there carried on among her "national monuments and ecclesiastical ruins," if we would gain that knowledge of how to proceed, which practical experience alone can give. It is one thing to know that our monuments should be protected, and another to decide on the wisest method of dealing with them. Nothing is more difficult than to draw the line between restoration, preservation, and protection, as we feel when reading the annual reports drawn up by Mr. Deane, of Dublin, upon the works executed in Ireland under the Commissioners of Public Works. Whatever questions may arise as to minor points, we thankfully acknowledge the energy and skill with which his labours are being pursued. The undertaking, of which he is superintendent, is for the preservation of those ecclesiastical structures, the guardianship of which was first entrusted to the Irish Church, and which has now passed into the hands of the Board of Works. We learn from the report in question that, since the commencement of the work,

---

[1] See Report of Mr. T. N. Deane upon the works executed under the Commissioners of Public Works in Ireland for the Preservation of National Monuments.
[2] See prospectus of the Society for the Preservation of National Monuments.

CHRONOLOGICAL TABLE OF THOSE EXAMPLES (
WORK THE DATES OF WHICH

A.D.	ARCHITECTURE.	NAMES OF BUILDERS.
807	Columba's house at Kells	
904	Cathedral of Clonmacnois [1]	King Flann Sinna and Abbot Colman
917	Cashel and Belfry of Seirkieran [2]	Donnchadh, son of Flann Sinna, and Queen Saba
919	Belfry of Castledermot [3]	Abbot Cairbre, son of Feradach
952 to 964	Tempul Cillen, Clonmacnois	Cormac O'Cillen, Abbot of Clonmacnois and Tuaim G[r]
952 to 964	Church and belfry of Tuaim Greine [4]	Cormac O'Cillen, Abbot of Clonmacnois and Tuaim G
1007	Church of Killaloe [5]	King Brian Boruma
1007	Church of Iniscaltra [6]	King Brian Boruma
1015	Belfry of Kinneth [7]	Abbot Mocholmog
1027	Church and belfry of Aghadoe (commenced) [8]	Maenach
1089 to 1103	Cathedral of Clonmacnois rebuilt [9]	Flaherty O'Longsy and Cormac, son of Conn of the Po
1100	Church and belfry of Dungiven [10]	O'Cahane
1123	Tomb of King Murtogh O'Brien [11]	
1124	Belfry of Clonmacnois finished [12]	Abbot O'Malone
1126	Basilica of SS. Peter and Paul consecrated [13]	Imar O'Aeducain, anchorite, and tutor of St. Malachy
1127 to 1134	Cormac's chapel built [14]	King Cormac M'Carthy
1127 to 1134	Two churches at Lismore built [15]	King Cormac M'Carthy
1127 to 1134	Monastery in Iveragh built [16]	King Cormac M'Carthy and St. Malachy
1142	Mellifont consecrated [17]	Donagh O'Carroll, King of Oriel, and St. Malachy
1146	Bective consecrated [18]	Murchard O'Melaghlin, Prince of Meath
1148	Baltinglass consecrated [19]	Dermot M'Murrough, King of Leinster
1148	Church of Knock na Sangean built [20]	St. Malachy and Bishop O'Ceallaidhe and Donogh O'C
1161	Cathedral of Tuam built [21]	King Turlough O'Conor and Abbot Aed O'Hoisin
1151	Church of Kilbarry [22]	Cucaille MacScolaighe and Gillacoimhdhe O'Anli
1151	Boyle consecrated	
1151	Nenay in Limerick [23]	Turlough O'Brian, King of Munster
1168	Church of Dervorgilla built [24]	Queen Dervorgilla
1158	Church of Aghadoe finished [25]	Auliffe Mór O'Donoghoe
1164	Cathedral of Derry built	Flathbert O'Brolchan and Murtogh M'Laughlin
1167	Church of O'Kelly's, Clonmacnois	Conor O'Kelly, chief of Hy Many
1167	Tempul Kieran	Conor O'Kelly, chief of Hy Many
1166	Clonfert rebuilt [26]	Conor O'Kelly, chief of Hy Many
1166	Twelve churches in Galway and Clare built	Conor O'Kelly, chief of Hy Many
1238	Belfry of Annaghdown built	

[1] Annals Four Masters, Annals Clonmacnois, A.D. 901.
[2] Keatinge, History of Ireland. MS. Trinity College, Dublin, H. 5, 26, p. 149. See also History and Antiquiti[es] of St. Canice's Cathedral, pp. 8, 13. Foundation of the round tower still remains, and has been examined by the Re[v.] James Graves.
[3] Tradition that it was built by Abbot Cairbre, who died A.D. 919.
[4] Chronicum Scotorum, p. 217.
[5], [6] MacLiag's Life of King Brian Boruma, MS. Library, Trinity College, Dublin.
[7] Tradition. Smith, History of Cork, vol. ii. p. 416.
[8] See Notes on Irish Architecture, vol. ii. p. 36.
[9] Annals Four Masters, Annals Clonmacnois, A.D. 1100.
[10] Archdall Monasticon, p. 92, Allemande.
[11] Annals Four Masters, A.D. 1119.
[12] Chronicum Scotorum, Annals Four Masters.
[13] Annals Four Masters.

IRISH ARCHITECTURE, SCULPTURE, AND METAL AN BE APPROXIMATELY FIXED.

A.D.	SCULPTURED CROSSES AND TOMBSTONES.	A.D.	METAL WORK.
806	Tuathgal, Abbot of Clonmacnois		
914	Terminal cross erected by Abbot Colman in memory of King Flann Sinna	904	Bronze bell of Cumascach, son of Ailill.
921	Fiachra of Eagles Beg at Clonmacnois		
921	Muredach, Abbot of Monasterboice		
932	Uallach, chief poetess of Ireland		
944	Guare, priest of Clonmacnois		
948	Rechtar, priest of Clonmacnois		
955	Diarmait		
953	Dunadach, Bishop of Clonmacnois	954	Bell shrine of Maelbrigde.
991	Maelfinia, Bishop of Clonmacnois		
994	Odran Ua h-Eolais, Scribe of Clonmacnois		
1002	Flannchad, Bishop of Clonmacnois	1001 to 1025	St. Molaise's cumdach or case of the gospels.
1013	Corpre Mac Athail		
1025	Muiredach, Bishop of Clonmacnois	1023 to 1052	Cumdach of Stowe missal.
1028	Maelphatraic, Priest of Clonmacnois.		
1032	Dubinse, Lector of Clonmacnois		
1056	Mael-finnia, Bishop of Clonmacnois	1047	Crosier of Maelfinnia of Kells.
1059	Conn na-mbocht, founder of the Culdees at Clonmacnois		
1066	Fogartach, anchorite and sage at Clonmacnois		
1079	Maelchiaran, Bishop of Clonmacnois		
1080	Muiredach		
1085	Gillachrist, student at Clonmacnois	1098	Cathach of the O'Donnells.
		1091 to 1105	Shrine of Armagh bell.
		1101	Crosier of Lismore.
		1106 to 1126	Shrine of St. Lachtin's arm.
1123	Cross of Tuam erected by King Turlough O'Conor	1123	Cross of Cong.
		1150	Cumdach of Dimma's book.
		1166	Shrine of St. Manchan.
		1353	Domnach Airgid.
		1376	Fiachail Phadruigh.
		1381	Part of the cumdach of the Stowe missal.
1403	Tomb of Finola O'Conor at Knock-moy		

[14] Annals Four Masters.
[15] Annals of Inisfallen.
[16] Life of St. Malachy, by St. Bernard of Clairvaux.
[17] Archdall Monasticum, p. 479 (no remains of the original building).
[18] Archdall Monasticum, p. 516, War. Mon.
[19] Archdall Monasticum, p. 761, War. Mon.
[20] Annals Four Masters.
[21] Petrie, Ecclesiastical Architecture, p. 311. Ware, Annals Four Masters.
[22] Annals Four Masters, 1151.
[23] Built by Turlough O'Brian.
[24] Annals Four Masters.
[25] Annals Inisfallen, Lanigan, vol. iv., p. 168.
[26] Built by Conor O'Kelly (see Cambrensis Eversus, vol. iii. p. 321). (Celtic Society.)

REFERENCES TO BELFR[IES]

			TIGHERNACH.	CHRONICON SCOTORUM.	ANNALS OF INISFALLEN.	
			Compiled at close of the eleventh century. Tighernach O'Braoin, abbot of Clonmacnois, died A.D. 1088.	Compiled by Gillachrist O'Malone, Abbot of Clonmacnois, who died A.D. 1123.	Compiled about A.D. 1215. Commenced two centuries earlier.	
950	Slane	County Meath		A.D. 949. The belfry (*cloigtech*) of Slane was burned by the Gentiles, with its full of people in it, including Conecan, Lector of Slane.		A. was The a be Lec alon
966	Tomgraney	County Clare		A.D. 964. Cormac Ua Cillin, of the Ui Fiachrach Aidhne, comarb of Ciaran and Coman, and comarb of Tuaim-greine, by whom the great church of Tuaim-greine, and its *cloigtech* (belfry), were constructed, sapiens et senex, et Episcopus, quievit in Christo.		
987	Louth	County Louth				
996	Armagh	County Armagh	A.D. 996. Ardmacha was burned, both houses and *daimliag*, and *cloictech*, and *fidnad*—a complete destruction such as occurred not in Erin before, and that will not occur till doomsday.	994. Ardmacha was burned; houses, churches, and its belfry (*cloigtech*).		
1017	Down	County Down				A Chu i.e.
1020	Armagh	County Armagh	A.D. 1020. Ardmacha was burned on the third of the kalends of May, with all its *dertechs*, save only the *teach screptra*. And a great many houses were burned in the *Trians*, and the great *daimliag* was burned, and the *cloigtheach* with its bells, and *daimhliag na togho*, and *daimhliag int sabauill*, and the Preaching Chair, and a great quantity of gold and silver, and jewels besides.	A.D. 1018. Ard-Macha was burned, together with the Rath, except the *Teach-Screaptra* (library); and the great stone-church (*damliag*) was burned, and the belfry (*cloigtech*), and the *carbad* (chariot), and a great deal of gold and silver.		I viz. with thac the abb thir befc of t the libr chu pitt golc
1040	Clonard	County Meath				
1049	Roscommon	County Roscommon		A.D. 1049. Ross-Comain was entirely burnt, both Damhliag (stonechurch) and Regles (abbey-church), by the men of Breifne.		
1052	Rostalla	Westmeath		A.D. 1052. A tower (*cloictech*) of fire was seen at Ross-Deala, on the Sunday of the festival of George, during the space of five hours; black birds innumerable going into and out of it, and one large bird in the middle of it; and the little birds used to go under its wings when they went into the tower.		
1059	Emly	Tipperary			A.D. 1058. Turlough, son of Teige, son of Brian, at the head of the Lagenians, Ossorians, and Danes of Dublin, marched into Munster and burnt most of the country all along to Limerick.	A dair fry)

ANNALS OF ULSTER.	ANNALS OF THE FOUR MASTERS.	ANNALS OF LOCH CE.	ANNALS OF CLONMACNOIS.
at Senait MacManus by Cathal oge McManus. Died A.D. 1498.	Compiled by Michael, Conary, and Cucogry O'Clery, with Ferfeasa O'Mulconry. Written principally by Michael Teige O'Clery, born 1575, died 1635.	Compiled by Brian MacDermot, who died 1592.	Original lost. A compilation, made in English in 1627.
The *cloictheh* (belfry) of Slane by the Foreigners of Dublin. of the Patron was burned, and best of bells. Caenechair the burned, and a great number him.	A.D. 948. The belfry (cloictech) of Slaine was burned by the foreigners, with its full of relics and distinguished persons, together with Caineachair, Lector of Slane, and the crosier of the patron saint, and a bell, the best of bells.		A.D. 945. The steeple of Slane was burnt by the Danes, which was full of worthy men and relics of saints, with Kennyagher, lector of Slaine.
	A.D. 964. Cormac Ua Cillene, successor of Ciarain, a bishop and a wise man of great age, died.		
	A.D. 986. Great and unusual wind, which prostrated many buildings and houses, and among others the Oratory of Lughmagh (Louth), and many other buildings.		A.D. 981. There was such boysterous stormy winds this year that it fell down many turretts, and among the rest it fell down violently the steeple of Louth, and other steeples.
	A.D. 995. Ard-Macha was burned by lightning, both houses, churches, and cloicteaca (belfries), and its sacred wood with all destruction.		A.D. 989. Ardmach was also burnt, both church, house, and steeple, that there was not such a spectacle seen in Ireland.
16. Dunlegh-glais all burnt. Nois, Clonfert, and Ceananus, burnt.	A.D. 1015. Dunda-leathghlas was totally burned, with its stone church and belfry (cloictheach), by lightning.	A.D. 1016. Dun-lethglaise was entirely burnt. Cluainferta and Cenannus were burned.	
rd-macha was altogether burned, *mhliag mor* (great stone-church), of of lead, and the belfry (*cloic-* its bells, and the *sabhall*, and nd the chariot (*carbad*) of the l the old preaching chair, on the e kalends of June, the Monday itsuntide. Ardmach, the third ends of June, was burnt from id to the other; save only the the houses were burnt, the great ple, the church of Savall, the pul- of preaching, together with much ooks, were burnt by the Danes.	A.D. 1020. Ard-Macha was burned, with all the fort, without the saving of any house within it, except the library only, and many houses were burned in the Trinns; and the great stone-church was burned, and the belfry (*cloictech*) with its bells; and Daimhliag na Toe, and Daimhliag-an-tsabhaill; and the chariot of the abbots and their books in the houses of the students, with much gold, silver, and other precious things.	A.D. 1020. Ard-Macha was altogether burned; viz. the great stone-church with its roof of lead, and the belfry with its bells, and the Sabhall, and the Toai, and Carbad-na-nAbbaid, and the old preaching chair, on the 3rd of the kalends of June, the Monday before Whitsuntide.	A.D. 1013. Kildare, Glandalougha, Clonard, Aron, Swords, Clonvicknose, were throughly burnt by Danes. Ardmach the third of the Kalends of June was burnt from the one end to the other, save only the library; all the houses were burnt, the great church-steeple, the church of the Sanal, the pulpit or chair of preaching, together with much gold, silver, and books, were burnt by the Danes.
	A.D. 1039. The belfry (*cloictech*) of Cluain Iraird fell.		A.D. 1039. The steeple of Clonard fell down to the earth.
	A.D. 1050. Doire-Caelainne and the belfry of Ros-Comain were burned by the men of Breifne.		
	A.D. 1054. A steeple (cloicteach) of fire was seen in the air over Ros-Deala, on the Sunday of the festival of George, for the space of five hours; innumerable black birds passing into and out of it, and one large bird in the middle of it; and the little birds went under his wings when they went into the steeple.		
8. Imlech-Ivair all burnt, both tone-church) and *cloictech* (bel-	A.D. 1058. Imleach-Ibhair was totally burned, both daimhliag and steeple (*cloictheach*).	A.D. 1058. Imlech-Ibhair was entirely burnt, both stone church and steeple (*cloictech*)	

REFERENCES TO BELFRI
(Con

TIGHERNACH.	CHRONICON SCOTORUM.	ANNALS OF INISFALLEN.
Compiled at close of the eleventh century. Tighernach O'Braoin, Abbot of Clonmacnois, died A.D. 1088.	Compiled by Gillachrist O'Malone, Abbot of Clonmacnois, who died A.D. 1125.	Compiled about A.D. 1215. Commenced two centuries earlier.
A.D. 1076. Murchadh, grandson of Flann Ua Maeilsechlainn, was slain in treachery by Amlaibh son of Maelan, king of the Gailenga, in the belfry (*cloictech*) of Cenannus (Kells); and he (Amlaibh) was slain immediately after, through the miracle of Colum Cille.	A.D. 1073. Murchadh, son of Conchobhar Ua Maeilsechlainn, was killed by Amhlaibh, son of Maelan, *i.e.* the King of Gaileng, in the *cloictech* (belfry) of Cenannus (Kells), and he himself fell by Maelsechlainn, son of Conchobhar.	A.D. 1076. Murcha O'Maolseachlin was murdered in the steeple of Kells (*cloiccteach* Cenanais) by Auliff, son of Maolan O'Lochain, king of Gailenga.
	A.D. 1093. The *cloigtech* (belfry) of Mainistir was burned, with the writings (*scriptuir*, "scripture") in it.	
	A.D. 1120. The great belfry (*cloictech*) of Cluain-muc-Nois was finished by Gillachrist Ua Maeleoin and by Toirdelbuch Ua Conchobhair.	
		A.D. 1127. A great hosting by Connor MacFergall O'Loghlinn, together with the people of the North of Ireland, to Meath; they burnt Trim, both *cloictech* (steeple), and church, and these full of people.
	A.D. 1131. Lightning knocked off the head of the steeple (*cloichtech*) of Cluain-muc-nois, and pierced the steeple of Ros-cre.	
A.D. 1156. A hosting by Murtogh Mac Neile into Ossory when they plundered the entire country, and burnt four principal churches, including Durrow of Idough and Aghmacart, and he burnt Eochy O'Cuinn the lector in the cloicctech (belfry).		A.D. 1156. Mortogh, son of Niall Mac Lochlainn, marched into Ossory; and they plundered and laid waste the whole country, and burnt four principal churches, among which were the church of Durrow in Hy Duagh, and Achy-mic Airt; and he burned Eochaidh O'Cuinn, the Lector, in the *cloictech* (belfry).
		A.D. 1171. The belfry of Tulach-Ard-Connallain, with its full of people in it, was burnt by the same fierce warrior O'Ruairc.
		A.D. 1238. The belfry of Eanach-duin (Annadown, Co. Galway), was built.

IN THE IRISH ANNALS

d).

NALS OF ULSTER.	ANNALS OF THE FOUR MASTERS.	ANNALS OF LOCH CE.	ANNALS OF CLONMACNOIS.
Compiled A.D. 1498.	Compiled by Michael, Conary, and Cucogry O'Clery with Ferfeasa O'Mulconry. Written principally by Michael Teige O'Clery, born 1575, died 1635.	Compiled by Brian MacDermot, who died 1592.	Original lost. A compilation, made in English in 1627.
1076. Murchadh, son of Ua Mailsechlainn, king 'a during three nights, in in the *cloictech* (belfry) is, by the son of Maelan, f the Gailenga.	A.D. 1076. Murchadh, son of Flann Ua Maeleachlainn, at the expiration of three days and three nights after his having assumed the supremacy of Tara, was treacherously killed in the Belfry (Cloicthech) of Kells by the lord of Gailcanga, i.e. Amlaoibh, the grandson of Maelan.	A.D. 1076. Murchadh, son of Flann Ua Maelscchlainn, King of Temhair (Tara), during the space of three nights, was slain in the *cloicteach* (belfry) of Cenannus (Kells), by the son of Maelan, King of Gailenga.	A.D. 1073. Murrogh, son of Flann O'Melaghlin, the reigning king of Moate but three dayes and three nights, was killed by Awly, son of Moylan, prince of Gailenga, in the borders of Leinster; he was killed in the steeple of Kells.
1097. The *cloictech* (belf Mainister, with its and various treasures, rued.	A.D. 1097. The Cloicthech (belfry) of Mainister, with its books and many treasures, was burnt.		
1121. The *cloictech* (bel- Telagh Inmayne (Tulla- in Ossraighe, split by a rbolt, from which a stone ll down killed a student church. . . . A great happened on the nones ember, which tore off the :hopar, (or cap,) of the ŧ (belfry) of Armagh, used great destruction of all over Ireland.	A.D. 1121. A great wind storm happened in the December of this year, which knocked off the cap of the cloictech (belfry) of Ardmacha, and caused great destruction of woods throughout Ireland. The cloictech of Tealach n-Inmainne in Osraighe was split by a thunderbolt, and a stone flew from the cloictech, which killed a student in the church.	A.D. 1121. The steeple (*cloictech*) of Telach-n Inmuine (Tullamaine) in Osraighe was cleft by a thunderbolt, and a stone flew from it which killed a student in the church. A gale of wind occurred on the nones of December which knocked off the cap of the steeple (*cloictech*) of Armagh, and caused a great destruction of trees throughout all Erinn.	
	A.D. 1124. The finishing of the cloicthech of Cluain-mic- -Nois by Ua Maeleoin, successor of Ciaran.		.
		A.D. 1128. The burning of Ath-truim (Trim) with its churches; and a great number *of persons* suffered martyrdom in them.	
	A.D. 1135. Lightning struck off the head of the cloicthech of Cluain mic Nois, and pierced the cloictheach of Ros Cre.		A.D. 1137. There was boysterous, tempestuous wind this year; by it fell down many trees, houses, turrets, steeples, and other things, and whirled them into the sea.
	A.D. 1147. A thunderbolt fell this year upon the cloicthech of Daimhliag Chianain (*i.e.* Duleek), and knocked off its beannchobhar (*i.e.* cap).		
	A.D. 1156. Eochaidh Ua Cuinn, the chief master, was burned in the cloictheach of Ferta.		A.D. 1153. Murtogh, son of Neale, was king of Ireland 14 yeares; he with his forces went to Finglas and gave the kingdom and government thereof and the province to Dermott Mc Murrough, for yielding him hostages of obedience and allegiance—they wasted and spoyled Ossory without respect of church or chapel.
			A.D. 1182. The steeple of Ardbreakan fell this yeare.
	A.D. 1171. The cloicthech of Telach-aird was burned by Tighearnan Ua Ruairc with its full of people in it.		
	A.D. 1238. The cloictheach of Enachduin was erected.	A.D. 1238. The belfry (*cloictech*) of Enachduin (Annaghdown, Co. Galway) was erected.	

the ecclesiastical ruins at Ardmore, Ardfert, Monasterboice, the rock of Cashel, Columba's house at Kells, the churches of Gallarus and Donaghmore, the towers or bell-houses of Ardmore, Killala, and Donaghmore, and the crosses of Donaghmore, Killamery, Kilkeeran and Kilcleshin, have been placed in a condition of comparative safety, and that provision has been made for the effectual maintenance of such guardianship as will insure them from injury. The works now in progress are for the preservation of the ruins at Devenish and Glendalough.

Such works may be classed under two heads—preservation and diggings. In the carrying out of the first, Mr. Deane's care has been to see that all stones in the buildings entrusted to him, which have been loosened by storm, are fixed; that cement is laid on the tops of the walls to prevent infiltration of moisture; that the roots of dangerous trees are removed; that the upper portions of the walls are grouted with concrete, and fallen stones reset. Thus, rent and tottering walls have been made good; arches long built up have been reopened; fences and gates have been repaired or supplied where wanting, and the noble tower, or bell-house, of Glendalough, which was on the very verge of falling, is now in such a condition that, having already stood eight hundred years, there is no reason why it should not stand eight hundred longer.

The other work involved in these labours, that of digging and clearing, has already led to much valuable discovery. Within these buildings lay the accumulated rubbish of centuries, débris that tells the story of the rage of the iconoclast of former times, or the still more mournful indifference of the present day that leaves these sacred temples to be turned to cattle sheds.

In the necessary clearing away of such sad growth, and the levelling of the church floors, discoveries of no small value have been made. At Glendalough alone, seven windows have been unearthed, one belonging to the little church upon the Rock, or Tempul na Sceilig, the other six to the beautiful Irish Romanesque church of St. Saviour's; the decorated chancel arch of the same building; the staircase leading to the upper chambers in the roof; the foundations of another church; the stones which formed the conical roof and apex of the bell-house; one entire high cross richly sculptured, with the shaft and base of another; carved tombstones, one bearing an Irish inscription, and an ancient road or causeway, leading from one of the two lakes to the church of the rock. At Devenish, crosses and sculptured stones have been found and put in a place of safety; at Monasterboice, a third of the termon, or high crosses, has been found and set up again.

In the difficult but necessary task of pointing the walls, we hear from those who have seen Mr. Deane's work, that admirable care has been taken to avoid disfiguration by keeping back the cement in the joints from the face of the wall, as well as by toning down its raw fresh colour.

The question as to the instances in which it is or is not legitimate to remove features which do not belong to the original building, has come before Mr. Deane twice in dealing with Cormac's chapel. The first in the case of the two windows in the south wall of the nave; the second, that of the wall which partly concealed the fine doorway of the same building. In the first instance he decided on leaving the more modern windows, and his reasons for so doing are well explained when he asks whether such changes may not "mark certain epochs in the history of the building, indicative of habits and customs, times of peace and war, which add a charm and tell a tale which a more perfect structure would fail to do." In the second instance, the later work was removed for the very justifiable reason that it concealed a great part of the finest portal of the chapel. A like fine distinction had to be drawn by Mr. Deane in dealing with the lancet windows of the cathedral of Cashel: the filling of the lower portions of the lancet windows was taken out, but not the curtailing done in the fourteenth century.

If we may offer a suggestion, it would be that the work of preservation can hardly be worthily carried out until descriptive catalogues of each of these various classes of monuments be prepared. Such lists are now being drawn up by the ladies of Alexandra College Archæological Society, who have commenced by using the Ordnance Survey letters as the foundation for their work.

The following table supplied by them shows the number and situation of the prehistoric sepulchral monuments or cromleacs of Ireland, so far as they have yet been catalogued. It will be perceived that there are 55 cromleacs mentioned in Leinster, 46 in Ulster, 82 in Connaught, and 43 in Munster, making in all 226.

Province	County	Monuments
Leinster	Carlow, 3	Aghade. Haroldstown. Kernanstown.
	Dublin, 10	Ballybetagh. Ballybrack. Brennanstown. Ballymonduff. Tallaght. Bally-na-scorny. Kippure. Howth. Phœnix Park. Shanganagh.
	Kildare, 2	Kilcullen. The Curragh.
	Kilkenny, 6	Derry-na-hinch. Fiddown. Whitechurch. Ballyhenetry. Tubbrid. Kilmogue.
	King's County, 1	Old Croghan.
	Louth, 3	Monasterboice. Castle-ring. Prolcek.
	Longford, 1	Cloonker.
	Meath	Broad Boyne. Newgrange Dowth.
	Westmeath	Carn. Lickblay. Hill of Cearna. Dysart.

Appendices.

PROVINCE	COUNTY	MONUMENTS
LEINSTER, *continued*	Wexford, 3	St. Vogues. Kilcavan. Kilgorman.
	Wicklow, 19	Baltinglass. Kilruddery. Delgany. Calry. Castleruddery. Leitrim. Kilcoo. Athegrany, No. 1. Athegrany, No. 2. Athegrany, No. 3. Sugarloaf. Ballycarrigeen. Powerscourt. Moya Comb. Powerscourt Mountain. Glaskenny. Annacrivey. Enniskerry. Maletia.
ULSTER	Antrim, 14.	Ballycarngraney. Ballintoy. Glegnagh. Cloughnaboghill. Fairhead. Ballyvennagh (2). Cloghs. Craigs (2). Ticloy (2). Island Magee. Mount Druid. Layd. Ballyalbanagh. Drumagorgan.
	Armagh, 1.	Cairn, near Newry.
	Down, 14.	Magheralin. Scarva. Drummillen. Rathfryland. Drumbo. Kempestone. Mount Stewart. Loughmoney. Sliddery-ford. Legannanny. Cloghmore. Kilkeel. Kilfeagan. Annadorn.
	Monaghan, 3	Calliagh (Aghaboy). Latuamard. Lennan.
	Fermanagh, 2	Slieve Betha. Slieve-dha-Chou.

PROVINCE.	COUNTY.	MONUMENTS.
ULSTER, *continued*	Tyrone, 5	Loughrey. Tullyhog. Castlederg. Drumnakilly. Trillick.
CONNAUGHT	Galway, 9	Marble hill. Knockroe (Diarmait's bed). Loughrea. Loughnee (circle). Mohar (Aran Islands). Knockma. Ballymagibbon. Carn an cluith. Carn meenain uisge.
	Mayo, 6	Cogaula. Doonfeeny. Duncarton. Glencastle. Ratheskin. Kilmore.
	Sligo, 67	Ardnaree. Ballyglass. Rathfran. Carbad. Carrowmore (63).
MUNSTER	Clare, 14	Cragballyconnell. Coolamore. Knockalassa. Kiltumper. Bally-cum-marga. Cahir-mac-crusheen. Kilnaboy. Commons, north. Knocknaglaise. Teeshagh. Shallee.
	Cork, 3	Castlemary. Macroom. Labbagally.
	Kerry	Lohert.
	Limerick, 6	Cromwell's Moat (2). Ballynagalliagh (2). Knockadown. Grange.
	Tipperary, 8	Doon. Foil-mahonmore. Doon-Kilgrant. Doon-Kilgrant, No. 2. Doon-Kilgrant, No. 3. Glengar. Upperchurch. Killoscully.
	Waterford, 10	Fenagh (3). Ballindud. Gurteen. Gaulstown. Portlaw. Matthewstown. Tooreen, West. Ballynageeragh.

ON THE INTERCOURSE WHICH EXISTED BETWEEN IRELAND AND FRANCE IN THE REIGN OF CHARLEMAGNE.

THE records which exist in evidence of the relations between the kings of the Scots and those of France before the tenth century, have been so often misunderstood as referring not to the rulers of Ireland, but to those of North Britain, now Scotland, that it may be desirable to recapitulate the information already supplied on this question by Dean Reeves and other reliable authorities.

North Britain—to the south-western portions of which the names Alba and Pictland were also given—was not termed Scotland till the close of the ninth century; whereas the island of Ireland had borne the name of Scotia for many centuries before. Legend derives the name from Scota—a mythical Eastern princess, whose descendants were held to have led one of the first colonies from the East through Spain to Ireland—and foreign chroniclers of the ninth century speak of "Hibernia, island of the Scots," when referring to events in Ireland regarding which corresponding entries are found in the annals of that country.

The history of the transfer of the name Scotland to North Britain is as follows.[1] In the year 503 Fergus, son of Erc, lord of Dalriada, sailed from Ulster into Pictland or Alba, and there founded a kingdom whose inhabitants were first termed Albanian Dalriada. It was not till some centuries later that the final subjugation of this portion of North Britain was effected by these colonists. In the year 838 Kenneth MacAlpin, the thirty-fourth ruler of the Albanian Dalriada, ascended the throne. In 842 he subdued the Picts of North Britain, thus becoming master of the entire country between Edinburgh and Caithness. From this time the specific name of Dalriada began to fall into disuse, until at length the whole kingdom was called Scotia or Scotland, after the name of the race which had branched into it from Ireland, and to whose authority it had gradually submitted. This was at a period fully half a century later than that to which Eginhard alludes, the reign of Karl the Great having dated from A.D. 768 to 814. One of the kings alluded to by Eginhard was apparently Aed the Dignified, who reigned in Ireland from A.D. 793 to 817. It was under this king that the clergy of Ireland were first exempted from attending their chieftains in battle, and important developments in architecture and art seem to have been effected in his reign. The Calendar or "Song in praise of the Saints" of Oengus, the Culdee, is said to have been

---

[1] See Reeves's "Adamnan," pp. 433, 437.

written in his lifetime, as also the poem of Fothud of the Canon, wherein occurs the first reference to the Irish church towers, commonly called Round towers, as places of refuge. It is curious to find that we have the authority of Ariosto for the assertion that an Irish king of this period passed a portion of his youth in the Court of France. In the eleventh canto of "Orlando Furioso" we read—

> "Oberto sopraviene,
> Oberto il rè d'Ibernia, ch' avea inteso
> Che 'l marin Monstro era su 'l lito steso."—St. 59.

And the Irish king recognizes Orlando because he had been a page of honour in France.

> "Lo conoscea, perch' era stato infante
> D' onore in Francia, e se n' era parti
> Per pigliar la corona l'anno inante
> Del padre suo, ch' era di vita uscito
> Tante volte veduto e tante e tante," &c. &c.—St. 62.

In the dissertation of Dr. Matthew Kennedy on the family of the Stuarts, printed in Paris in the year 1705, this writer remarks at page 181, alluding to the "alliance of friendship" between the Irish king and Charlemagne :—

"Whoever doubts of the truth of this assertion, which requires a more ample debate than is fit to bestow upon't in this place, let him but cast an eye upon a very ancient piece of *Tapestry* in the inner hall of Audicience in Monsr de Chamillaris appartements at Versailles, and there he shal find the king of Ireland standing in the row of the Princes in amity with Charle-Magne, and drawn with the Irish harp by his right side as a marck of distinction, the Emperour himself being of the number."

The relationship between Ireland and the Franks is of a very early date. One of the foreigners who came to Ireland with St. Patrick was the Deacon Justus, "and he was of the Franks *ut quidam putant*," as we learn from the Felire of Aengus. He it was who baptized St. Ciaran, the founder of Clonmacnois.

One of the letters spoken of in the passage above referred to, of Eginhard as witnessing to the relationship between Ireland and France, appears to have been preserved in Ussher's "Epistolae Hibernicae" (Epist. xviii., Works, vol. iv. p. 466), written by Alcuin from the Court of Karl the Great, "from the humble priest Alcuin to the blessed master and pious father Colcu greeting," and concluding thus :—

"I have sent for thy charity some oil, which at present is scarcely found in Britain, that you may dispense it through the stations of bishops where it is required for the use of men or the honour of God. I have also sent fifty shekels for the brotherhood of the alms of King Charles. I adjure you to pray for him. And of my own alms fifty shekels, and to the brothers in the south at Baldhuinega thirty shekels of the king's alms and thirty of my own alms, and twenty shekels of the alms of the king to the family of Areides and twenty of my own alms, and to each of the anchorites three shekels of pure silver, that they all may pray for me and for our lord King Charles, that God may preserve him for the protection of His holy Church and for the praise and glory of His name."

The ecclesiastic to whom this letter was addressed was Lector of Clonmacnois, and himself the author of a remarkable devotional work. He died about the year 789. Many proofs exist of the friendship entertained for Karl the Great by the learned Irishmen of his day. The monks of the Irish Monastery of St. Gall were so attached to his person that they were accustomed to call him "our Karl,"[1] and the intimacy that existed between Ireland and France in the eighth century only increased in the ninth. We find that Cormac Mac Cuilennain, Prince of Cashel, born in the year 831, and Carroll, son of the King of Leinster, were foster-brethren and school-fellows. They were apparently educated at the school of Castledermot (*i.e.*, Disert Diarmata), for we read that Snedgus of that monastery was Cormac's tutor. Their nurse was Gelsherc, a Frankish princess; "hence," says the Irish annalist, "Cormac sang:—

"' Bring me my tympan, that I may play on it,
For my ardent affection for Gelsherc, daughter of Deirill,'

—*i.e.*, Gelsherc, daughter of Deirill, King of the Franks, nursed them both (unde forod Geilsheirce)."[2]

It is doubtful whether the place mentioned here as Geilsherc's seat be in Ireland or France, but if in the latter, it would suggest the idea that the kings of Ireland gave their sons training in the Frankish Court, an idea which seems borne out by the statement of Ariosto before alluded to. The Prince of Cashel, who was thus royally nursed, was afterwards bishop, and author of the *Sanas Chormaic:* he was slain in battle, A.D. 903, at Ballaghmoon in Kildare, and legend states that he lies buried at Cill-fine Cormaic, in that county. His glossary probably formed part of the great compilation called Saltair Chormaic, or Saltair Chaisil, which seems to have been made by Cormac Mac Cuilennain and added to by Brian Boruma.

The statements in the Irish Annals as to the victories achieved by the Irish over the Northmen in the beginning of the ninth century are corroborated by corresponding entries as to the achievements of the Scots in the Annals of Fulda and Regino's Chronicle,[3] as also in that of Hermannus Contractus; but that which bears most fully on the present subject is the passage in the Annals of Eginhard, at the year 812, where he distinctly mentions Hibernia as the island of the Scots. "The fleet of the Northmen," he says (A.D. 812), "having arrived at Hibernia, island of the Scots, after that a battle had been fought with the Scots, and after that no small number of the Northmen had been slain, basely took to flight and returned home." Thirty years later we find in the Chronicle of the Deeds of the Normans in France, a somewhat similar recognition of the services of the Irish, where the chronicler, describing the burning and wasting of a portion of Aquitania by the Northmen, adds:—"The

---

[1] Hallam's "Middle Ages," vol. iii. p. 529; Ekkehardus, "Vit. B. Notkeri," c. xxix. G., p. 277.

[2] See "Fragments of Irish Annals," p. 221. Edited by John O'Donovan, for Irish Archæological and Celtic Society.

[3] "Enhardi Fuldensis Annales," A.D. 812; "Hermanni Aug. Chron." ib. Mon. Germ. Hist. Ed. Pertz, tom. i. p. 335, and tom. v. p. 102; "Chronicorum Reginonis," lib. primus, p. 409 (Conradi Abb. Ursperg. Chron.).

Scots breaking in upon the Northmen, by God's help victorious, drive them forth from their borders. Whereupon the King of the Scots sends, for the sake of peace and friendship, legates to Charles with gifts;"[1] and we have the authority of Ware for stating that the Scottish king here alluded to was Malachy I., who sent legates to Charles the Bald, with presents, to acquaint him of his victory and desire liberty of passage to Rome.

---

[1] "Hist. franc. Script.," t. ii. p. 524 (Lutet. Par. 1636).

KEY TO THE MAP.

Irish Name.	Translation.
Achaidh-biorair	Aghavuller.
Achaidh dá Eó	Aghadoe.
Achaidh-fobhair	Aghagower.
Achadh Úr	Freshford.
Airgialla	Oriel.
Airthir Maighe	Armoy.
Anteriores Maugdorni	District in Co. Monaghan.
Ara	Aranmore Isd. (Co. Donegal).
Ara airthir	Inishere.
Aramór	Aranmore (Co. Galway).
Ard-ferta	Ardfert.
Ard Brecain	Ardbraccan.
Ard Ceannachte	In Louth.
Ard Macha	Armagh.
Ard Mór	Ardmore.
Ard rathain	Ardrahen.
Ard Phatraicc	Ard patrick.
Ard Uladh	Heights of Ulster (near Bangor).
Ath Truim	Trim.
Baile beg	Ballybeg.
Baile Mhuirne	Ballyvourney.
Balla	Ballagh.
Banna	Bann.
Beannchor	Banagher.
Bearba	Barrow.
Beirre	Bearhaven.
Benn Edair	Howth.
Boinn	Boyne.
Boirce	Mourne (Co. Down).
Brigobhann	Brigoone.
Cahir Gel	Caher Gal.
Caiseal	Cashel.
Caisel Ban	Cashel bawn.
Campus Breg	Plain of East Meath.
Campus Eilni	Plain between the Bann and the Lee.
Carrigeen	Carrigeen.
Ceannanus	Kells.
Ceann-eich	Kinneth.
Charybdis Brecani	Strait near Rathlin.
Cianacta	Keenaght.
Ciarraige Luacra	Kerry.
Cill alaidh	Killala.
Cill Ausaille	Killossy.
Cill Beanain	Kilbannon.
Cill Chainnigh	Kilkenny.
Cill Cuillen	Kilcullen.
Cill dara	Kildare.
Cill inghine Boeth	Kilnaboy.
Cill Maelchedair	Kilmalkedar.
Cill mic Duach	Killmacduach.
Cill mo Cealloch	Killmallock.
Cill Molaise	Lorum.
Cill Osnadha	Kellistown.
Cill Ree	Kilree.
Cill Ruaid	Kilroot.
Cill Sliebhe	Killeevy.
Cill Uissean	Killeshin.
Cinel Conaill	In Donegal.
Cinel Eogain	In Londonderry.
Cinel Luigdec	In Kilmacrenan (Donegal).
Cliara	Clare Island.
Cluain Cafa	Malin Head.
Cluain Caione	Clonkeen.
Cluain Dolcain	Clondalkin.
Cluain Eos	Clones.
Cluain Ferta	Clonfert.
Cluain Iraird	Clonard.
Cluain mic Nois	Clonmacnois.
Cluain mor	Clonmore.
Cluain Uamha	Cloyne.
Cnoc Brendain	Brandon Head.
Collum Bovis	Drumboe.
Conmaicne Mara	Connemara.
Corcach	Cork.
Corca Baiscinn	S. E. of Clare.
Corca Laegde	In Munster.
Cruthini populi	In Antrim and Down (Irish Picts).
Cuailgne	Cooley in Louth.
Cuan Mod	Clew Bay.
Cuan Snama Aigne	Carlingford Bay.
Daeminis	Devenish.
Daimhinis	Devenish.
Daimhliag Cianan	Duleek.
Dairbre	Valentia.
Daire Calgaigh	Londonderry.
Dalriada	Antrim and Down.
Dealbhna	Iar Connaught.
Deilginis	Delgany.
Deise	Decies (Waterford).
Disert Diarmata	Castledermot.
Disert Tola	Disert O'Dea.
Disert Oengusso	Dysart.

Key to the Map.

Irish Name.	Translation.
Doire Calgaigh	Londonderry.
Domnach Tortain	Donaghmore.
Dotair	Dodder.
Druim Cliabh	Drumcliff.
Druim Cliabh	Drumcliff.
Druim-in-easclainn	Dromiskin.
Druim leathan	Drumlane.
Dubh Cathair	The black fort.
Dun Aengusa	Fort of Aengus.
Dun Lonchobair	Dun Conor.
Dun da Lethglais	Downpatrick.
Dun Eochaill	Dun Ochill.
Dun Garbhain	Dungarvan.
Dun Geimhin	Dungiven.
Dun-na-mbeann	Dunaman.
Dun Sobairce	Dunseverick.
Eanach-duin	Annaghdown.
Eas Ruaid	Assaroe.
Eas ui Fhloinn	Assylin.
Eile	Ely.
Eoir	Nore.
Faoit	Whiddy.
Fearna	Ferns.
Fer Ceall	In Meath.
Feargus	Fergus.
Ferta fer feic	Slane.
Fearta na Caireach	Fertagh.
Fionn Traig	Ventry.
Firmanæ	Fermanagh.
Gall-rós	Gallarus.
Gaet Dobair	Gweedore.
Glinnedalocha	Glendalough.
Imleach	Emly.
Inber Domnann	Malahide river.
Inber Mor	Arklow.
Inber Naile	Inver Bay.
Inis-an-ghoill	Inchagoile.
Inis bo finn	Inisbofin (Co. Galway).
Inis Caein Dega	Iniskeen.
Inis Cathaig	Scattery.
Inis Celtair	Holy Island, Lough Derg.
Inis Cleire	Cape Clear.
Inis Clothrainn	Inis-cloran.
Inis Doimle	Little Island, Waterford.
Inis Eogain	Inishowen.
Inis Geide	Iniskea.
Inis Gloire	Inis Glora.
Inis Mac dara	Inis-Mac-dara.
Inis Medhon	Inismain.
Inis Mic Nessain	Ireland's eye.
Inis Muireadaig	Inis-murray.
Inis Mochaoi	Mahee Island.
Inis Mod	Inisgore.
Korkureti	Corkaree, in West Meath.
Labrann	Cashen river.
Lann Abhaid	Rams island.
Leim concúllain	Loop Head.
Liath	Lea.
Liphe	Liffey (river).
Loc Carman	Wexford Haven.
Loc da Caec	Waterford Harbour.
Loch Bricrenn	Loughbrickland.
Loch Cuan	Strangford Loch.
Loch Eachach	Loch Neagh.
Loch feabail	Loch Foyle.
Loch Rudraige	Dundrum Bay.
Loch Suilige	Loch Swilly.
Loch Lurgan	Galway Bay.
Loch Neatac	Lough Neagh.
Luacros	Loughrusmore Bay.
Lughmagh	Louth.
Luimneach	Limerick.
Lusca	Lusk.
Machaire ratha	Maghera.
Mainister Buite	Monasterboice.
Mide	Meath.
Miliuc	Mayo.
Muscraige Mitaine	Muskerry, in Cork.
Nepotes Tortrei	In Tyrone.
Nepotes fechureg	In Co. Tyrone.
Nua chongbhail	Nohoval Daly.
Ochter ard	Oughterard.
Oentreb	Antrim.
Osraighe	Ossory.
Port Muirbuilg	Ballycastle.
Rathain	Rahen.
Rath-both	Raphoe.
Rathluraigh	Maghera (Co. Londonderry).
Rath mhichil	Rathmichael.
Rath Tuaidh	Rattoo.
Recra (Co. Dublin)	Lambay.
Rechru	Rathlin Island (Co. Antrim).
Rinn Dubair	Waterford Point.
Rinn Seimne	Island Magee.
Ros Ailither	Rosscarbury.
Ruis Coeman	Roscommon.
Ruis Cré	Roscrea.
Ruis finglas	Rosenallis.
Saighir Ciaran	Seirkieran.
Samdoir	Erne.
Senan	Shannon river.
Sinainn	Shannon.
Siuir	Suir.
Sliabliac	Slieve League.
Sligeache	Sligo.
Sord Choluimcille	Swords.
Stagnum vituli	Belfast Lough.
Suc	Suck.
Tamlaght finlagen	Tallagh finlagen.
Tamlaght finlagen	Drumachose.
Teach Mochua	Timahoe.
Teach Tuæ	Teghadœ.
Telach Aird	Tullaghard.
Telach nionnuainne	Tullamain.
Tempull Croine	Iniskeragh (Co. Donegal).
Tempull C.c.	Inis Keeragh.
Tir Bogaine	In Donegal.
Tire da Loc	Iar Connaught.

Irish Name.	Translation.	Irish Name.	Translation.
Tir Enda	In Donegal.	Tulach thirne	Tullaherin.
Tir Aeda	Tirhugh, in Donegal.	Turlach	Turlough.
Toir Inis	Tory Island.	Ui Ceinsellaig	Hy Kinsela (Co. Wexford).
Torbuirg	Benmore, or Fair Head.	Uaran Mór	Oranmore.
Trumaire	Trummery.	Ui Fidgeinnte	In Co. Limerick.
Tuaim Greine	Tomgraney.	Uladh	Ulster.
Tuaim da Gualann	Tuam.	Umhall uacdrac	The Owles (Co. Mayo).

INDEX.

Aengus the Culdee, A.D. 780, 42.
Aghadoe Cathedral, Killarney, 55, 120, 126.
Alcuin, Epistle of, to Colcu of Clonmacnois, Appendix viii.
Annadown Abbey, 123.
Annalists, records by, of the foundations of early Churches, 6, 43-4, 48; see also table at end.
Aran, Islands of, 28; description of, 49 to 52.
Aranmór, Lakes in, 49.
Arch, true, date of buildings which show a knowledge of, 3, 4, 9, 10, 43, 47; no double-roofed buildings before the introduction of this knowledge, 120.
Architecture, earliest examples on the Isles of Aran, 14; innovations in, generally represent some revolution in the history of a country, 91, 92.
Ardmore, Romanesque arcade in, 121.

Banagher Church, Londonderry, 8, 46, 113, 116.
Bardic legends, announce advent of Christianity, 21.
Bede's account of Ecclesiastical Cashel, built by St. Cuthbert at Lindisfarne, 33, *note*, 34.
Bells, Early Irish, 81, 83; those of the tenth to the thirteenth century, small and light, *ib.*; bell-ringing as practised in the ninth and tenth centuries, illustrated from contemporary MS. and architectural ornament, 82; bell of St. Patrick, 83; bell of Cumascach, *ib.*; bell at Cashel, *ib.*; bell at Aughagower, tradition concerning, *ib.*; bell at Ferta, *ib.*; Ratto, *ib.*; bells as audible from top of round towers as at base, *ib. note*.
Belfries, 7, 53, 111; see also " Ecclesiastical Towers" and "Irish Church Towers."
BELFRIES :—
  Aghadoe, Kerry, 55.
  Annadown, 55.
  Antrim, 54, 57.
  Ardmore, 55, 56, 57, 86, 121, 123.
  Cashel, 7, 9, 55, 57, 83, 84, 129.
  Disert Aengus, Limerick, 55, *note* 7 *ib.*, 57.
  Disert O'Dea, 55, 56.
  Finan's (St.) Church, belfry of, 55; dimensions, masonry, joined to the church, 63.
  Glendalough, 55.
  Iniscaltra, 55, 109.
  Kells, 55, *note* 9 *ib.*, 57; St. Columbkille's house, 43, 120.
  Kevin's (St.) Church, Glendalough, 120; tower attached to the church and coeval with it, most perfect and oldest instance, 62.
  Killala, County Mayo, 55.
  Kilkenny, Round Tower of, important discovery of Christian interment below level of its foundations, 59.
  Kilmacduach, belfry of the group of churches in the Barony of Killtartan, County Galway, 55.
  Monasterboice, 55.
  O'Rorke's Belfry, Clonmacnois, 55.
  Roscrea, 55; carvings on, ship carved on side of doorway, *note* 2 *ib.*
  Timahoe, 55, *note* 8 *ib.*, 57.

Brendan, of Inisglora, date of his death (577), 39.

Brian Borumha, rebuilt churches, introd. 6; erected thirty-two round towers, 108.

Burton, F. W., on round tower at Dinkelsbühl, 65.

Byzantine workmen, influx of, into North Italy and the Court of Charlemagne, 100.

Caimin's (St.) Church, Iniscaltra, 109, 119, 120; remains of west doorway (fig. 83), peculiar capitals to pillars of chancel arch (fig. 82), Cashel (fig. 81); marks transition to the enriched round arch, 113.

Campaniles or bell towers, date of their construction on the Continent, 64, 66, 68, 70, 78, 100, 101.

Canice (St.), Church of, 60.

Carlyle, Thomas, quoted, 24, 94.

Cashel, County Tipperary, group of ruins in, 129; Cormac's chapel, 7, 9, 55, 57, 83, 84.

Cashels, or Ecclesiastical Forts, connected by tradition with introduction of Christianity, 1, 2, 21; outworks or *chevaux de frise* never observed outside, 33; features in masonry peculiar to them, *ib.*; special feature in their oratories and cells, which mark the dawn of Christian decorative art, 35; form and small size, probable origin of the type, 37.

Celsus, Archbishop of Armagh, 128.

"Celtic" art (see also "Irish Native Art"), a term applied to knotwork, &c., a misnomer, 125; Celtic decorative art died out in Britain during the occupation by the Romans; not so in Ireland, 5.

Cement, buildings without, 1; introduction of, 3.

Chalices, rude stone, 41.

Chancels, churches with, generally much later date than churches of one chamber, 4.

Charlemagne, ravages of the Vikings owing to his conquests in North Germany, 92.

Chisel, evidences of the early use of, 44.

Christian decorative art, early examples in the oratories of Cashels or Ecclesiastical Forts, 35.

"Christ's Saddle," or the "Garden of the Passion," St. Michael's Rock, 31.

Churches, early Christian, 43 (see "Early Christian Churches").

Clare, County of, cyclopean character of masonry here due to its geological formation, description of scenery, 51.

Clemens, a learned Irishman of Charlemagne's time, 100.

Cloicctech, or Bell House, name used for round towers by the Annalists, 77; original intention was "a keep" or place of safety, a term never used by the Annalists before A.D. 950, 103, 104.

Clonaltin, Romanesque ornament at, 115.

Clonfert Church, date of, 114.

Clonmacnois, Cathedral of, 121; herringbone masonry in tower, 120; belfries at, 55, 127; Northmen at, 97; heathen rites in Cathedral of, 97, 98, 108.

Clonmacnois, the Nun's Church (Queen Dervorgilla's), 129.

Clonmacnois, O'Melaghlin's Church at, erected as a mortuary chapel, 38, *note* 1.

Colman Mac Duach (St.), Church of Kilmacduach (Galway), tower of, 55.

Colman Mac Duach, Church of (Aranmôr), angle projections, 46; introduction of a rude impost in chancel arch, 47.

Columba, 23, 24.

Colum-cille's (St.) House, vault of, shows transition from the false to the true arch, 43; steep-pitched stone roof, 120.

Conroy, Dr., description of Aran, 49.

Cormac, King, 300 years before St. Patrick, refuses heathen burial, 21.

Cormac's Chapel, Cashel, built by Cormac M'Carthy, 129; barrel vaulted, 9; method of construction of the stone roof, *ib.*; Romanesque ornament at, 116, 117, 121; date of, 126.

Croziers, early, 41, 84.

Curoi, Son of Daré, legend of, 17.

Dahlmann's opinion on the missionary character of the early Irish Church, 24; Irish probably the first discoverers of America, *ib.*, *note* 1.

Dates of Irish buildings, cannot be determined by any comparison with English examples, 5; period of Romanesque style can be determined by historical evidence, 126.

Dervorgilla's (Queen) Church at Clonmacnois, beauty of chancel arch, 11, 129.

Dome-shaped roofs, universally adopted by early races, 27.

Double-roofed buildings, not only places of worship but dwelling-places, 121.

Druids, prophecies of, regarding Christianity, 21.

Drumkeat, Council of, in 590, 43.

Early Christian Churches, comprising those churches where grouting or cement has been used—cyclopean character, 27; restoration of which took place after the overthrow of Turgesius the Dane, 96.

Early Christian Monasteries, 29, 40.

Ecclesiastical Towers, classified according to average styles of their masonry and apertures (table of)—conclusions to be drawn from—their position with regard to the church to which they were attached—collateral evidence that most of these towers were erected in places where Christianity was already established—round towers which are attached to churches and coeval with them, nine in Ireland, two in the Orkneys—their probable date—examples of similar round towers on the Continent—the Irish tower not singular from its size and form, but from its isolation, 53, 111. (See also "Irish Church Towers.")

Eliot, George, quoted, 52, 131.

Farannan's (St.) Church, mouldings at, 120.

Fechin, of High Island, founder of monasteries, died A.D. 665, 39.

Ferguson, Mrs., "The Irish before the Conquest," 16, *note* 1.

Ferguson, Samuel, 19; *note* 2, *ib.*; quoted, 20, 21, 23.

Fergusson, James, quoted, 11, 77, *note* 2, 110.

Finan the Leper, founder of church on St. Michael's Rock—his dwelling on Church Island—lived at close of sixth century, 39.

Flannan (St.), Church of, Killaloe, situated alongside the cathedral, stone roofed and vaulted nave with chamber, 121.

FORTS :—

Forts, Pagan, similarity between, and first Christian monasteries, 2, 3; applied to Christian uses, 29, 40; tradition ascribes them to a period as early as the first century of the Christian era, *ib.*; attempt to establish a link between them and Christian forms of building, 25; reasons against the theory of their remote origin, *ib.*

Aengus, situation of—legendary history—size—plan of—doorway—platform—defensive outworks, 14, 16, 26, 130.

Black Fort, the, Aranmôr, name derived from colour of stone—consists of one great wall between two cliffs—stone houses with rounded roofs in interior—*chevaux de frise*, 26.

Forts on the South Island of Aran, the Great Fort—double enclosure—cells and cloghauns in enclosure—peculiar style of building, 27.

"Cashel Bawn," Sligo, size and form—built of limestone boulders—masonry, 26.

"Cahir Dún Fergus," horseshoe form in plan—roughly built—stones mostly in horizontal layers, 26.

France, communication between Ireland and, restored after the overthrow of Turgesius the Dane, 101.

Freeman, Edward, quoted, 8, 38, 48, 74, *note* 2, 112, 114, 118 *note*.

Freeman, Mr., opinion on Irish Romanesque, 8, 114.

Froude, Mr., opinions of, with regard to Irish art and culture, 12.

Galway, limestone district of, the character of the masonry in such districts, 49-52.

Garden of the Monks, St. Michael's Rock, 29, 32.

Glendalough Cathedral, 47.
Glendalough, Trinity Church, 47.
Glendalough, Our Lady's Church—chancel doorway—chancel arch, 46.
Graves, Rev. Ch., D.D., on Ogham Inscriptions, 19, *note* 1.

Hermits, character of, 3, 23; actual remains of their original buildings on the west coast of Ireland, 3.
Herring-bone masonry, rarity of, 118.

Inchagoile, capitals in church, 115.
Inchiquin, Lake of, 51.
Incised surface mouldings, a characteristic of Irish architectural decoration, 124.
Inisglora, Island of, St. Brendan's Oratory and Cell, 39.
Inismurray, Cashel of Monastery, 39.
Ireland, dawn of letters in, 18; history and antiquities of, errors with regard to, 41; period of steady progress in, politically and intellectually, between 6th and 9th centuries, *ib.*; colonized great part of Scotland and Isle of Man, 42.
Irish Church, founders of, teachers, mariners, and anchorites, 22; believed to have carried Christianity to Ireland, the Faroe Islands, and America, 24; engrafted their own faith on ancient objects of heathen veneration, *ib.*; non-prevalence of the diocesan system accounts for the small size of churches, 113.
Irish Church Towers, the type chosen not peculiar to Ireland, but derived from Western Europe, 6; five varieties, 7; Mr. Wilkinson's view concerning, 7; origin and use of, erected for defence and for the safe housing of bells and other sacred treasures, 77; not intended for hanging bells at their summits, 78; name used by the Annalists in referring to them, 77; Dr. Lynch's opinion of their comparatively late date, 85; Dr. Petrie's view of the towers as places of defence, 87; Colonel Montmorency, quotation from, 87; Giraldus Cambrensis mentions them, 87; recapitulation of arguments which point to the ninth century as the date of their erection, 88; external causes which led to the introduction of this defensive element in church architecture, 89, 91, 92; mark the effort made by Ireland in defence of her faith against paganism, 92; introduced into France about the same time, 101; erected in places most infested by the enemy, 106; motives which actuated the defenders in restoring them so persistently, 107; early recorded builders of towers, 108; three distinct periods to which they may be assigned, 109; those latest built show signs of development into work of greater beauty, 111. (Letters from Mr. Clark and M. Viollet-le-Duc, Appendix.)
Irish literature, early, 42, *note* 3.
Irish native art, epoch of, 21; lavish use of all the decorations of, 123; designs in Irish illuminated sacred writings all reproduced by the chisel in her church decorations, 5, 112; two designs specially characteristic of, 125; strongest mark of the individuality of Irish art, not the mere form, 126; gradual growth of, shown in metal-work and sculpture, *ib.*; period at which enriched style prevailed, *ib.* (See "Chronological Table" at end of vol.; see also "Romanesque in Ireland.")

Kells, Book of, 71, *note*; peculiarity of art in, 127; the most wonderful achievement of the Irish school, *ib.*; date of, prior to A.D. 1000, *ib.*; its perfection of execution and rich harmony of colour, *ib.*
Kevin's (St.), Glendalough, only church with chancel arch built in primitive style, 4.
Killbannon (Galway), monastic fort originally a pagan building, 32.
Kilmalkedar, Romanesque Church, pilasters, 46.
Kilmurvey, town of, in greater Island of Aran, 33; monastic fort originally a pagan building, *ib.*
Knights of the Red Branch, 17.

Legends, early builders', 15.

Leo the Isaurian, by his iconoclastic movement caused great influx of artists into Italy and France, 100.
Limestone districts of Ireland, cyclopean character of the masonry in Clare, Galway, and Isles of Aran, due to the geological formation, 44, 49, 119.

Maghera (Londonderry County), fine west door sculptured, 26, 130.
Malachy, King, victory over the Danes, 100; St. Malachy reforms disorders and rebuilds churches, 128.
Michael's (St.) Rock, situation and aspect — approach to the monastery — St. Michael's Church not the original building — cells — wells and crosses — cashel or enclosing wall — leachta and burial-ground — history of the Skelligs, 29-32.
Mochua, founder of Nendrum (died A.D. 497), 39.
Molaga of Leaba Molaga, founder of monasteries, tomb of, 39; died (A.D. 665), *ib.*
Molaise, Church of, Inismurray, 39; died (A.D. 560), *ib.*
Monasteries, Island, places of retreat, 2.
Monasteries, Early Christian, 29-39. (See "Early Christian Monasteries.")
Mouldings and ornaments, growth in use of, 4.
Moyra, battle of, 42.
Muredach, a contemporary of St. Patrick, 39.
Murtogh O'Brien (King), Tomb of, Killaloe, date of, 126.

Northmen (The) in Ireland, 91, 111.

Oghamic writing, 18, 61.
Oratories, their small size and peculiar form, copied possibly from an early type of church in Italy, 37.
Ornament, gradual growth in use of, 4.
Otta, wife of Turgesius the Viking, 98, 108.
Ought-Máma, County Clare — chancel arch — form of arch, 47.

Paganism and Christianity, Ireland the battle-field of a struggle between, 92, 96.

Patrick, St., traditions which imply that he was not the first missionary to Ireland, 22; hymn to the Holy Trinity one of the most interesting monuments of Celtic literature, 42, *note.*
Petrie, Dr., first investigator of history of Irish architecture, 5, 89; corroboration of his views by recent investigators, 58; views as to date of towered churches, 62; Dr. Hibbert's letter to, 72; on office of bell-ringer, 82; quoted, 83, 87, 91, 103, 104, 105, 107, 112; views corrected by Lord Dunraven, 111.

Rahen small church, limestone used in, 119.
Reeves, Rev. Dr. William, quoted, 22, 23, *note* 3, 99, 105, *note* 3.
Renaissance, development under Charlemagne, 100.
Retreat, Hermitages places of temporary, 23.
Rock of Woman's Wailing, St. Michael's Rock, 23.
Romanesque, development of Irish variety of, marked by continuous series of monuments, 1; date cannot be determined by comparison with English examples, 4-5; pre-existent and entirely independent of Anglo-Norman architecture, 11.
Romanesque, Irish, 112, 129; St. Caimin's, Iniscaltra, marks its introduction, 113; primitive architecture upon which it was engrafted gives it a distinctive character, *ib.*; features which determine this character, *ib.*; Mr. Freeman's views, 114; archaic character of ornament at Inchagoile, Clonaltin, and Banagher, 115; cultivation of arts not confined to ecclesiastics, 127; sudden arrest of its development by civil war, 129. (See also "Irish Native Art.")
Romanesque in England, Westminster Abbey marks the transition, 112; distinctive character of, 113.
Round Towers in France, 100; M. Viollet-le-Duc on their origin, 6; their origin, 102; intended to protect their churches from Northmen, 103; introduced into

Ireland at same time, *ib.*; examples from early bas-reliefs, manuscripts, and frescoes, 102. (See also Appendix.)
"Runic" and "Celtic," terms applied to knotwork, &c., a misnomer, 125.

Schliemann, architectural remains at Hissarlik found by, 27, *note* 1.
Sepulchral monuments, pre-Christian, carvings in, 1.
Skelligs, The. See "St. Michael's Rock."
Sons of Umor, legend of the migration of, 16.
Stanley, Dean, description of Palestine, 50, 51.
"Stone of Pain," St. Michael's Rock, 31.
Stone churches with cement, 41-52; probably erected after the Council of Drumcheat, 43; Tomgraney Church an example with historic evidence for date, *ib.*; distinctive features, 47.
Stone-roofed buildings, important achievement of Irish architecture, 8, 9; Mr. Fergusson's remarks upon, 10; bold and lofty, as at St. Flannan's, King Cormac's, and St. Doulough's, an original conception in Ireland, 110.

Temple Martin, Kerry, doorway exhibits earliest and simplest style of moulding, 44.
Todd, Rev. James, D.D., quoted, 22, 24, 96, 97, 98, 114.
Tomgraney Church, County Clare, first example of stone church with cement, for whose date there is historic evidence, 43; chancel originally ten feet shorter, 47.
Traditions of early builders, 15-16.

Tuam, cross at, 126; chancel arch, 115; date of church, 126; curious inscriptions on stone crosses which belonged to this church, *ib.*
Turgesius, Viking, invades Ireland and establishes himself at Armagh, 96; condition of Ireland during his rule, 98; his overthrow and death, as recorded by Keatinge, 99.

Vere, Aubrey de, quoted, 20, 21.
Vikings, descent of, on the British Islands, its cause, 92; only from the period of Charlemagne, showing evidence of preconcerted plan and energy, 93; characteristics of their religion, 94; the Christianity by which it was confronted, *ib.*; record of the first attack upon Irish shores, 95; invasion by Turgesius (A.D. 818), 96; course taken by the invaders, 106. (See Map.)
Viollet-le-Duc, opinion upon origin of church towers in France, 6, 77; primitive ramparts in Gaul, 25, 101.

Waagen on Celtic illumination, 124.
Way of the Cross, religious ceremony on St. Michael's Rock, 31.
Wells, holy, in Aran, 49.
Westminster Abbey as rebuilt by Edward the Confessor marks the transition to the enriched round arch in England, 112.
Wilkinson, George, quoted, 26.
Willis, Professor, on ancient plan of St. Gall Monastery, 66.
Windows, nave, when introduced, 47, 48.
Wood, early Irish churches not generally of, 35.

CHISWICK PRESS:—C. WHITTINGHAM, TOOKS COURT, CHANCERY LANE.

Fig. 1.

Doorway, Dún Aengus.

Fig. 2.

STEPS IN CAHER GEL, CO. GALWAY.

Fig. 4.

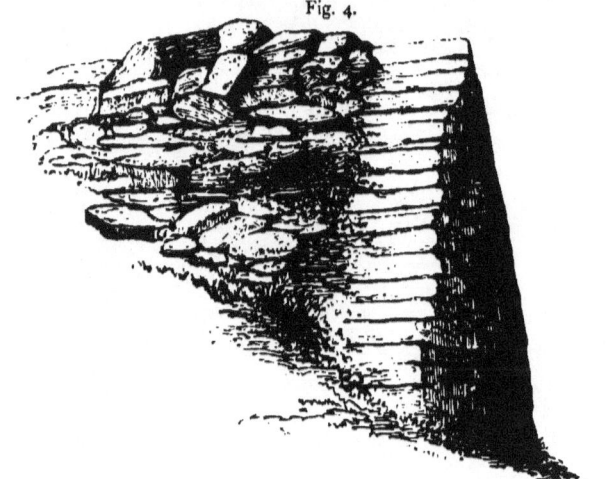

PORTION OF WALL, CAHER GEL, CO. KERRY.

Fig. 3.

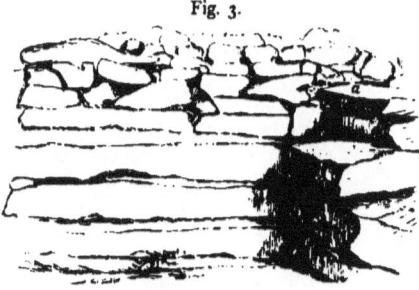

STEPS, DÚN OONACHT.

Fig. 5.

CAHER GEL, ON LOUGH CORRIB.

Fig. 6.

DOORWAY OF CLOCHÀN IN CAHIR NA-MAC-TIRECH.

Scelig Mhichil, St. Michael's Rock, Co. Kerry.

Fig. 8.

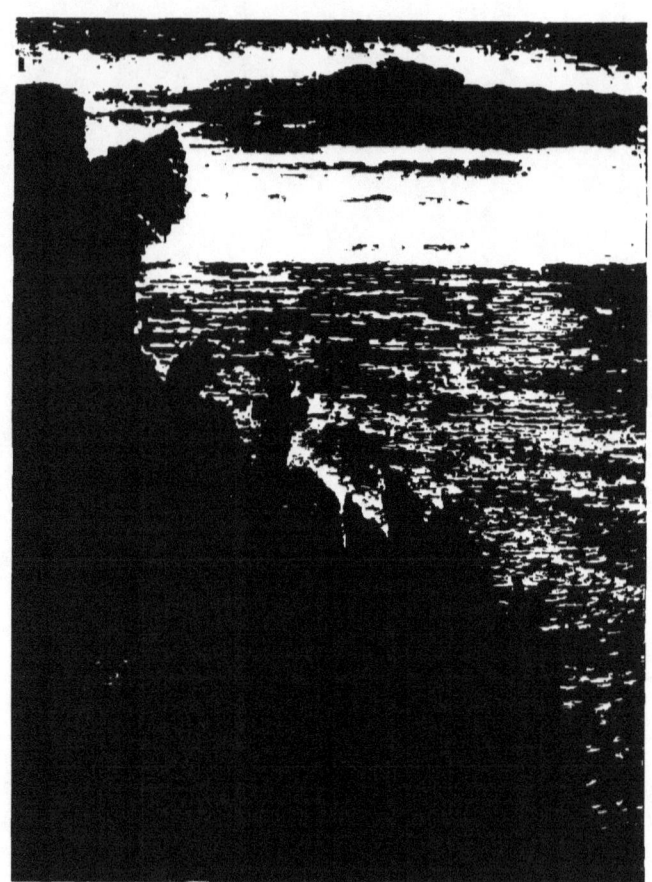

THE WAY OF THE CROSS, SCELIG MHICHIL.

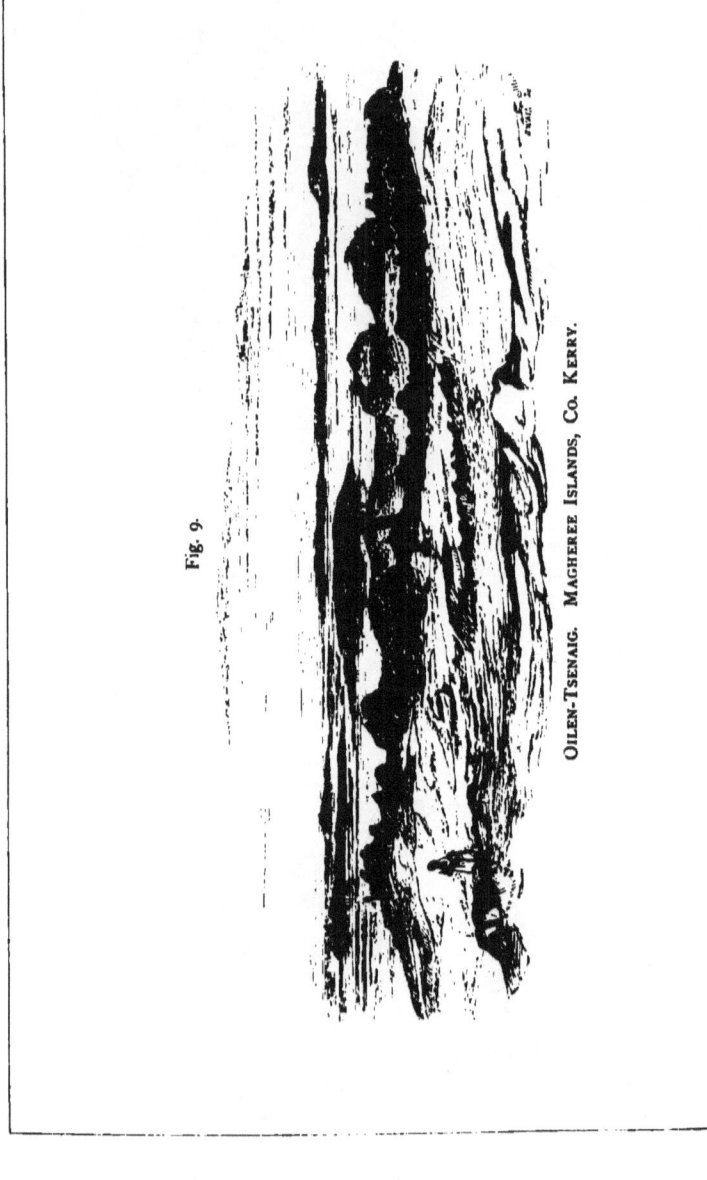

Fig. 9. OILEN-TSENAIG. MACHEREE ISLANDS, CO. KERRY.

Fig. 10.

OILEN-TSENAIG, DOORWAY OF CELL.

Fig. 11.

DOORWAY OF ST. FINAN'S CELL, INTERIOR.

Fig. 12.

INTERIOR OF ST. BRENDAN'S ORATORY, INISGLORA.

Early Christian Monasteries.

PL. IX.

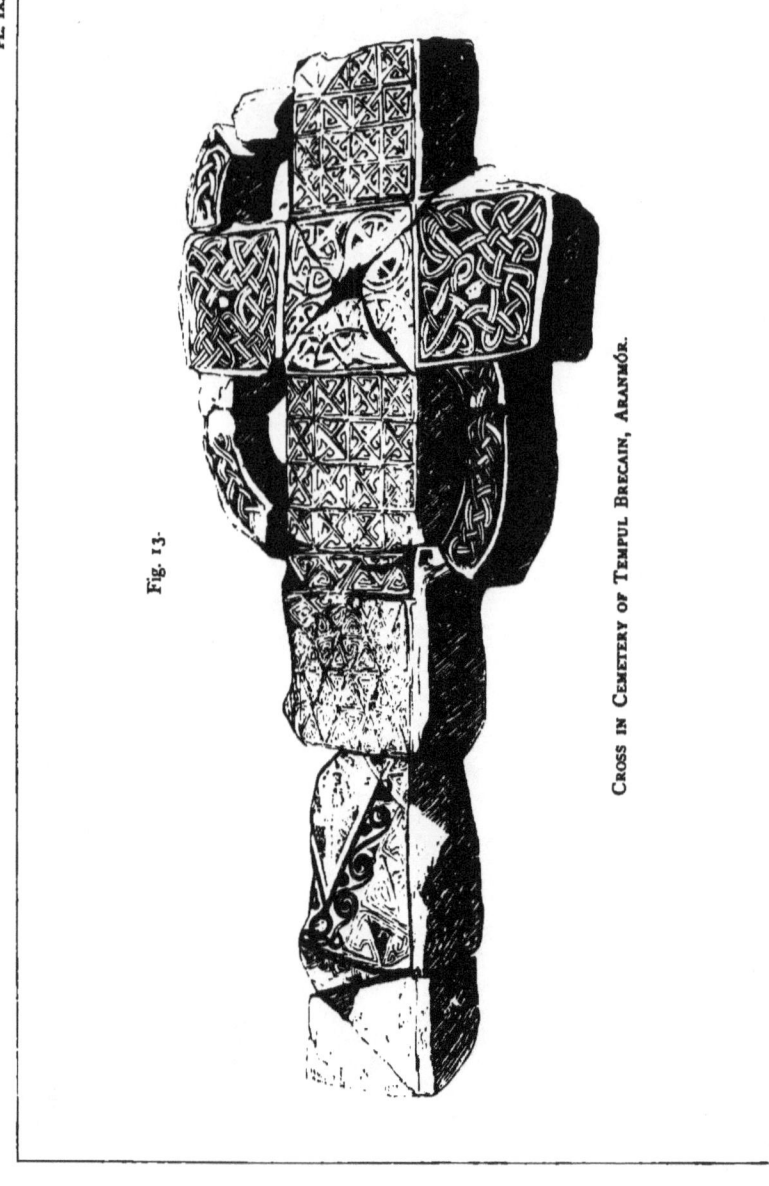

Fig. 13.

CROSS IN CEMETERY OF TEMPUL BRECAIN, ARANMÓR.

Stone Churches with Cement.

Pl. X.

Fig. 14.

East Window in Mac Dara's Church.

Fig. 15.

South Window in Kill Enda.

Fig. 16.

Doorway, Mac Dara's Church.

Stone Churches with Cement.

Fig. 17.

DOORWAY OF ST. CAIMIN'S CHURCH, INISMAIN. INTERIOR.

Fig. 18.

SOUTH WINDOW, ST. CAIMIN'S CHURCH, INISMAIN.

Stone Churches with Cement.

Fig. 19.

TRINITY CHURCH, GLENDALOUGH.

Fig 20.

DOORWAY OF ST. CAIMIN'S CHURCH, INISMAIN. EXTERIOR.

Fig. 21.

WINDOW IN KILMORE MOY CHURCH.

Fig. 22.

DOORWAY OF KILFRAUCHEN.

Fig. 23.

WINDOW IN ST. BRECAN'S CHURCH.

Fig. 24.

KILCRONY, CO. WICKLOW.

Fig. 25.

DOORWAY, MUNGRET CHURCH.

Fig. 26.

DOORWAY OF KILLANNIN CHURCH.

Stone Churches with Cement.

Fig. 27.

EAST WINDOW, ALTANNIN.

Fig. 28.

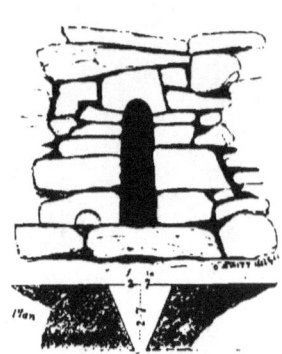

SOUTH WINDOW, ST. KEVIN'S.

Fig. 29.

SOUTH WINDOW, ST. KEVIN'S. INTERIOR.

Fig. 30.

DOORWAY, ST. KEVIN'S.

Stone Churches with Cement.

PL. XVII.

Fig. 31 KILLCANANACH, INTERIOR OF DOORWAY.

Fig. 32. TEMPLE MARTIN.

Fig. 33. DOORWAY OF BANAGHER CHURCH. INTERIOR.

Fig. 34. DOORWAY OF BANAGHER CHURCH. EXTERIOR.

Stone Churches with Cement.

Fig. 35.

WEST DOORWAY OF MAGHERA CHURCH.

Ecclesiastical Towers.

Pl. XX.

Fig. 36.

SCATTERY. DOORWAY OF TOWER.

Fig. 37.

ORAN. DOORWAY OF TOWER.

Ecclesiastical Towers.

PL. XXI.

Fig. 38.

Fig. 39.

WINDOWS IN LUSK TOWER.

Fig. 40.

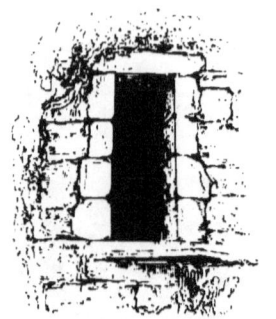

Fig. 41.

DOORWAY OF CLONDALKIN TOWER.   DOORWAY OF TAGHEDOE TOWER.

Fig. 42.

INTERIOR OF DOORWAY, LUSK TOWER.

Fig. 43.

DRUMCLIFF TOWER.

Fig. 44.

AGHAVULLER.

Fig. 45.

DOORWAY OF AGHAVULLER TOWER.

Fig. 46.

KILLREE TOWER.

Fig. 47.

DOORWAY OF KILLREE TOWER.

Ecclesiastical Towers.

PL. XXV.

Fig. 48.

INISCELTRA.

Fig. 49.

DOORWAY OF TOWER, INISCELTRA.

Ecclesiastical Towers.

PL. XXVI.

Fig. 50. DOORWAY OF TOWER, MEELICK, CO. MAYO.

Fig. 51.

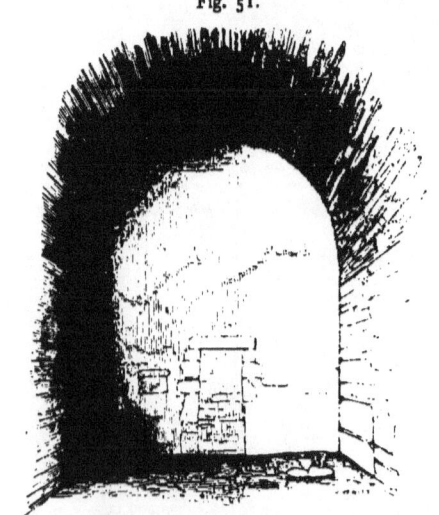

NAVE OF ST. KEVIN'S CHURCH, SHOWING ENTRANCE TO TOWER IN THE ROOF.

Ecclesiastical Towers.

Fig. 52.

WINDOW IN MONASTERBOICE TOWER, EXTERIOR.

Fig. 53.

MASONRY IN ROOF OF TEMPLE FINGHIN.

Fig. 54.

ROSCREA TOWER IN 1835.

Fig. 55.

DOORWAY OF CASHEL TOWER.

Fig. 56.   Fig. 57.   Fig. 58.

WINDOWS IN DYSERT AENGUS TOWER.

Fig. 59. Doorway in Dysert Aengus Tower.

Fig. 60. Dysert Afngus Church and Tower.

Ecclesiastical Towers.

Pl. XXX.

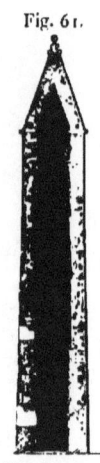

Fig. 61.
SECTION OF DEVENISH.   Fig. 62. DOORWAY OF KILKENNY TOWER.   Fig. 63. DEVENISH.

Fig. 64.   GLENDALOUGH.

Fig. 66.

DOORWAY OF BELFRY, KELLS.

Fig. 65.

DISERT O'DEA, DOORWAY IN TOWER.

Fig. 67.

WINDOW OF BELFRY, KELLS.

Fig. 68.

KELLS.

Ecclesiastical Towers.

Fig. 69.     Fig. 70.

CORBELS IN ARDMORE.

Fig. 71.

ARDMORE TOWER.

Ecclesiastical Towers.

PL. XXXIV.

Fig. 72.

WINDOW IN TOWER OF TIMAHOE.

Fig. 73.

DOORWAY, KILDARE.

Fig. 74.

TORY ISLAND. ST. COLUMBA'S CHURCH, TOWER, AND CROSS.

Ecclesiastical Towers.

Fig. 75.

DOORWAY OF DROMISKIN TOWER.

Fig. 76.

DROMISKIN TOWER, CO. LOUTH.

Ecclesiastical Towers.

Fig. 77.

KILBANNON TOWER.

Fig. 78.

ABERNETHY.

Fig. 78a.

SCHENESS.

Irish Romanesque.

Fig. 79. EXTERIOR OF DOORWAY, KILMALKEDAR.

Fig. 80. INTERIOR OF DOORWAY, KILMALKEDAR.

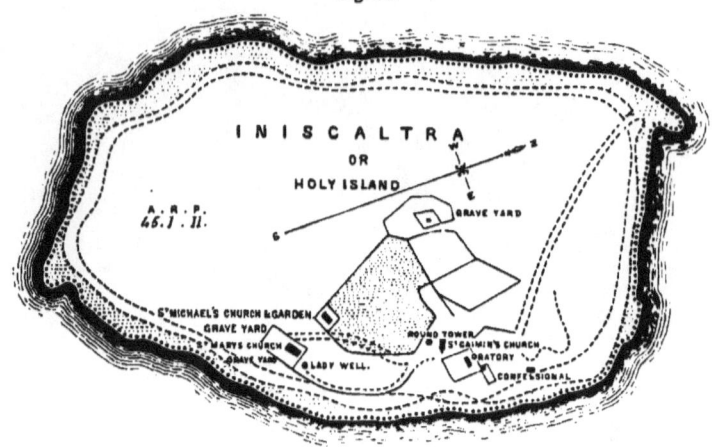

Fig. 81.

GROUND PLAN OF MONASTERY ON INISCALTRA.

Fig. 82.

CAPITALS OF PILASTERS IN CHANCEL ARCH,
ST. CAIMIN'S CHURCH, INISCALTRA.

Fig. 83.

DOORWAY OF ST. CAIMIN'S CHURCH,
INISCALTRA.

Fig. 84.

Fig. 85.

CAPITALS, CHANCEL ARCH, RAHEN.

Fig. 86.

PORTION OF WEST DOORWAY, SAINTS' CHURCH, INCHAGOILE.

Fig. 87. Interior of Cormac's Chapel, Cashel.

Fig. 88.

NORTH DOORWAY, CORMAC'S CHAPEL, CASHEL.

Irish Romanesque.

PL. XLII.

Fig. 89. CHANCEL, CORMAC'S CHAPEL, CASHEL.

Fig. 90. CORMAC'S CHAPEL, CASHEL.

Irish Romanesque.

Pl. XLIII.

Fig. 91.

KILLESHIN DOORWAY.

Fig. 92.

KILLESHIN DOORWAY.

Irish Romanesque.

Pl. XLIV.

Fig. 93.

FRESHFORD. WEST DOORWAY.

Irish Romanesque.

PL. XLV.

Fig. 94.   Fig. 95.

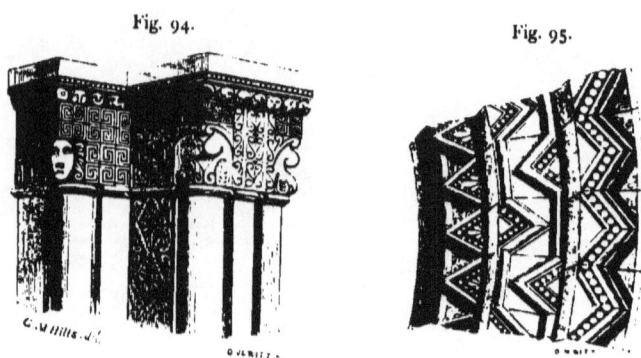

QUEEN DERVORGILLA'S CHURCH, CLONMACNOIS.

Fig. 96.

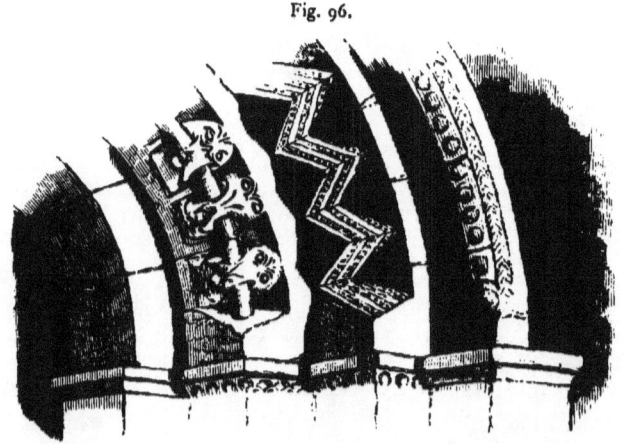

QUEEN DERVORGILLA'S CHURCH, CLONMACNOIS.

Irish Romanesque.

PL. XLVI.

Fig. 97.

WEST FRONT, ST. CRONAN'S CHURCH, ROSCREA.

Fig. 98.

Chancel Arch, Mona Incha.

Irish Romanesque.

Fig. 99.

KILLESHIN.

Fig. 100.

TOMGRANEY.

Fig. 101.

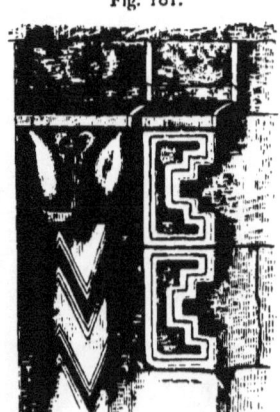

PORTION OF DOORWAY, AGHADOE.

Fig. 102.

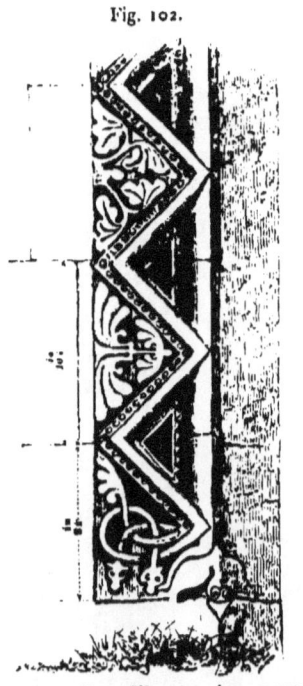

MOULDING, EAST WINDOW, ANNADOWN.

Irish Romanesque.

PL. XLIX.

Fig. 103.

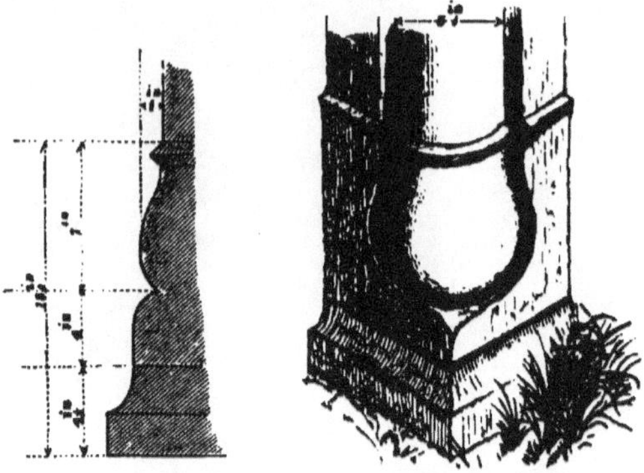

QUEEN DERVORGILLAS CHURCH, CLONMACNOIS.

Fig. 104.

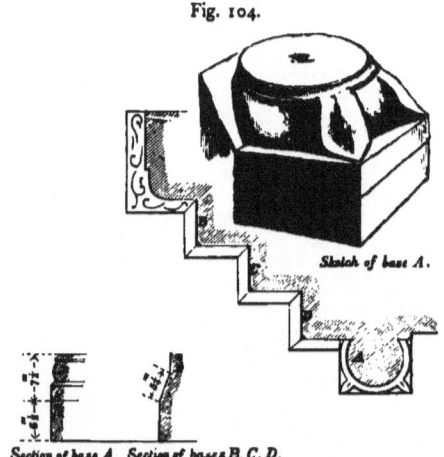

Sketch of base A.

Section of base A. Section of bases B. C. D.

WEST DOOR OF CATHEDRAL, CLONMACNOIS.

Irish Romanesque.

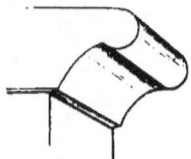

Fig. 105.

CORNER PROJECTION, CLONMACNOIS.

Fig. 106.

CAPITAL, CLONMACNOIS.

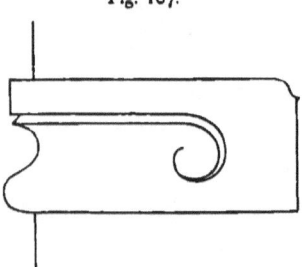

Fig. 107.

IMPOST OF WEST DOOR, CLONMACNOIS.

Fig. 108.

TOMGRANEY. QUOIN SHAFT.

Irish Romanesque.

PL. LI.

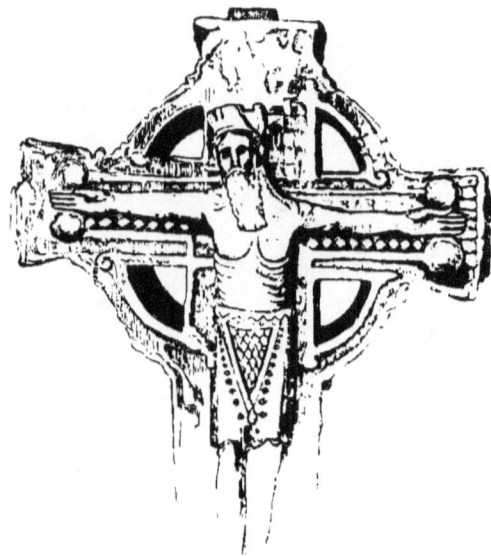

Fig. 109. High Cross, Tuam.

Fig. 110. Base of High Cross, Tuam.
OR DO THOIRDELBUCH U CHONCHOBUIR DONT..UR....IARLATHE
....S IN DERNAD IN SAE....
for Turlogh O'Conor, for the .... of Iarlath, by whom was made this ....

Corner Shafts of Churches.

Fig. 111.

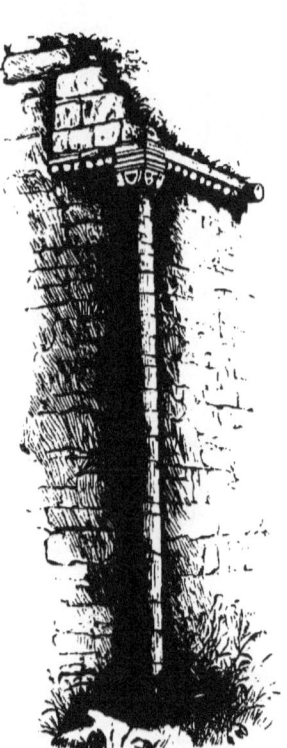

Tempul Muire, Ardfert.   Tuaim Greine.

www.ingramcontent.com/pod-product-compliance
Lightning Source LLC
Chambersburg PA
CBHW032103220426
43664CB00008B/1120